Analysing Political D

Analysing Political Discourse is a must for anyone interested in the way language is used in the world of politics.

Invoking Aristotle's idea that we are all political animals, able to use language to pursue our own ends, the book uses the theoretical framework of linguistics to explore the ways in which we think and behave politically.

Domestic and global politics come under the linguistic microscope. What do politicians really do in a radio interview? What verbal games do they play in a parliamentary knock-about? Contemporary and high-profile case studies are used, including an examination of the dangerous influence of a politician's words on the defendants in the Stephen Lawrence murder trial.

International in its perspective, *Analysing Political Discourse* also considers the changing landscape of global political language post-September 11, focusing on self-legitimising language and the increasing use of religious imagery in political discourse. Bill Clinton's address persuading his country to go to war in Kosovo is analysed, and speeches by George Bush and Osama bin Laden are examined in relation to each other.

Written in a lively and engaging style, *Analysing Political Discourse* offers a new theoretical perspective on the study of language and politics, and provides an essential introduction to political discourse analysis.

Paul Chilton is Professor of Linguistics at the University of East Anglia, where Critical Linguistics was pioneered. His previous publications include *Orwellian Language and the Media* (1988), *Security Metaphors* (1996) and (co-edited with Christina Schäffner) *Politics as Text and Talk* (2002).

Analysing Political Discourse

Theory and practice

Paul Chilton

 Routledge
Taylor & Francis Group

LONDON AND NEW YORK

First published 2004
by Routledge
11 New Fetter Lane, London EC4P 4EE

Simultaneously published in the USA and Canada
by Routledge
29 West 35th Street, New York, NY 10001

Routledge is an imprint of the Taylor & Francis Group

© 2004 Paul Chilton

Typeset in Perpetua by Graphicraft Limited, Hong Kong
Printed and bound in Great Britain by TJ International Limited, Padstow, Cornwall

British Library Cataloguing in Publication Data
A catalogue record for this book is available from the British Library

Library of Congress Cataloging in Publication Data
Chilton, Paul A. (Paul Anthony)
  Analysing political discourse : theory and practice / Paul Chilton.
    p. cm.
Includes bibliographical references.
  1. Language and languages – Political aspects.   2. Great Britain –
Languages – Political aspects.   I. Title.

  P119.3.C48 2004
  306.44–dc21   2003011976

ISBN 0–415–31471–2 (hbk)
ISBN 0–415–31472–0 (pbk)

To my father and to the memory of my mother

Contents

Figures and tables

Figures

Tables

Preface

Remember that politics, colonialism, imperialism and war also originate in the human brain

Vilayanur S. Rmachandran

The analysis of political discourse is scarcely new. The western classical tradition of rhetoric was in its various guises a means of codifying the way public orators used language for persuasive and other purposes. The Greco-Roman tradition regarded humans as both creatures who are defined by the ability to speak and creatures defined by their habit of living together in groups. For writers like Cicero the cultivation of the power of speech was the essence of the citizen's duty. For others it was the essence of deception and distortion. In eighteenth-century Europe, the new scientific minds began to distrust deeply the things language could do. Rhetoric as the study of the forms of verbal persuasion and expression declined. But of course orators, politicians, preachers and hucksters of all sorts continued to use their natural rhetorical talents as before. Rhetorical practice, in the form of public relations and 'spin', fuelled by the media explosion, is now more centre stage than ever.

In the last half of the twentieth century, linguistics took enormous strides, largely through the realisation that language must be seen as an innate part of all human minds. Chomsky's influence is undoubted, as is the impact of the generative model of language with which he is associated. The research questions were essentially scientific. This is not to say that linguists in this tradition have not raised their voices in matters of domestic and foreign politics, both in the United States and Europe, but their research agenda was not directed towards theorising any relationship there might be between the human language faculty and the social nature of humans. The language faculty was largely identified with syntax and viewed as sealed off from other mental capacities.

Scholarly interest in the public *uses* of language was another matter, pursued by other scholars, mainly in Europe. The Frankfurt School and proponents of critical theory (including Benjamin, Adorno, Horkheimer, Marcuse, Habermas, Stuart Hall, Bourdieu) were among the most distinguished to link language, politics and culture. Some linguists and scholars in the humanities were aware of this current of thought. In England, socially concerned linguists (Fowler *et al.* 1979; Kress and Hodge 1979 revised as Hodge and Kress 1993; Fowler 1991, 1996) produced Critical Linguistics. They were followed by socially and politically oriented linguists from a variety of backgrounds, networking broadly under the banner of Critical Discourse Analysis (for example, Mey 1985, 2001; Fairclough 1989, 1992, 1995a, 1995b; van Dijk 1984, 1987, 1993b, 1997a, 1997b, 1998, 2002; Wodak 1989, 1996, 2002; Reisigl and Wodak 2001; Blommaert and Bulcaen 1997; Blommaert and Verschueren 1998, and many others). Scholars in this movement have tended to work not with the generative model of the Chomskian tradition but with the systemic-functional linguistics associated with M. A. K. Halliday (van Dijk and Verschueren are exceptions). This theoretical perspective does not investigate language as a mental phenomenon but as a social phenomenon. Starting from single issues such as racism, or from political categories such as ideology, scholars in this tradition have tended to use linguistics as a tool kit and have not tried to tell us more about the human language instinct. Worthily, they have sought to fight social injustice of various kinds. I do not know if discourse analysts can have any serious impact on the genocides, oppressions and exploitations we are still witnessing.

The generative revolution in linguistics was also a cognitive revolution, one that generated a further cognitive revolution that went off on its own in the 1980s. This group of linguists and philosophers, mainly in North America (Fillmore, Langacker, Lakoff, Mark Johnson, Turner, Fauconnier, and in a slightly different mode Jackendoff, among others) but also increasingly in Europe, deliberately linked the mental capacity of language with the other mental capacities. These linkages have included spatial cognition, for example. More importantly, cognitive linguistics has told us a great deal about the nature of cognitive creativity through research on conceptual metaphor and blending. Once such linkages begin to be studied, social and political cognition comes into the frame, sometimes in a distinctly critical mode (Lakoff 1996 and his Internet papers on the Gulf War, the events of 11 September 2001 and the second Gulf War, and in Europe, Chilton 1996, Dirven 2001). In parallel, cognitive science in general has explored social intelligence, the nature of communication and the evolution of language (among others, Sperber and Wilson 1986; Sperber 2000; Cosmides and Tooby 1989; Leslie 1987; Hurford *et al.* 1998). The cross-fertilisation among these currents of thought now offers the most exciting paradigm for exploring the nature of the human mind in society.

Rhetoric, generative linguistics, critical theory, cognitive linguistics – all these contexts are reflected in the present book, but most of all the last two. The book has come about through a long engagement in the analysis of, and commentary on language used in the domain of politics and international relations. It has equally come about through research and teaching in linguistics. Behind the book is a question: what does the use of language in contexts we call 'political' tell us about humans in general? The question shows how much we lack anything like a *theory* of language and politics. What I have tried to do in this book is to move the debate towards a *linguistic* and rather more broadly a *cognitive* theory of language and politics, one that will take account of the most probing speculations on semantics, pragmatics, evolution and discourse processing. At bottom there may exist a deep link between the political and the linguistic. I do not pretend to have demonstrated it but several sections of this book have that thought in mind.

The first two chapters seek to explain why we should bother at all with the relationship between language and politics, especially as some non-linguists, even some political scientists, might be tempted to open the book. Chapter 2, in particular, is meant to provoke speculation regarding the evolution and functioning of language in relation to political behaviour. Chapters 3 and 4 separate two complementary dimensions of what people do with language – interact with one another and exchange mental pictures of the world. I hope that the bits of linguistic theory that I introduce will provide techniques that people can and will use in order to make themselves aware of what the talk and text that surrounds us is doing. That is Part I of the book, the theoretical groundwork.

Parts II and III of the book contain practical analyses of actual specimens of political text and talk, using and developing various analytic techniques. Artificial though it may be, the two parts distinguish between internal domestic politics and the international environment. Part II selects three types of political communication in the domestic arena. Chapter 5 takes the case of the institutionalised media genre of the political interview, in its surrounding context of constitutional party politics. Chapter 6 moves to parliamentary discourse, again looking at the fine detail of what political actors are doing in using language. In Chapter 7, I turn to types of domestic discourse that characterise a community's anxieties about the 'others', the 'outsiders', the 'foreigners' that are the counterpart of its own sense of identity. Here I am concerned not primarily with the institutional context of a type of political interaction, but with the continuity over time of certain kinds of political representation.

Domestic political communication is complicated enough. On the global scale communication is almost inconceivably complex, and I do not attempt to tackle the issues of global communication head on. I have simply analysed texts associated with particular international events. These are events that have threatened the domestic security of millions of people beyond the English-speaking world – as well as within it, most appallingly on the 11 September 2001.

Chapter 7 is a kind of transition, since it attempts to get inside the mind, via the language they use, of those who fear or hate people they perceive as alien and threatening. The three chapters in Part III of the book develop a particular model for the analysis of discourse, based on spatial conceptualisation. At the same time, we encounter the problem of 'background knowledge' – the fact that in order to 'make sense' human communicators do not just encode information in signals, but actively (though unconsciously) draw on 'background' knowledge of all sorts. In analysing political language behaviour, the problem takes on interesting forms for the analyst. Chapter 8 investigates the means whereby western leaders represent, through language use, the world beyond their borders, and how they justify going to war to their electorates. Going to war is such a serious enterprise that it requires extraordinary communicative efforts, and a variety of presumptions about background knowledge, norms and values. Chapters 9 and 10 address texts that were part of the reaction to 11 September 2001. In many ways, this is hazardous territory; the effects are still with us and the full consequences still unknown. Chapter 9 begins to look at the way the world is represented in an international arena that has acquired a new kind of polarisation. Using the spatial model, it looks on the one hand at a public address by George W. Bush, and on the other it looks at a text issued by Osama bin Laden. The point? In this newly polarised world, we need at least to start to try to understand how different human minds imagine the world and communicate their imaginings. Chapter 10 seeks to open up another area for discourse enquiry – the role of religious conceptualisation. The analysis of religious discourse has been a neglected area of research, as has its overlap with politics. It poses challenges for a cognitive-linguistic approach, as well as for our understanding of contemporary politics more generally.

As will be evident, there is a theoretical agenda underlying the chapters of this book, and I attempt to draw together some of the threads in Part IV, in the hope that other scholars will explore them further. Perhaps there is a case now for pursuing a more coherent theory of language and political behaviour.

A final word. During the course of our explorations we will come across the crucial question of discourse, and discourse analysis, across cultures, across languages and through translation. These encounters pose more intriguing, and politically urgent, challenges for scholars in a world that is both more global and more fragmented.

Acknowledgements

As always, it behoves an author to express gratitude and love to their family, and I do so most heartily to Tricia, Jonathan, Emily and my wider family. Books do not get written without personal debts to those closest to them. So for once, this should be said first and not least.

This book has evolved over several years, during which time I have benefited from the ideas and writings of many colleagues and contacts. I hope I have not misrepresented their ideas; if I have, the responsibility is mine and I crave their indulgence. Throughout the preparation of this book I have been indebted to an international community of intellectuals. I cannot list them all here, but among those who have been generous with their ideas, their support or both, over a number of years, I would mention, in alphabetical order: the late Pierre Achard, Jan Blommaert, Patricia Chilton, Teun van Dijk, Norman Fairclough, Cornelia Ilie, Mikhail Ilyin, George Lakoff, Frank Liedtke, Luisa Martin Rojo, Jacob Mey, Christina Schäffner, Viktor Sergeev, Jef Verschueren, Ruth Wodak, Rüdiger Zimmermann. I would like to express my thanks to Alan Durant for helpful criticisms of an earlier draft of this book, and for the constructive points made by other reviewers. My thanks are due also to Louisa Semlyen and Kate Parker of Routledge for promoting this project, for their practical advice and for seeing it through the publication process.

The book was prepared and written while I was working at three different universities. At Warwick University I was fortunate for a long time to have the intellectual space to lay the groundwork, and I am grateful to former colleagues who made that possible, not least among them Christopher Thompson and the late Donald Charlton. At Aston University, Christina Schäffner, was a supportive critic, as she has been over many years. At the University of East Anglia, I am glad indeed to have found a creative environment for the exploration of an area of thought pioneered by the late Roger Fowler in collaboration with Gunther Kress, Bob Hodge and others in the 1970s. The final stages of writing this book benefited too from stimulating discussions on many matters with my colleagues Bill Downes and Clive Matthews.

Various parts of the book adapt short extracts from some of my previous publications, including in particular the following:

Chapter 3 uses about one page from Chilton and Schäffner, 'Discourse and Politics' in T. van Dijk (ed.), *Discourse as Social Interaction*, Sage, 1997.

Chapter 3 also uses about a page from Chilton and Schäffner, 'Introduction: themes and principles in the analysis of political discourse' in P. A. Chilton and C. Schäffner (eds) *Politics as Text and Talk*, Benjamins, 2002.

Chapter 9 uses some paragraphs from my article, 'Do something! Conceptualising responses to the attacks of 11 September 2001', *Journal of Language and Politics*, 1 (1): 181–95, 2002, published by Benjamins.

I am grateful to all the publishers and editors involved.

Permissions have been granted for the use of certain other published texts and documents. The author and publisher of the present book wish to thank the following for permission to use copyright material in this book:

Mouton de Gruyter for two diagrams and some text from my chapter 'Deixis and distance: President Clinton's justification of intervention in Kosovo' in *At War with Words*, edited by Mirjana N. Dedaic and Daniel N. Nelson, Mouton de Gruyter, Berlin, 2003.

BBC *Today* programme for permission to transcribe and reproduce of the interview by John Humphrys of Margaret Beckett, MP, June 2001.

BBC News Online for the text 'bin Laden's Warning' originating from BBC News South Asia, 7 October 2001.

Her Majesty's Stationery Office for the licence to use extracts from the Stephen Lawrence Inquiry Command Paper, 4262, Appendix 10, Sequence 11, 3 December 1994, 23:25:28 to 23:28 (http://www.official-documents.co.uk/document/cm42/4262/sli-ap10.htm).

The publishers apologise for any errors or omissions in the above list and would be grateful to be notified of corrections for incorporation in any future reprintings.

Part I

Political animals as articulate mammals

1   Politics and language

How can politics be defined? It is not the business of this book to answer this question definitively. We shall, however, say that politics varies according to one's situation and purposes – a political answer in itself. But if one considers the definitions, implicit and explicit, found both in the traditional study of politics and in discourse studies of politics, there are two broad strands. On the one hand, politics is viewed as a struggle for power, between those who seek to assert and maintain their power and those who seek to resist it. Some states are conspicuously based on struggles for power; whether democracies are essentially so constituted is disputable. On the other hand, politics is viewed as cooperation, as the practices and institutions that a society has for resolving clashes of interest over money, influence, liberty, and the like. Again, whether democracies are intrinsically so constituted is disputed.

Cross-cutting these two orientations is another distinction, this time between 'micro' and 'macro'. At the micro level there are conflicts of interest, struggles for dominance and efforts at co-operation between individuals, between genders, and between social groups of various kinds. As Jones *et al.* (1994: 5) put it,

> [a]t the micro level we use a variety of techniques to get our own way: persuasion, rational argument, irrational strategies, threats, entreaties, bribes, manipulation – anything we think will work.

Let us assume that there is a spectrum of social interactions that people will at one time or another, or in one frame of mind or another, think of as 'political'. At the macro extreme, there are the political institutions of the state, which in one of the views of politics alluded to above serve to resolve conflicts of interests, and which in the other view serve to assert the power of a dominant individual (a tyrant) or group (say, the capital-owning bourgeoisie, as in the traditional marxist perspective).[1] Such state institutions in a democracy are enshrined in constitutions, in civil and criminal legal codes, and (as in the case of Britain) in precedent practice. Associated with these state institutions, are parties and professional politicians, with more or less stable practices; other social formations – interest groups, social movements – may play upon the same stage.

What is strikingly absent from conventional studies of politics is attention to the fact that the micro-level behaviours mentioned above are actually kinds of linguistic action – that is, discourse. Equally, the macro-level institutions are types of discourse with specific characteristics – for example, parliamentary debates, broadcast interviews. And constitutions and laws are also discourse – written discourse, or text, of a highly specific type. This omission is all the more striking as students of politics often make statements like the following:

> Politics involves *reconciling differences* through discussion and persuasion. Communication is therefore central to politics.
>
> (Hague *et al.* 1998: 3–4)

And Hague *et al.* cite Miller (1991: 390), who says that the political process typically involves persuasion and bargaining. This line of reasoning leads to the need to explain how use of language can produce the effects of authority, legitimacy, consensus, and so forth that are recognised as being intrinsic to politics. What is the role of force? What is the role of language? As Hague *et al.* (1998: 14) point out, decisions, reached (as they must be, by definition) through communication, i.e. persuasion and bargaining, become *authoritative* – a process that involves force or the threat of force. However, as they also point out, 'politics scarcely exists if decisions are reached solely by violence but force, or its threat, is central to the execution of collective decisions'. If the verbal business of political authority is characterised by the ultimate sanction of force (fines, imprisonments, withholding of privileges and benefits, for example), it needs to be also pointed out that such force can itself only be operationalised by means of communicative acts, usually going down links in a chain of command. However politics is defined, there is a linguistic, discursive and communicative dimension, generally only partially acknowledged, if at all, by practitioners and theorists.

Politics and language: what's the connection?

Political animals and articulate mammals

Embedded in the tradition of western political thought there is in fact a view that language and politics are intimately linked at a fundamental level. It is not generally pointed out that when Aristotle gives his celebrated definition of humans as creatures whose nature is to live in a *polis*, in almost the same breath he speaks of the unique human capacity for speech:

But obviously man is a political animal [*politikon zoon*], in a sense in which a bee is not, or any other gregarious animal. Nature, as we say, does nothing without some purpose; and she has endowed man alone among the animals with the power of speech.

But what does Aristotle mean by 'speech'? Aristotle's next sentence distinguishes 'speech' from 'voice'. The latter is possessed by all animals, he says, and serves to communicate feelings of pleasure and pain. The uniquely human 'speech' is different. Aristotle sees it in teleological terms, or what might in some branches of today's linguistics be called functional terms:

> Speech, on the other hand, serves to indicate what is useful and what is harmful, and so also what is just and what is unjust. For the real difference between man and other animals is that humans alone have perception of good and evil, just and unjust, etc.
>
> (*The Politics*, 1253a7, translated by T. A. Sinclair 1992)[2]

Of course, the ability of individuals to have a sense of the just and the unjust might logically mean that there could be as many opinions as there are individuals. Such a state of affairs would probably not correspond to what one understands as the political. Not surprisingly, therefore, Aristotle's final point in this significant section, is that '[i]t is the sharing of a common view in *these* matters [i.e. what is useful and harmful, just and unjust, etc.] that makes a household and a state'.

What we can hold onto from this is the following. It is *shared* perceptions of values that defines political associations. And the human endowment for language has the function of 'indicating' – i.e., signifying, communicating – what is deemed, according to such shared perceptions, to be advantageous or not, by implication to the group, and what is deemed right and wrong within that group. Almost imperceptibly, Aristotle states that the just and the unjust is related to what is (deemed) useful and harmful, in the common view of the group. In addition, while Aristotle places the state above the household, we may note that the domestic and the public are defined in similar terms. This is important because it suggests that it is not only the public institutions of the state that depend on value perceptions and shared 'speech', but also other social groupings, not least what Aristotle's society understood as the 'household', which included, in subordinate positions, slaves and women.

Aristotle does not pursue in detail the connection between the linguistic and political make-up of humans, but the implications have a fundamental importance. In linguistics it is now widely accepted that the human capacity for speech is genetically based, though activated in human social relations. What is controversial is how the genetic base itself evolved. Did it evolve as part of social intelligence?

This might be the Aristotelian view, for language would have evolved to perform social functions – social functions that would in fact correspond to what we
understand as 'political'. Or did it evolve by a random mutation, providing
neural structures that led to the duality and generative characteristics of human
language? In this view the language *instinct* would not be intrinsically bound up
with the political instinct.[3] However, two things need to be noticed in this
regard. First, this view does not entail that the social and/or political behaviour
(as in Aristotle's political animal) is not itself genetically based. And second,
even if the language instinct is itself politics neutral, so to speak, one has to
assume that the cultural and culturally transmitted characteristics of human
language observably serve (though of course not exclusively) the needs of the
political.

What is clear is that political activity does not exist without the use of
language. It is true, as noted earlier, that other behaviours are involved and, in
particular, physical coercion. But the doing of politics is predominantly constituted in language. Conversely, it is also arguably the case that the need for
language (or for the cultural elaboration of the language instinct) arose from
socialisation of humans involving the formation of coalitions, the signalling of
group boundaries, and all that these developments imply, including the emergence
of what is called reciprocal altruism. This is not of course to say that language
arises *exclusively* out of these motives or functions.

Just semantics

What about the political animals themselves, especially the expert ones? Does
language matter to politicians? At the level of use of language, at the level, say,
of wording and phrasing, political actors themselves are equivocal. Here are two
examples.

In 1999 the UK Labour government was introducing legislation to reform the
House of Lords. Interviewed on BBC Radio 4's *Today* programme, a government spokesperson, when asked about the future composition of the second
chamber, said that it would be 'properly representative'. The interviewer observed
that she had not said 'properly democratic', to which the spokesperson replied
dismissively: 'we're talking about semantics now'. British politicians habitually
use the word *semantics* to dismiss criticism or to avoid making politically sensitive
specifications. In this instance, it was of interest to know whether 'properly
representative' meant that members of the reformed chamber would be appointed
by government to represent sectors of the population or whether the members
would be democratically elected by the population. In the linguistic sense of the
term, the *semantics* is actually politically crucial, because 'representative' may
mean 'claimed or believed to be representative by the drafters of the new
constitution' and not 'representative' in the sense of 'representative by popular

election'. Somehow, one aspect of the semantics of the term *semantics* in English makes it possible to take it for granted that people think seeking the clarification of meaning is a bad thing. We need not explore here what it is in popular English culture that can be invoked by politicians when it comes to the discussion of ideas. The point is that the interviewer's concern to clarify meaning had sufficient political significance for the politician to fend it off, and to do so by implicitly challenging the very validity of inquiry into the speaker's meaning.

Views may vary depending on political ideology. An example that illustrates the extremes is the following. In 1999, at a UK parliamentary Select Committee on Public Administration a Labour MP was questioning a certain Sir David Gore-Booth, a former British High Commissioner in India and ambassador to Saudi Arabia, about, among other things, his use of the phrases 'company wives' and 'one of yours' (i.e. 'one of your employees'). While ambassador to Saudi Arabia, Sir David had used this expression in a letter to the chief executive of British Aerospace, on the subject of a complaint made by an Aerospace employee against British consular staff, a complaint that had led to the employee's being asked to resign. The Parliamentary Ombudsman had enquired into and criticised various cases of undiplomatic language. At one end of the spectrum of attitudes towards language were two women Labour MPs (Helen Jones and Lynda Clarke) and the Labour chairman Rhodri Morgan, who regarded the expression 'company wives' as 'insulting' and 'incredibly disrespectful'. At the other extreme was Sir David himself, who retorted that the offending phrase was no worse than 'FO wives' ('Foreign Office wives') and was merely 'convenient shorthand'. For the Labour members, the phrasing mattered, presumably because it embodied social values which they did not share and which had manifestly contributed to the bad relations between the Foreign Office and a British company overseas. For Sir David (Eton educated, of an older generation, and probably old Conservative in outlook), the concentration on 'language' was 'bizarre'. He also observed that he was 'not a particularly politically correct person'.[4]

This minor example tells us several things. The different actors have different views of the significance of phrasing and wording, although the referent is constant. 'Company wives' versus, for example, 'wives of employees of the company': both have the same referent, refer to the same individuals, but the different syntax can be arguably related to different conceptualisations. For example, the noun-plus-noun construction could be said to prompt the interpretation that the wives in some sense belong to the company, or have no other independent definition. Some speakers would deny that alternative phrasing changes the meaning in any way; such speakers may or may not also deny that, for example, it matters whether wives are thought of or portrayed as company property. While some speakers are sensitive to such possibilities and integrate them with their political ideology, others do not.

In fact, Sir David's moves illustrate two commonplaces in political argumentation of a certain kind. The politician (and particular political ideology may not be relevant here), when questioned about some verbal formulation, will frequently respond with some version of the formula 'do not concentrate on words' or, as it is often put, 'this is just semantics'. A similar move involves the notion of 'political correctness'. Anyone challenging a verbal formula that can be said, when its meanings are attended to in relation to political values, to contravene certain political values, may be countered with some version of the objection 'you are just being politically correct', where 'political correctness', is expected to be taken as referring to something undesirable. Of course, since politics is partly about priorities, it may be justifiable, whatever one's political values, to claim that attention to linguistic detail in ongoing discourse is an inappropriate prioritisation. But, unless one wishes to argue that alternate referential formulations are indeed arbitrary and neutral (in which case one also has to explain why they occur at all), there may also be very good reasons to relate wording and phrasing to concepts and values. Challenging verbal formulation on such grounds is a part of doing political discourse, as is refusing to do so. Some political actors regard it as legitimate, others attempt to delegitimise it. As will be seen later in this book, legitimising and delegitimising are important functions in political discourse.

Furthermore, despite the tendency of politicians to deny tactically the significance of 'language', the importance of 'language', in the sense of differential verbal formulation, is tacitly acknowledged. Political parties and government agencies employ publicists of various kinds, whose role is not merely to control the flow of, and access to information, but also to design and monitor wordings and phrasings, and in this way to respond to challenges or potential challenges. The terms 'spin', 'put a spin on' and 'spin doctor' are terms that reflect the public belief in the existence of and significance of discourse management by hired rhetoricians. The proliferation of mass communication systems has probably simply amplified the importance of a function that is found not only in contemporary societies but in traditional societies also.

Language, languages and states

If politicians, through their very denials, suggest that wording and phrasing is important at the level of micro-interaction, what about language at the macro level? Or rather *languages*, in the sense that English and Spanish are separate languages. Many people take it for granted that the political entities we call states have their own language. This is not a state of affairs that comes about naturally, so to speak; it is deeply political (Haugen 1966).

The 'standard' language of the state is the medium for activity yielding the highest economic benefits. The role of the state in providing instruction in the prestige standard can be viewed not only as the part of the construction of nationhood and national sovereignty, but also as a part of the institution of democracy. This is so not only because the standard may provide equal potential access to economic benefits, but because the standard may be demanded (openly or tacitly, rightly or wrongly) for participation in political life. If one could not speak Greek, one would not de facto be able to participate in the deliberations of the city state. If one cannot speak French, one cannot, in the French Republic, be regarded as fully French; in the United States, the defining character of American English causes controversy about the use of Spanish. What is true of national languages is also true for literacy in modern societies. The ability to use the standard writing system is even more basic. Even with a command of the spoken standard, the range of economic opportunities open to non-literates will be highly restricted. Yet states are not linguistic monoliths.

What is a language?

We have already introduced an important distinction between *a* language (say English, French or Arabic) and language, the universal genetically transmitted ability of humans to acquire any language, and often more than one. However, even this distinction can be misleading, since it gives the impression that *a* language, let us say French, for example, is a uniform system that is spoken the same way throughout a whole territory. In fact, what are conventionally referred to as 'languages' show a great deal of internal variability across geographical and social space. Not only do different regions that speak the 'same' language show greater or lesser degrees of variation in one or more levels of language structure (pronunciation, word-forms, syntax, vocabulary), but so also do different social strata and different ethnic groups.

Furthermore, if one considers the language that people speak over a geographical area, one frequently finds one speech community shading off gradually into another, without a sudden break. Such linguistic spaces are known as 'dialect continua'. In so far as it is possible to isolate distinct dialects in the linguistic flux, one can say that dialect d_1 overlaps with dialect d_2 which overlaps with dialect d_3. Adjacent dialects are usually mutually intelligible, although speakers often perceive differences that may be exaggerated, associated with feelings of hostility and politicised. Between certain points along the chain mutual intelligibility decreases and ceases. There are well-known examples of such linguistic continua. One example is north-western Europe, where Germanic dialects merge into one another; another case is the west Romance continuum, and a third the Slavic continuum. What is significant for present purposes is that such continua override political boundaries between the historic nation states, but interact with them in complex ways.

Linguistic closeness does not necessarily imply social or political closeness. Small differences can become hugely significant from a political point of view.

In the former Yugoslavia, for example, this was certainly the case for eastern and western varieties of Serbo-Croat used in Bosnia–Hercegovina. The varieties differ in relatively minor ways, and are certainly mutually intelligible, despite the fact that one difference is salient – the use of the Cyrillic alphabet by Orthodox Serbs in the eastern regions, and the use of the Roman alphabet in the Catholic western regions. There are other differences on the level of phonology, morphology and syntax, and to some extent the vocabulary itself differs slightly. These differences are in themselves minor, but all differences are capable of being politically indexed. The differences in the Serbo-Croat dialect continuum were seized upon and politicised by nationalist movements during the violent disintegration of Yugoslavia that began in 1991. Previously, under the structures of Tito's communist state, there had been a pluralistic mixture and alternation of linguistic forms in educational institutions and in the media in Bosnia–Hercegovina, but different nationalist discourses emphasised eastern or western variants, or words of Turkish origin, according to their perceived ethnic or religious allegiance (Levinger 1998; Carmichael 2002). Linguistic 'cleansing', went along with 'ethnic cleansing'. This example is a clear case of linguistic difference being selected in a particular political situation for particular political ends formulated by an elite, specifically to create identity through difference. It shows that the process of codifying differences that occur 'naturally', through social and geographical differentiation that have little to do with the politics of states, can contribute to the production of structures maintaining violence and warfare. Another such case is that of the form of Rumanian spoken in the former Soviet republic of Moldavia, now known as Moldova. From 1945 the Cyrillic writing system was administratively imposed in order to distance 'Moldavian' from Rumanian, and local linguistic variants were codified into the descriptions – actually, prescriptions – of the standard (Trudgill 1999: 176).

Relatively small linguistic differences can be exploited in politically different ways. Blommaert and Verschueren (1998: 135–8) contrast and compare the Belgium situation with that of the Balkans in the 1990s. The situation is similar only in so far as the close varieties of the same language are involved. In the Balkans Serbia, Croatia and Bosnia-Herzegovina use varieties that are mutually intelligible, varying only in some pronunciations, word-forms and syntactic structures. In Belgium, there is a similar relationship between the Dutch spoken in the northern part of the country, Flanders, and the Dutch spoken in the neighbouring Netherlands. The major linguistic division of Belgium is between the Dutch-speaking north and the French-speaking south (Wallonia), while there is a bilingual enclave in the north constituted by Brussels. The significant contrast between the Belgian situation and that of the Balkans lies in the fact that in the Balkans nationalist ideologies have led to the magnification of linguistic variants and to claims that close varieties are separate 'languages', while in Flanders the political argument has been the reverse – Flemish nationalists seek to emphasise the similarities between Flemish varieties and standard Dutch.

The role of language in the construction of states, though variable, is more crucial than many historians and political scientists are wont to acknowledge (but see Deutsch 1953; Anderson 1991; Hobsbawm 1990; Barbour and Carmichael 2000; Wright 1996 and 2000). There have been many periods of history when linguistic borders – and such borders, as we have noted, are generally not distinct lines – have not at all coincided with the borders of government. For Europe, one can make the generalisation that a language became criterial for ethnic and political identity only through discourse processes that occurred in the nineteenth century. That is to say, there emerged among literary elites in different countries talk and texts which promoted the notion that linguistic identity was essential to political identity. There were different forms of this kind of thinking, both supporting linguistic centralisation and the suppression of minority languages. Intellectuals of German Romanticism such as Herder and Fichte, expressed a quasi-mystical bond between language and social belonging, between the *Volk* and the *Volksprache*.

A somewhat different case is that of France, a unitary state in the making since the sixteenth century that had remained multilingual until the eve of the 1789 Revolution. It is worth recalling how a multilingual situation can become monolithic. Perhaps only 50 per cent of the population inhabiting territorial France in the eighteenth century spoke anything close to the standard of the court that had been codified by the Académie Française, although many of the non-standard French speakers spoke closely related Romance variants. The remainder spoke distinct languages: Breton, regarded as particularly threatening by the Revolutionaries because Brittany was a conservative feudalist region, and German, regarded as representing alien political entities. The language policy of the French Revolution was not inconsistent with already existing centralising linguistic tendencies, but inscribed itself as part of a democratic–revolutionary programme aimed to root out reaction and deliver equality of citizenship. The *Comité du salut public* deputed Bertrand Barrère, who supported the Terror of 1793–4, to report on the linguistic state of the nation, which he did in February 1793. The abbé Grégoire – a constitutional revolution-supporting cleric – had already been charged in 1790 to prepare a similar report based on a national questionnaire, and his report was returned in June 1794 to the National Convention. Grégoire's famous document was entitled 'On the Necessity and the Means of Annihilating the *Patois* and Universalising the Use of the French Language'.[5] This was not transitory revolutionary madness; the policy was effected over a long period of time and different constitutions through educational policy, curriculum planning, media control and legislation on linguistic 'correctness' that continued throughout the twentieth century.

These details give some indication of the explicit and deliberate way in which regimes can approach language policy. In the early nineteenth century we have the cultural avant-garde in German-speaking territories lending legitimacy to the notion of a monolingual nation state, arguing that there is an essential *natural* and *organic* bond between national, ethnic and linguistic identity. This is an ethno-linguistic or ethno-cultural view of nationhood (Brubaker 1999: 113–14) that subsequently united with an ethno-territorial conception and the construction of the German Reich in 1870–1. In the case of France we have a revolutionary bur-eaucratised ideology partly arguing in instrumental terms for national linguistic unity on the grounds of democratisation, but also partly inspired by a rationalist ideology and belief that the French language was inherently more rational *qua* symbolic system than other languages. In England the same general tendency towards linguistic unification and purism was not the less powerful for being less obviously enshrined in the organs of the state.

Implications for political philosophy

The existence of a social group speaking a language different from the language of the majority, or different from the official language of the state, or in a variety of the majority or official language that is perceived as significantly deviant, gives rise to questions of minority rights in political theory. Ronald Dworkin proposed two fundamental inalienable rights of citizens: the right to be treated equally and the right of citizens to have their human dignity respected (Dworkin 1977). The right to life, liberty, property and the pursuit of happiness is not absolute in this philosophical framework. Equality and human dignity are prior, though Dworkin argues for specific liberties such as the right to free expression. All we need to note here is that the general principles (equality and human dignity) make speaking the language of one's social group at least a very good candidate to be a human right.

The debate about which minority groups have (or should be recognised as having) particular rights is complex and controversial. One problem identified by political scientists is how to circumscribe a minority group. Some groups (e.g. women, widows, mothers, senior citizens) have or can be given clear legal definitions. Cultural groups on the other hand are said to be more difficult to define. One solution is to regard all rights as essentially individual rights. Members of both sorts of groups thus have rights. But what sort of rights? The notion of 'positive rights' makes it feasible to say that individuals have rights to, for example, family allowances or pensions in the clear-cut groups. What rights might be claimed by minority cultural groups? As Birch (1993) notes, the claim is usually for special protection of language and culture. Several conundrums arise from putting the matter in this way. One of them – the argument that 'language and cultures are not right-bearing entities' (Birch 1993: 126) – can be easily disposed of. The issue does not have to be stated in the form of a sentence such as 'languages and cultures have rights'. Languages and cultures are not entities. It can be formulated, as above, in the sentence: 'individuals have the right to speak the language of the social group with which they primarily identify', in which case the problem returns to the domain of individual rights, and arguably to the domain of the right to free expression. Two other problems are less soluble. Should the taxpayers of a polity be required to pay for the protection of a minority language? Should a minority language be protected when parents who speak it want their children to learn the majority language?

The answers to these questions require more argument. Birch, who raises them, seeks to clear the ground by distinguishing between four different types of right claimed by cultural minorities. First, the 'right to be in' confers the right of individuals belonging to groups that do not speak the majority or official language to receive instruction in that language, as a precondition for economic rights. Alternatively, it can lead to the right to speak one's language in the work-place and as part of the work process, as has happened in the case of Canada for French speakers. Such situations can lead to arguments about 'affirmative action' and 'positive discrimination'. Should French speakers be favoured as against English speakers, especially if qualifications are not equal? Such language cases are analogous to contentious cases concerning discrimination in favour of blacks claimed to have inferior qualifications.

Birch's second and third categories, the 'right to be out' and the 'right to stay out', concern the right of cultural minorities to retain cultural identity, however that is defined. A non-linguistic example is the celebrated 1989 case of the *foulards islamiques* (Islamic headscarves) in France, which brought claims to traditional dress code into conflict with principles of the secular state. The affair, which led to a wide and protracted media debate involving France's intellectual personalities, involved three Muslim schoolgirls whose wearing of traditional scarves was deemed to be an infringement of school rules and French law, in particular the constitutional principle that education is secular. If the issue of headscarves is replaced by that of languages, the problems for political theorists are even more contentious, as Birch's discussion shows. Suppose, for example, that some cultural minority wants support for the maintenance of a bilingual system. Birch argues as follows:

> It is clear that bilingualism is not a natural state of affairs and that if two languages are spoken in a given area the stronger of them will normally drive out the weaker. A weaker language cannot be expected to survive over a long period unless it receives government help.
>
> (Birch 1993: 129)

There are several misconceptions here. What does it mean to say bilingualism is 'not a natural state of affairs'? It is certainly not unnatural for the human brain:

individuals grow up as natural bilinguals in many regions of the world. To say that it is not natural for societies or polities is to beg some very serious questions of political philosophy. Nor can languages seriously be conceived as individuals, more or less 'strong', in a state of nature characterised by the survival of the fittest. Moreover, to say that a language cannot 'survive' without government help makes precisely the point that we made above in discussing the role of language in the emergence of states. The term 'a language' cannot be taken for granted; a language, such as French or German or Japanese, is the product of a political process in which that language is defined, codified and promoted – in short, given 'government help'. 'Strong' languages are the ones that have been bound up in the state's production of itself.

To ask whether languages have rights can easily lead to the conclusion that the political discourse of rights is simply inappropriate – that, for example, because motives and goals are diverse among individuals, it is impossible to identify a group claim to minority cultural rights to language protection. The problem arises because of the confusion of individual and group perspectives. A language is clearly a group phenomenon; but the discourse of rights is generally couched in terms of the individual. Instead of personifying languages, the question could be formulated as follows: Do individuals have the right not to have a language imposed upon them which they do not wish to speak?

This may seem to be simply a negative reformulation of 'Do individuals have a right to speak their own language?' In fact, however, the negative formulation avoids the pitfalls of the first formulation. It is based on the individual rather than the group. It allows for individuals who do not want to continue to speak a minority language, and for the numerical decline that may arise from such individual choices. The issue of assuming rights for collective entities does not arise; a language as such, cannot have rights, only the individuals who speak it. Although the formulation is syntactically negative, it can be seen as equivalent to other concepts in rights discourse that have to do with 'freedom from'. This perspective also puts in question the legitimacy of the imposition of a particular language by groups and polities on their members or citizens.

So what next?

We have moved rapidly from Aristotle to the modern period, from micro aspects of political intercourse to macro aspects of languages in states. At every stage we have seen that politics comes up against questions of language, and that these questions range from the choice of words to the choice of language – in other words, from fine detail of phrasing and wording to large-scale issues of national language policy. Political actors recognise the role of language because its use has effects, and because politics *is* very largely the use of language, even if the converse is not true – not every use of language is political. The point has been to try to convince you that language is important for political life and that it is worth spending time looking more closely at language from this perspective. In this book we cannot, however, look at *all* aspects. Languages (in the plural) are implicated in politics, as we have seen. But for the rest of this book we focus on language. How do we use its complexities, fluidities and rigidities in doing what we call 'politics'? One final caveat: we are approaching these questions in English, and with a necessarily limited collection of English-language examples.

2 Language and politics

In the last chapter we illustrated the kinds of complexities – political complexities – that attend everyday references to 'languages' or 'a language'. Up to now we have not defined the broader sense of the word 'language', or what in the Aristotle quotations is referred to as 'speech'. We also introduced another everyday notion – the *use* of language in politics, suggesting that political actors themselves are well aware of the importance of how language is used even in the act of denying the fact. What the present chapter aims to do is twofold – first to consider further the nature of *language* (we will sometimes refer to it as *language$_L$*, for clarity) and second to consider ways in which its *use* can be meaningfully studied in relation to what we call politics. Throughout this discussion, then, it is important to distinguish the human capacity for language (language$_L$) from *a* particular language (which we will call *language$_l$*), such as Dyirbal, Chinese or French, and from *use* of a language (*language$_{l/u}$*), which we shall often refer to as 'discourse'.

The co-evolution of language and politics?

If it is granted that language is an innate organ of the human mind/brain, we can ask how it evolved, and whether this casts any light on how we might think about possible links between language, society and politics. There are two views as to how this 'language organ' has arisen. Both views have consequences for thinking about the relationship between language and politics. Speculation about the origins of language was banned by the Paris Linguistics Society in 1866, so wild and ill-founded had it become, just six years after the publication of *The Origin of Species*. However, the present re-emergence of Darwinian evolutionary theory, and new computational, archaeological, neurological and philosophical methods of investigation, have given rise to renewed and more rigorous enquiry into how language evolved in homo sapiens (see for example, Bickerton 1990; Hurford *et al.* 1998; Jackendoff 2002: 231–64). While the debate remains very much open, two clear lines of thought have been established, and both have implications for thinking about the relationship between language and politics.

According to the first line of thought, language evolved from an arbitrary genetic mutation that was beneficial to evolving humans. It does not build on prior properties of emerging human brains, but is an entirely novel and species-specific ability. This is the position apparently taken by Chomsky (e.g. Chomsky 1975, 2000). What are the implications of such a view for question of the relationship between language and political behaviour? It is possible to sketch possible conceptual links between this view of the evolution of language and important ideas that are familiar in the tradition of political thought. If this version of the emergence of a language$_L$ ability in the human brain were correct, language would have no direct genetic or neurological link with social grouping or social manipulation. It would be a free-standing ability, not predictable from human social behaviour, uninfluenced by it. We could then think of it as generative and creative in a very wide sense; we could go further and say that it is reminiscent of ideas about human autonomy and freedom. Presumably, similarly independent modules of the mind would co-exist alongside language$_L$. One would then have to ask what relationships could exist, in a functioning mind, in a real social context, between the language module and, say, a social intelligence module. We return to issues of language and freedom below.

According to the second current of thought, language did evolve from existing structures in the primate brain. More specifically, it is social intelligence that provides the basis for language (e.g. Humphrey 1976). Social intelligence itself is taken to be a specialised 'module' of the early human brain. Unsurprisingly, there are variants of the theory that language emerged out of social intelligence. One school of thought maintains that there is plenty of evidence to suggest that language evolved for specifically social purposes.[1] It replaced grooming (which chimpanzees, and other animals still do, of course), which itself has a primarily social function, because who is seen to be grooming whom, and for how long, signals social relations, coalitions and hierarchies. Though anthropologists call it 'social', it is a short step to seeing it as 'political', or proto-political (Dunbar 1993; Mithen 1996).

Another approach, which we will now explore in more detail, starts with the assumption that early human individuals would be 'machiavellian' in all behaviours (i.e., seek strategies of maximum individual advantage), including communicative behaviours.[2] There is a prima facie problem with this kind of view of the evolution of linguistic communication. If human behaviour is indeed fundamentally machiavellian, and if communication involves sharing information, then why would it be advantageous for early humans to wish to share information any more than to wish to share food? The answer given by proponents of this kind of perspective is twofold. On the one hand, the answer may be given that Darwinian inductive reasoning can explain the apparent contradiction in terms of 'reciprocal altruism' – that is to say, it can be argued that individual interest can be maximised by the *strategic* sharing of information, and would be selected in evolution, though precisely when and how has not been explained. On the other hand, it may be argued, and this argument is partly linked to the previous one, that language is not only about sharing information but is also to do with signalling *group identities*. If a group of us code and share information in our own language, people outside the group cannot get the information, and, as an extra benefit, we all know who is in the group and who isn't. Some accounts argue that group ritual is at the origin of the sort of reciprocal altruism that is needed if individuals are going to be willing to share information. Others emphasise the emergence of 'mind reading' abilities in primates – that is, the ability to infer other individuals' plans and goals (see Humphrey 1976; Hurford *et al.* 1998). If you can guess other individuals' intentions, then machiavellian intelligence can make counter plans, though this in itself does not explain the emergence of language.

So, we can say that in reciprocal altruism individuals behave in a machiavellian way to get maximum individual benefit, and the group becomes selfish or machiavellian as a collective system. Is machiavellian and individual advantage the *only* sort of altruism humans have? Perhaps, but it is perhaps also capable of detaching itself to become a free-wheeling ethical ideal – a line of thinking that we can't pursue here. What we do have to pursue is the question *how* exactly, assuming that reciprocal altruism existed, could that fact favour the evolution of human language? Why should language, given this basis, afford an evolutionary advantage?

Part of the answer to these questions lies in *representation* and *meta-representation*. It also lies in replacing the notion of reciprocal altruism with that of *cooperation* – a move that has the effect of making us focus on a crucial aspect, working together for individual gain. Animals have the ability to *represent* things, happenings, actions, etc., whether they are aware of them or not. Humans have the ability to *meta*-represent things (Sperber 2000). What is important is that humans can generate *detached* representations of things as well as *cued* representations, while animals most likely generate only cued ones (Gärdenfors 2002). Cued representations take place in a physical situation where there is or has just been a stimulus, but detached ones can occur in the human mind without a co-present stimulus – what Gärdenfors calls 'inner worlds'. If you can simulate the outer world by inner worlds, you are an animal with an advantage, because you can map places, objects and predators, and you can make plans for future actions, e.g. by choosing between alternative simulations. It seems that the only animal that can do this is the human. Where does language come into the picture? Language is, as Hockett pointed out, a system that among other things provides symbols which are *detached* from their referents (Hockett 1960). Language makes it possible to communicate about things past, future, possible and impossible, permissible and impermissible – from the point of view, that is, of some speaker or group of speakers. These are important dimensions, as will be seen throughout this book.

Let us now see how this ability is intrinsically entwined with what we would intuitively call 'politics'. Humans show a vastly evolved ability to plan for future cooperative group action. Even if some humans are machiavellian, they can only be machiavellian if they have common cooperative activity to work on. The main point, however, is that planning for future cooperative goals can surely only be possible if there is a medium of communication that can be detached from immediate contextual referents.[3] Individuals thus have a capacity to communicate, compare, align or dissent from one another's mental representations of the present, future and possible worlds. Evaluations of representations can be assigned and agreed upon, or not agreed upon. In Gärdenfors's words, 'language makes it possible for us to *share visions*' (Gärdenfors 2002: 5, his italics), by which he means, for example, that

> the chief of a village can try to convince the inhabitants that they should co-operate in digging a common well that everyone will benefit from or in building a defensive wall that will increase the security of everybody.

Or the goals may be more nebulous:

> An eloquent leader can depict enticing goals and convince the supporters to make radical sacrifices, even though the visionary goals are extremely uncertain.

(Gärdenfors 2002: 5)

Both examples suggest forms of human action that could be called 'politics'. There is presumably a strong evolutionary advantage in being able to plan cooperative action to achieve goals detached from immediate stimuli. This can plausibly only be achieved in and through a system of symbolic communication that has properties such as those of human language. If so, Gärdenfors's argument provides an argument for the co-evolution of language and politics – which is not to say that language was not also evolving for other adaptive advantages at the same time.

Communication as cooperation

This evolutionary story of language and politics brings to mind key ideas that have arisen in the study of the language and communication of modern humans in modern societies. In particular, Grice's influential argument that a 'co-operative Principle' (CP) must underlie human communication looks as if it ought to be consistent with this paradigm (Grice 1975, 1989). However, theoretical debate surrounding the Gricean approach means that we need to make some qualifications.

Communicative cooperation: a minimalist view

Grice's formulation of cooperation has caused controversy because, on the face of it, a lot of human talk is either apparently aimless, i.e. has no coordinated purpose as in chat and banter, or else it seems completely uncooperative, as in quarrelling, browbeating, lying, and the like. So it is necessary to try to be clear what we mean here by 'cooperative principle'. What I mean here by 'cooperative principle' is that whenever humans linguistically communicate they do so on the basis of a tacit assumption that each will cooperate with others to exchange meanings. We might call this the minimalist interpretation of Grice's cooperative principle. Without this kind of minimal, primary cooperation quarrelling, browbeating or lying are not even possible. It is helpful to set aside the connection with Grice's 'conversational maxims', which we can interpret as ways of conducting rational talk-exchanges at a *secondary* level of cooperation, where particular kinds of talk-exchange (e.g. weather reports as distinct from selling a second-hand car, etc.) are defined by specific variants of the maxims.

Sperber and Wilson (1986: 161f.), who have criticised Grice, seem to have the same sort of thing in mind when they say that 'the only purpose that a genuine communicator and a willing audience have in common is to achieve successful communication'. They think this underlying cooperative agreement is not very interesting or significant. However, I would want to say that in some respects it is the most crucial point of all. This becomes clear if one bears in mind what we have said earlier about reciprocal altruism, which is simply cooperation driven by self-interest. The existence of altruism cannot be explained (in an evolutionary framework), unless it is reciprocal, but it is necessary to postulate that humans do in fact have this mode of behaviour. Grice's cooperative principle is reciprocal altruism in the domain of linguistic communication. It has to be postulated in order to get communication off the ground, against the objection that revealing information through language would have no survival benefit for the individual. Humans cannot help communicating, apparently: the cooperative principle seems to be innate. Communicators expect to receive benefit in return, and do; communication is not naturally one way. So cooperation is fundamental, although there is more to the story as we shall see below.

Of course, saying that humans cooperate in communicating, or communicatively cooperate, does not mean that individuals cannot still be machiavellian in communication. Grice himself, in his reassessment of his earlier work, makes the point that 'collaboration in achieving exchange of information or the institution of decisions may coexist with a high degree of reserve, hostility, and chicanery' (Grice 1989: 369). The point he does not quite make is the one I am emphasising here: that it is impossible to lie or be devious *unless* the group makes a collective assumption about communicative cooperation. One cannot lie if everyone believes all the time that all communication is mendacious. Such a view of the evolution of language is consistent with a view of social and political life in which cooperation and exploitation go hand in hand.

Language use and politics are both cooperative and uncooperative. Moreover, one might argue that the structure of human linguistic communication is related to precisely these functions: it makes what we recognise as 'political' inter-actions possible. One should in this sort of perspective expect some of the structural components of language to have a functional role. It should be possible to see a connection between what we can interpret as political discourse and the use of particular features of language. However, it would be foolish to argue that *all* language use is political, though one might do so if a sufficiently broad definition of the term 'political' were adopted. Certainly, not all linguistic structures need have a socio-political function, but when we examine recognis-ably 'political' discourse, we shall repeatedly encounter certain uses of certain linguistic structures. There is no need to assume that the structures of language have to be inherently and necessarily political. This is not to say that such structures, particularly in their semantic aspects, did not first evolve from socio-political needs – for instance, deictic systems that signal self or self's group as distinct from non-group member. Other structures of language, for example thematic roles like 'agent' and 'affected', could also be seen as having social-cognitive origins, while the abstract computational systems of syntax (e.g. 'move alpha', 'c-command' in generative theories), with which such structures interact, need have no grounding in social, or political, functions at all.

Truthfulness and the checking of cheaters

The account minimal communicative cooperation that we have just roughly sketched has a sequel. According to Grice, truthfulness (the 'maxim of quality') is assumed under the cooperative principle. Wilson and Sperber (e.g. 1986, 2002) argue, contrary to Grice, that the fundamental convention, norm or assumption in linguistic communication is not truthfulness but relevance. The latter is defined as individuals getting the best cognitive return on the effort they put into processing linguistic material. Both cognitive effect and processing effort can be interpreted in terms of the circumstances, interests and desire of the moment – which means that the theory could have something to tell us about political language behaviour. We shall return to the cooperative principle in Chapter 3, but for now we shall just note the following point regarding truthfulness in human communication.

Humans do not, or do not *have to* process incoming messages as already true or real. Sperber (2000: 135f.), takes up Cosmides and Tooby's (1989) argu-ment (developing Axelrod's (1984) argument about the logical structure of human cooperation) that the human mind possesses an innate 'cheater detection' ability. Sperber goes one step further: humans, he hypothesises, also have a 'logico–rhetorical' module which checks for consistency and for deceptive manipulation in communication. Consistency here means self-consistency, that is, the internal logical consistency of an incoming representation, and also consistency of the incoming representation with the receiving mind's own existing representations. The argument for the existence of logical checking and cheater checking abilities rests on reciprocal altruism: it is worth giving information to others because I can get information in return, and we all benefit. But, so the argument goes, the risk of deception and manipulation remains, and social exchange, social contracts, social cooperation could not develop. So humans have acquired a natural back-up – the ability to detect exploiters and deceivers. As Sperber puts it, the importance of linguistic communication in human social groups must have led to a logic of persuasion–counter-persuasion – a kind of spiralling communicative 'arms race'.[4]

If this is the case, then in one sense truthfulness has not in fact gone away; it is still there as the ground rule, only supplemented and enabled by the parallel checking modules and the ability to meta-represent. Communication is useful to individuals in a group; it is useful to be able to take what you are told as representing what is real (useful, harmful, right, wrong, as Aristotle might have put it), but you do need to be able to check to be sure. Humans have, if the claims are correct, acquired a natural ability to do such checking.

An interesting aspect of this ability is *meta-representation*, a species-specific ability. The ability to meta-represent means that humans can decouple representations of the world from any inherent truth claim they may have. For instance, 'propositional attitude' markers suspend truth, reference and existence: contrast 'P is the case' with 'Jill *thinks* that P is the case', 'Jill *heard* that P is the case', 'Jill *hopes* that P is the case', etc. Natural language clearly has the structural and semantic capacity for meta-representation. One reason why this potential exists could be that the ability to meta-represent constitutes a significant part of our ability to detect communicative deception. This idea helps to elaborate the point made by Gärdenfors, which we summarised above. It is also useful to see meta-representation in relation to evidential expressions – the presentation in language of sources, evidence or authority for the truth of a representation. Thus Cosmides (2000: 70) thinks that 'source-tagging' must have been important in the evolution of communication as a guard against deception or error, and meta-representation can be seen, precisely, as a kind of source-tagging. Of course, the source can either increase or decrease the credibility of the embedded proposition, and this is a matter that becomes significant when we enter the realm of the political, because it has to do with what is called 'credibility'. Consider, for instance, the different degrees of truthfulness that different people from different backgrounds might attribute to expressions such as: '*The Times* says that *p*', 'the *Sun* says that *p*', 'the President of France says that *p*', 'the Bible says that *p*' or 'the *British Medical Journal* says that *p*'.

Language and representation

To repeat in other terms what we said above about cooperation, humans expect linguistic communication to be both truthful and untruthful. Veracity and mendacity are somehow intertwined: the one in some form implies or presupposes the other. We have arrived at this conclusion by asking: 'why would the human genome have selected for language in the first place?' We can do no more than make reasoned guesses but one answer has to be that it is advantageous for survival to give and receive information about the environment which the communicator believes to be accurate and which does indeed turn out to be objectively accurate enough to be advantageous. So far, so good. But the *expectation* of truthful communicative behaviour, and thus the receiving of reasonably accurate and useful information about the social and physical environment, make it possible for individuals to deceive or distort. This we expect already from even the non-linguistic behaviour of primates: they are sometimes machiavellian, and so are their human descendants. The point is that the sequence, in evolution and in logic, has to be this way round: the expectation of truthfulness has to precede the possibility of deception. In evolution it is obviously advantageous for an organism to get and transmit accurate information, but it is not so obvious that it is advantageous to develop a highly complex and dedicated system of communication specifically for deception. In all logic, I cannot arrive at the conclusion that you are deceiving me unless I want and expect that you will be telling the truth. At least most of the time, for if I believe you are *always* deceiving me the concept of 'deception' makes no sense, since there can be no expectation of truth-telling to contrast it with. Such a fundamental expectation of truth is consistent with the way perception works. The world that one perceives (and constructively conceives) is taken to be prima facie accurate. Sure, appearances can be deceptive, but we have to meta-represent that assertion and code it as a monitory dictum in social intercourse.

We shall see throughout this book that political discourse involves, among other things, the promotion of representations, and a pervasive feature of representation is the evident need for political speakers to imbue their utterances with evidence, authority and truth, a process that we shall refer to in broad terms, in the context of political discourse, as 'legitimisation'. Political speakers have to guard against the operation of their audience's 'cheater detectors' and provide guarantees for the truth of their sayings.

Language and freedom

Noam Chomsky's impact on twentieth-century linguistics is well known, and in the domain of politics his radical critique of American foreign policy is equally well known (e.g. Chomsky 1969, 1972, 1973, 1989, 1999; Chomsky and Herman

1988). To many people any connections between Chomsky's political ideas and actions and his linguistic theories is absent or invisible (Salkie 1990). There is relatively little in Chomsky's successive theoretical writings that can be directly applied to the study of discourse in, for instance, the 'critical discourse' school. This seems curious to some, because the critical analysis of discourse has its roots in Marxism and Chomsky is generally seen as on the left of the political spectrum.

However, there are links, albeit at an abstract level. They are important links, ones that are instructive for a general exploration of the relationship between language and politics. The common ground between Chomsky's linguistics and his politics becomes clear when one notes that his political philosophy is essentially a form of anarchism.[5] Putting the matter at its most general, anarchist political thought views humans as rational individuals, capable of governing themselves without authority. Chomsky's rationalism is well known: language is viewed as a form of innate knowledge, alongside other forms of innate knowledge, or knowledge schemata (see, among other writings, Chomsky 1966, 1968). Further, anarchistic politics asserts freedom as a basic value: individuals are free to join or not to join in social combination, without constraint from social authorities. This core concept is present in at least two crucial aspects of Chomsky's linguistics – aspects that Chomsky has repeatedly defended in such a way that a space is always preserved for a compatibility with anarchist principles.

First, the bedrock of Chomsky's linguistic theories, whatever their theoretical mutations have been, is the principle of generative creativity. The human language ability, and the uniqueness of the design of human language when contrasted with other systems in the biological sphere, is that in a human language indefinitely many different well-formed sentences of that language can be generated given only a finite set of principles and rules. This capacity is innate to individuals, and universal for all humans. Two political or ethical principles are embodied here: the generative creativity of language is a form of freedom, and all humans are in this respect, a rather fundamental and serious respect, equal.

Second, Chomsky preserves the anarchist principle within his linguistics in another but related way. Empiricists have always objected to Chomsky's rationalism, or even suggested that his philosophy is Platonist. A key claim in this complaint is that language self-evidently has communication as its function, and that Chomsky's linguistics does nothing to relate language structure to language function. Given Chomsky's radical critique of the mass media, of government and commercial propaganda, given his admiration too for George Orwell's writing, it might seem perverse that he does not view language as part and parcel of socio-political processes. However, his position is understandable and consistent. Chomsky has repeatedly insisted that language does not just have communication as its function. For example:

communication is only one function of language, and by no means an essential one. The 'instrumental' analysis of language as a device for achieving some end is seriously inadequate, and the 'language games' that have been produced to illuminate this function are correspondingly misleading. In contemplation, inquiry, normal social interchange, planning and guiding one's own actions, creative writing, honest self-expression, and numerous other activities with language, expressions are used with their strict linguistic meaning irrespective of the intentions of the 'utterer' with regard to an audience; and even in the cases that the communication theorist regards as central, the implicit reference to 'rules' and 'conventions' . . . seems to beg the major questions . . .

(1975: 69)

The response to these points from functionalists would be that too much is taken for granted. One might, for instance, argue, that even in 'private' language, social models of communicative function, along with their 'rules' and 'conventions', could well still be operative. But what Chomsky is saying here makes sense nonetheless, if one bears in mind the anarchist impulse to remain free of social (socio-political) constraint. If individual freedom is the fundamental principle, then individuals must have freedom of thought. Taking this further, freedom of thought must involve freedom to use cognitive representations without constraint. This does not necessarily mean that Chomsky, in the above passage, is equating language and thought, but language is one major part of human cognitive processes. The crucial point is that Chomsky is claiming that language is used by humans for activities that are not primarily communicative. Here I assume 'communicative' means communicative according to the conventions of some social group. In this respect, he is in accord with Bertrand Russell, who also never went with the trend in the philosophy of language which favoured the later Wittgenstein's focus on socially embedded language games. In general, Chomsky, in viewing language as a genetically transmitted component of the human brain (and also an accident of, rather than a functional product of evolution), views language as free of social and political constraint. It should be clear, however, that this does not invalidate the notion that use of language, and the manifestation of language$_L$ as a language$_l$, is intrinsic in the social and the political.

In the last section I gave the arguments for thinking that language and the political might have an intimate connection, in fact that human sociality and human language might have co-evolved. In this section, I have presented an account that keeps language$_l$ separate from social behaviour, and presumably from any mental faculties related to it. It is not necessary to decide between these two views in the present context and for present purposes. One can make the two complementary, or integrate elements from both. Take the view that language and political nous co-evolved. We have seen that deception detection and meta-representation have to be postulated as an intrinsic part of such co-evolution. If this is accepted, then we also get a guarantee that humans are not constrained by the linkage between language and social behaviour, for meta-representation provides decoupling, and space for critical distance. Further, meta-representation seems closely linked to syntactic recursivity, a central design feature in the Chomskian view of syntax. If recursivity related to creativity, then creativity is, one could argue, related to critique. In any case, once the potential for generative recursion exists, for whatever the evolutionary adaptive reason, it can cut loose from its 'proper', or original, domain, as Sperber (1994) argues for mental modules in general. Thus we could view language as having closely co-evolved with socio-political behaviour, developing the capacity for recursive meta-representation, but becoming available in other quite different domains.

Language and unfreedom

But many people have felt, and have argued that somehow 'language' did not give freedom but was a prison house. There are some versions of this idea that we do not need to spend time on – for instance, those that don't say what is meant by 'language', like the last sentence. But one should perhaps not dismiss the question completely as Pinker (1994: 59–64) does. The question is: can a language$_l$ (say, Hopi, Spanish or Urdu) influence or even determine the way their speakers think and act? The assumption that they can is, of course, contained in what is known as the Sapir–Whorf hypothesis – the claim drawn from the writings of Edward Sapir (1970) and Benjamin Lee Whorf (1973) that the formal characteristics of a language govern the kinds of conceptions of the world that its speakers have. Another version of this line of argument, and a more plausible one, is that it is language$_{l/u}$, i.e. the *use* of a language$_l$, or discourse, especially in a repeatable, institutionalised form, that governs the way people think, or perhaps rather the meanings that are least effortfully exchanged (Lucy 1996).

The classic approach to the Sapir–Whorf hypothesis is interested in morphological structures, and whether different sets and arrangements of morphemes in different languages are isomorphic with different sets and arrangements of thoughts. However we do not have to view the morphological elements of a language as a static set of constraints that determine, or influence perception, cognition and behaviour. Rather, we might think in terms of a 'relative relativity' which is pragmatic in nature, or realised through language in use, through discourse. The grammatical and lexical resources of a language$_l$ are, to use Verschueren's (1999: 180) expression, 'put to work' at the level of linguistic interaction among individual human utterers and interpreters, where language practices of various kinds are elaborated and sometimes institutionalised. Looked at in this way, it is patterns of *language-in-use*, language *practices*, that might be said to play a role, through processes of socialisation, in establishing conceptual frameworks. The idea is that people would exchange certain kinds of conceptualisation more frequently (in association with certain kinds of affect, too, perhaps) because of a social and political nexus of interaction. Such conceptualisations would have language as their vehicle; they would not be *caused* by the language. They could be said to be facilitated by social and political practices in language use; even then, nobody is absolutely bound by such uses, and the issue becomes a political or ethical one.

There is another way one can view the problem. Even if one maintains that the structure of a language, or different discourses in the same or in different languages, might constrain their speakers, yet *in principle at least* they do not, since paraphrase, so it may be argued, can always yield alternative or new conceptual constructs. This argument is also an argument for the principle of cognitive freedom, and since we are talking here of *linguistic* knowledge, there is a compatibility with the Chomskian position – since it is precisely the generative creativity of language that makes it possible to overcome any supposed Whorfian constraint. Orwell's nightmare of a totalitarian, necessarily thought-constraining language, what he calls 'newspeak' in the novel *Nineteen Eighty-Four*, remains that – a nightmare not a serious possibility in linguistic or in psychological terms.

Nevertheless, Orwell may have had a point, if we interpret him in the following way. There are perhaps conditions in which we could speak of an Orwellian *effect* being produced. Above, I used the phrase 'in principle', and I did so because humans do not always, or are not always able, to resist the constraints of social conventions or political ideologies for the use of language, the ready-made moulds for the thinking of thoughts. What is important, is that *in principle* it is possible to use language creatively, independently of socio-political and linguistic constraint.

The ideal of free communication

There is a further domain of thinking about language, in this case specifically about language and society, that involves a similarly idealised 'in principle' kind of argumentation. It comes not from linguistics but from the social theorist Jürgen Habermas (1971, 1973, 1979, 1981). It is valuable to consider this kind of thinking here by way of conclusion to this chapter, since it has been often mentioned by analysts with a commitment to the politically oriented analysis of discourse (e.g. Fairclough 1989; Wodak 1996).

Let us approach the matter by way of Chomsky's suggestive reflections on language and freedom. In the quotation given in the previous section, Chomsky refers intriguingly to 'normal social interchange' and 'honest self-expression'. What might we take such modes of language use to be? Surely, these sorts of language$_{l/u}$ activity, so Chomsky's critics might argue, are despite appearances to the contrary subject to social and political control? To suppose the existence of such activities, the argument might run, is a form of self-deceiving idealism. Moreover, what is meant by 'expressions used in their strict linguistic meaning'? Can expressions be used, even in the privacy of one's own head, 'irrespective of the intentions of the "utterer" with regard to an audience'?. In any case, are 'linguistic meanings', strict or otherwise, ever undetermined by the social convention? These questions have considerable force. What is interesting, however, is that such charges are also often levelled at Habermas's type of language philosophy, since it too operates with an idealised 'in principle' yardstick. Habermas himself speaks of 'universal pragmatics', while Chomsky speaks of 'universal grammar'.

There are intriguing similarities here that are not often mentioned. First, there is a common ground in a form of philosophical rationalism, and in the insistence on universal individual freedom. These themes are found in both thinkers and in both have anarchist foundations. Second, Habermas posits precisely the ideal of free use of language in society apparently adumbrated by Chomsky in the passage we quoted. Habermas argues that communication is skewed by interests, and gauges this actual state of affairs against the abstract criterion of what he calls the 'ideal speech situation'. There is no need to accuse Habermas (or, *mutatis mutandis*, Chomsky) of utopianism: the point is that the 'ideal speech situation', in which individuals are able to engage in what could be termed 'normal social interchange' or 'honest self-expression', is not supposed to exist in actuality, but be achievable only in principle. This can mean two possibilities: (a) it can be claimed that it is sometimes achieved locally in specific situations, in, for example, certain kinds of social group or association; (b) it is a universally acknowledged principle, a kind of ethical principle or criterion underlying all communication, that makes it possible to discern distorted communication, that is, communication distorted by power and interests. The Habermasian perspective thus seems to have something in common also with the themes of truthfulness cooperation and cheater detection that we have seen appearing in pragmatics and cognitive science.

The argument so far

This chapter has been largely speculative, with the aim of shifting the study of language and politics into a more theoretical – and controversial – mode. One or two principles have emerged that will be taken as a platform for the next chapter. The first is that language and political behaviour can be thought of as based on the cognitive endowments of the human mind rather than as social practices. The second is that, despite this point, language and social behaviour *are* closely intertwined, probably in innate mechanisms or innately developing mechanisms of the mind and probably as a result of evolutionary adaptations. The third principle, again despite what the last point might be taken to imply, is that human linguistic and social abilities are not a straitjacket; rather language is linked to the human cognitive ability to engage in free critique and criticism.

What we have not done so far is consider the mechanisms of language in detail and how they might be used. We have, however, seen two broad roles for language – interacting with other individuals in social groups and representing states of affairs. These are two types of what people call 'meaning'. Interaction will be the organising theme of Chapter 3, representation of Chapter 4. In examining some of the ways in which linguists and others have approached these two roles, we shall also assemble some descriptive instruments for the practical dissection of political text and talk.

3   Interaction

In the preceding chapter we considered the possibility that there is a fundamental connection between the language faculty and the social, in fact political,
nature of human beings. Language is not the only way humans interact with one
another, but it is the most distinctive and most developed. When humans
interact by way of language there are many things they can be doing – philo-
sophising, flirting, informing, preaching or quarrelling, for example – but since
this book is about language and politics, we shall focus on the type of interaction
that has the sort of social dimension that intuitively we would call political.

Political action as language action

Only in and through language can one issue commands and threats, ask questions,
make offers and promises – provided one has convinced one's interlocutors that
one has the requisite resources to make the speech act credible. And only through
language tied into social and political institutions can one declare war, declare
guilty or not guilty, prorogue parliaments, or raise or lower taxes. Speech acts
have been treated by 'ordinary language' philosophers and some pragmaticists
within linguistics as a largely technical problem. It is clear, however, that the
non-logical parts of meaning-making cannot be easily separated from social
and political interaction, its conventions and institutions. Mey (2001: 115–16)
captures this point nicely in pointing out that language$_{l/u}$ always reflects 'the
conditions of the community at large':

> Among these conditions are institutions that society, that is, the social
> humans, have created for themselves: the legislative, the executive, the
> judiciary, and other organs of the state; the various religious bodies such as
> faiths and churches; human social institutions such as marriage, the family,
> the market and so on. In all such institutions and bodies, certain human
> agreements and customs have become legalized, and this legalization has
> found its symbolic representation in language.

Mey is evidently assuming democratic institutions in which there exists a separation of powers, but of course the same point can be made for other forms of governance. It might appear on closer inspection that the argument is viciously circular, for it can be said, and in fact has to be said, that it is precisely the use of language that creates institutions. For example, swearing an oath is a specific institution, because it is a specific speech act, and it is a specific speech act because it is a specific institution. However, the circularity is partly dissolved if we take seriously the observation that institutionalised speech acts – i.e., what could conversely be called speech-enacted institutions – are in fact embedded in *interconnected* speech-enacted institutions. In the case of oath-swearing, the institution depends on the presence of a lawyer as well as the use of a form of words, and the lawyer herself or himself is legitimated through a chain of speech institutions embedded in training and registration, as well, ultimately, as in the constitutional institutions of the polity mentioned by Mey above. This network of interlocking institutions may also, of course, in the long run be circular: all social and political speech-enacted and speech-enacting institutions are interdependent.

Classical speech act theory as proposed by Austin (1962) and developed by Searle (1969) sought to make generalisations about the conditions under which speech acts would 'fire' or 'misfire', or 'come off' or not, be 'felicitous' or not. The felicity conditions elaborated by Searle for such acts as 'promising' involve specifying the conditions under which a promise can be properly enacted. These can be summarised as follows (after Levinson 1983: 238–9):

(a) the utterer makes an assertion about a future event e of which (s)he is the agent;
(b) the utterer sincerely intends to execute e;
(c) the utterer believes (s)he is capable of executing e;
(d) e is not believed to be likely to happen as a matter of course;
(e) the receiver of the promise desires e;
(f) the utterer intends to put (her) himself under an obligation to execute e.

Without pursuing all possible avenues of explication and critique here, it is relevant to note two points that apply to many if not all speech acts, particularly when viewed within a social and political perspective. First, several of these 'felicity conditions' depend on assumptions about the utterer's intentions and abilities, and about the wants of the recipient. Second, viewing these matters within a political framework, as distinct from the decontextualised framework of ordinary language philosophy, it is impossible to avoid far-reaching questions about the political notion of *credibility*, the notion of utilities or wants and the notion of power and distribution of resources. Consider, for example, felicity conditions (b) and (c) in the above list, the criteria of intention and capability.

This pair are at the heart of political interaction. In international relations, strategists note that nation has military capability, and ask whether, or more likely assume that, nation has intention to use it. There is no *logical* reason to assume that capability implies intention, but there is an interesting *pragmatic* tendency to make the assumption.

Conversely, does having an intention mean that you must have capability? Well, logically that would seem to be the case, so we find felicity conditions (b) and (c) listed together as both being necessary. However, one may wonder whether pragmatically and psychologically capability is always present, even believed by the speaker to be present, in some actual political utterances. All this is saying, quite simply, that politicians (and other people, for that matter) are well known for, or suspected of, making glib promises – ones that they cannot keep. There are two ways that 'glib promises' might work. In the first case, the hearer believes that the speaker intends to and can perform *e*, and the utterer calculates that the hearer believes that (s)he, the utterer, has the resources and the intention to perform *e*. That would certainly be a case in which a speech act of promising works, but is issued deceptively, in bad faith. The second case, is not so easy to be sure about. It might be one of the odd cognitive states Orwell had in mind when he talked about 'doublethink'. In this case, intention is decoupled from capability. The utterer sincerely commits to (b), but either does not believe (c) or believes it on insufficient evidence.

In both cases, what matters, from a political point of view, is whether the speaker has 'credibility' (Fetzer 2002). Whether an utterer is believed, 'has credibility', is presumably a product of a complex chain of social and psychological circumstances. As we have noted in Chapter 2, the tagging of believable sources is an intrinsic part of human language and communication processing. It is easy to see that similar considerations apply to such speech acts as 'threatening' and 'warning', which have a prominent role in political discourse. Physical resources backing up the capability are clearly important, but, since such resources are not always visible, it is the verbal communication that becomes crucial in political interaction.

Cooperation again

We argued in Chapter 2 that human language, as a system of communication, must rest on reciprocal altruism in the analogous form of self-interested communication. The primary expectation is that individuals will truthfully intend to communicate representations of the environment, with the back-up that everyone also has the ability to check for consistency and cheating. If we accept this much, we can go on to ask, at a secondary level, what communication-specific cooperation actually looks like. Grice's tentative answer was that communication involved four types of 'maxim' (Grice 1989: 26–7), which he outlined thus:

i   *Maxim of Quantity.*
    Make your contribution as informative as is required (for the current purposes of the exchange).
    Do not make your contribution more informative than is required.
ii *Maxim of Quality.* Supermaxim: Try to make your contribution one that is true. Specific maxims:
    Do not say what you believe to be false.
    Do not say that for which you lack adequate evidence.
iii *Maxim of Relation.* Be relevant.
iv *Maxim of Manner.* Supermaxim: Be perspicuous. Specific maxims:
    Avoid obscurity of expression.
    Avoid ambiguity.
    Be brief (avoid unnecessary prolixity).
    Be orderly.

How are these maxims grounded?

> [I]t is just a well recognised empirical fact that people do behave in these ways.
>
> (Grice 1989: 29)

Let us reformulate this as follows:

> it is an empirical fact that people do seem to assume that they will be assumed to be behaving in these ways.

One reason for this reformulation is that it allows us to accommodate deception and lying as also an empirical fact. Indeed, lying and deception could not work or be attempted if the above assumption were not made. This point does of course give particular status to the maxim of quality (truthfulness), and perhaps also of quantity. The ethical basis of this particular maxim is not discussed at length by Grice. On the one hand, he points out that the CP (cooperative principle) and its maxims could be construed as contractual – a contract to which parties assent because they have a common interest in the current purpose of a talk exchange. On the other hand, and this is Grice's preference, the basis of the CP can be understood as being grounded in a rational choice:

> anyone who cares about the goals that are central to conversation/communication (such as giving and receiving information, influencing and being influenced by others) must be expected to have an interest, given suitable circumstances, in participation in talk exchanges that will be profitable only

on the assumption that they are conducted in accordance with the Cooperative Principle and the maxims.

(Grice 1989: 29–30)

In terms of political philosophy, broadly speaking, this way of grounding the CP is utilitarian. The idea is not, of course, that there is some superordinate authority 'governing' communication along the lines of the CP. Whatever kind of arrangement the CP is, it is not a social institution in the sense that the terms are normally used; rather, along the lines suggested earlier, it appears to have a natural basis in some evolutionary conjuncture of human language$_L$ and human social intelligence. However, at a secondary level, at the level of the particular maxims, it does make sense to suggest that social regulation and institutionalisation are active. Readers will have noted in passing that the formulation of the maxim of quality begs a few questions. 'Required' by whom? What are 'current purposes'? And for which 'exchange'? Intuitively, participants in different kinds of exchange will require or expect different quantities of information. With regard to the maxim of quality, the sub-maxim may well be fundamental, as we have suggested, but the second will surely vary between different types of communicative exchange. Different kinds or amounts of evidence may be 'adequate' in, say, a scientific report, a newspaper report or a ministerial statement to parliament. Similar points can be made for the other maxims, and in particular for the maxim of relation. What is interesting is that propositional attitude, meta-representation and 'source tagging' seem to be properties of language that are crucial here,[1] although their particular deployment is dependent on expectations in localised types of exchange. This is further reflected in the fact that, depending on the type of exchange, people often demand or negotiate particular types of evidence, or refer to institutionalised norms.

One way of interpreting the maxims, then, is to think of them as the social arrangement of natural tendencies – variable ethical norms applied on top of some underlying, fundamental expectation of cooperative truthfulness. The many forms of political exchange reflect variable expectations, but, however machiavellian the interaction, some schematic form of the CP is a precondition. Now this has rich consequences for interaction and for the mechanics of communication.

One might choose to dissent from the primary principle of communicative cooperation but one would have to remain silent or, what is virtually impossible for humans, refuse to understand verbal input – i.e., opt out of human intercourse.[2] On the other hand, it is easier to choose to depart from the particular maxims in different types of communicative exchange. It is possible, partly following Grice, to draw distinctions between *abandoning*, *violating* and *flouting* the maxims. Abandoning the maxims, and indeed the CP, would be the case of refusing to communicate. Violating the maxims would be infringing the regulatory maxims or norms for a particular exchange type. Such a case might be, in a highly institutionalised setting at one extreme, refusing to answer questions in a court of law; at the other extreme of generalised conversational exchanges, purposely telling somebody the wrong time when asked. In principle one could violate the maxims either overtly, as in refusing to give information in court (infringing the quantity maxim), or by covertly attempting to circumvent the hearer's cheater detection, by, for example, telling a half-truth or the opposite of the truth and calculating that one will not be found out. But covert violations, in the present sense, of the maxims of relation and manner seem to be impossible in principle. It is not easy to see what it would mean to speak of being irrelevant (in the appropriate sense) without being noticed, and thereby achieve some communicative mischief. The same for the maxim of manner. What would it mean to be obscure without anyone noticing? In general, violating the maxims means violating the expectations relating to truthfulness, the maxims of quality and quantity, and is subject to normative constraints integrated in human communication – and thus also subject to the human ability to monitor veracity, evidence and authority.

Neglecting numerous subtle special cases, we can now look at the those where one expects (a) that one's infringement of the maxims in some exchange type will be noticed, and (b) that the hearer will calculate that the speaker has the intent to communicate something thereby. Such cases more or less correspond to what Grice means by *flouting* the maxims. The speaker is assumed to be *not* violating the maxims (nor abandoning the CP) and therefore to be intending some communicative effect. These effects are termed *implicatures*.[3]

However, implied pragmatic meanings, implicatures, do not only arise through perceived flouting. Many more instances arise through the interaction between the conventional meaning of words and the operation of particular maxims and CP in local linguistic exchanges. They are crucial to all forms of communicative exchange, and involve complex cognitive mechanisms. It is accepted that they take different forms, some being general, others being for the nonce, i.e. once-off computations. They are of particular interest in political interaction, since they enable speakers to do such things as convey meaning without taking explicit responsibility, and to convey in-group meanings, where only members 'in the know' might be able to work out the intended implicatures.

Generalised and particularised implicatures and their uses

Grice distinguishes 'generalised' from 'particularised' implicature and the distinction is theoretically explored by Levinson (2000). An example of generalised implicature occurs in the following:

Some MPs are in favour of the policy.

If the speaker is perceived to be observing the maxim of quantity ('Make your contribution as informative as is required (for the current purposes of the exchange)'), then he or she expects to be understood as meaning 'not all the MPs favoured the policy'. The point is that in terms of propositional logic, if it is true that 'all the MPs are in favour, then it is true some of the MPs are in favour'. The pragmatic meaning – language as it is used – always implicates 'not all'. Sometimes, however, speakers may equivocate between pragmatic and logical meaning.

Another example, this time one where the implicature arises simply because it is assumed the speaker is observing the sub-maxim of manner ('be orderly') is:

the president declared war and attacked Afghanistan

which contrasts with

the president attacked Afghanistan and declared war.

From a logical point of view the two word orders would be semantically equivalent.

Since generalised implicatures apply in all kinds of language use, and we are concerned here with examining particular instances of language, we shall focus on particularised implicature. Particularised implicature occurs when a hearer's knowledge of the context and of some background knowledge is required to connect inferentially the semantic content of an utterance with a composite meaning in such a way that the local maxims (and the CP) are saved. The process may or may not involve obvious flouting. It depends on contingent contextual knowledge, as well as more long-term institutional knowledge. For example:

The MP is looking pleased.

Given a particular institutional context, i.e., location, time and event, together with particular knowledge frames, likely implicatures might be: he's been made a minister; his party's won the vote, etc. This is one kind of particularised implicature. A particularised implicature arising from flouting might be the following. The context in which the above sentence 'the MP is looking pleased' occurs might be such as to lead a hearer to perceive that the speaker is breaching the maxim of quality. Suppose, for instance, that the hearer knows that the MP's party has just *lost* the vote. Then, 'the MP is looking pleased' will actually mean (for the hearer) the opposite of its semantic content – that is, 'the MP is *not* looking pleased'. This is, of course, one way in which irony works.

The politics of particularised implicatures

Why is implicature of interest in considering political language in use? The answer is not surprising: it enables political actors to convey more than they say in so many words. In political discourse it can often happen that the inferences that save the maxims and the CP can only arise if the hearer adopts a particular ideology or set of attitudes and values. Here is an example (edited) from the political interview discussed in more detail in Chapter 6:

A: Mr X said that he should sack Mr Y
B: well he's been saying that for a long time
A: doesn't make him wrong

On the face of it, B's response to A's assertion is no more than a specification of the relative length of the period of time within which Mr X has made occasional assertions equivalent to A's embedded clause. There is also a (generalised) implicature that the aspect of the verb 'say' here is not continuous but repetitively punctual. More interestingly, there may be a perceptible flouting of one or more maxims – the maxim of quantity because B's utterance does not appear to be as informative as required for the current purposes of the exchange, and the maxim of relevance because the relation between A and B does not appear to be grounded in the semantic meaning of the current exchange.[4] To 'make sense' of this, the hearer assumes that nonetheless, at a fundamental level, speaker B is observing the appropriate maxims for the context and the CP. The implicature constructed by the hearer might then be that speaker B does not accept the truth of the assertion 'he should sack Mr Y', or perhaps more accurately, that speaker B does not accept that the point being implicated by A in making his assertion is of significance. The precise mental computations that a hearer goes through to arrive at the implicature are not well understood – but they presumably involve quite complex stores of knowledge about political behaviour. In this example, the implicature is clearly available, however it is arrived at, for speaker A explicitly averts to it when he says 'doesn't make him [Mr X] wrong'. That is to say, speaker A formulates the implicature in his own words as including something like 'Mr X is wrong' and 'Mr X is proved wrong because he repeats himself'.

The kinds of implicature we have been looking at are what Grice called 'conversational' – that is, they are produced during the course of interactive language use. Grice distinguished these from 'conventional' implicatures, which are not the product of a particular ongoing use. Grice himself is interested in words like 'but' and 'and', but the notion can be expanded by bearing in mind Levinson's point that conventional implicatures are 'simply attached by convention to particular lexical items or expressions' (Levinson 1983: 127) and

Mey's point that 'No matter how conventional the implicature, the very conventions which govern its use are basically historically developed, culture-specific and class-related' (Mey 2001: 50–1). An example that makes the point would be:

(a) The president made an announcement.
(b) A man made an announcement.

If (a) conventionally implicates (b), it is entirely in virtue of a historically and culturally local convention that presidents are not women. We are here on the border of interactive pragmatics and cognitive representation. The 'convention' in question can be understood as a 'stereotype', a cognitive construct concerning the properties of a social category.

There exists a similar kind of implicature that is liable to slip through one's fingers, but which is fairly fundamental in political discourse, and which I shall call 'deontic implicature'. Certain utterances seem to make sense – i.e., save some local maxims and CP in relation to the ongoing exchange – only if a certain value orientation or 'oughtness' is adopted. Consider the following extract from Enoch Powell's 'Rivers of Blood' speech which is examined in detail in Chapter 8. Powell is telling a story[5] of an old woman who

> went to apply for a rate reduction and was seen by a young girl, who on hearing she had a seven-roomed house, suggested she should let part of it. When she said the only people she could get were Negroes, the girl said, 'Racial prejudice won't get you anywhere in this country.' So she went home.

One possible conventional implicature (defined the way I am now suggesting) appears to arise from 'young girl', and to involve claims such as 'has no authority', 'should show respect to the elderly'. Another is the conventional implicature attached to 'Negroes'. The reported utterances are presumably:

Young girl: Why don't you let a room in your house?
Old woman: The only people I can get are Negroes.

The old woman's reply lacks coherence – conformity to the maxim of relation – if taken in truth-conditional terms. It can only make sense against a background of conventional social assumptions and stereotypes. The young girl's 'why' conventionally implicates the expectation that a reason will be given. The old woman implicates that one cannot let one's rooms to 'Negroes'. The referential semantics (labelling of a category of persons also picked out by terms such as 'blacks', 'Afro-Asians', 'immigrants from the British Commonwealth') in itself does not enable the hearer to 'make sense'. If 'Negroes' simply denotes a class of people, why cannot one let rooms to them? But all interlocutors expect the

CP to be preserved, together with specific maxims. For this to be so in the present example what is needed? What seems to be needed is a conventional implicature attached to the particular morpheme *negro*. At a minimum, this implicature has to be something *undesirable*. Incidentally, suppose that a hearer does not, in his or her idiolect, have this conventional implicature for *negro* – they will nonetheless be induced to supply it by abduction, accommodating to the language being used in order to conserve the CP (Levinson 2000: 60–3; Werth 1999: 253–7).

This is a complicated little narrative, however, which can be seen to involve even more layers of implicature:

Young girl: Why don't you let a room in your house?
Old woman: The only people I can get are Negroes.
Young girl: Racial prejudice will get you nowhere in this country.

The young girl now implicates, by the maxim of relation, that the old woman's utterance is categorised as 'racial prejudice', indicating that she has computed the implicature *undesirable* mentioned above, since 'racial prejudice' is conventionally undesirable, by further implicature, given another set of values. Implicature involving the maxim of manner may also account for the communication of meaning via 'get you nowhere', though this expression might be regarded as an encoded idiomatic block by some analysts.

We thus have an embedded conversational exchange that hinges on implicature. However, the sentence is in fact embedded in a larger stretch of talk in a particular setting and context. There are many implicatures that could be teased out and which are perhaps fleetingly used and represented in the mind of anyone who is listening to and processing Powell's speech. For example, in the narrative, the old woman is said to have gone home after the girl's last utterance. What is implicated is that the girl's utterance *caused* the woman's departure. In addition, it is deontically implicated that the girl was acting wrongly, that she was wrong in invoking racial prejudice and that the old woman was right in refusing to rent rooms to black people. The general point here is that the inclusion of the story, in all its detail, is subject to validation under context-specific maxims, specifically the maxim of relation, and the CP. The inserted anecdote is only made relevant by accommodating a series of evaluations of particular social categories.

Being politic

The cooperative principle appears to interact with other principles of human social behaviour (Leech 1983; Mey 2001). Earlier, we looked at speech acts. Now, speech acts may be perceived to be 'impolite' or 'polite', depending on the situation of utterance and the roles, including the social roles, of the participants. We can interpret the complex cultural notion of 'politeness' in terms of the production of some sensation of insecurity in the receiver. A further breakdown of the concept of politeness is provided by Goffman (1967) in terms of the idea of 'positive face' and 'negative face'. In interpersonal communication, Goffman argued, people pay attention to, and have to achieve a balancing act between, the positive need to be accepted as an insider and to establish 'common ground' on the one hand and on the other hand the negative need to have freedom of action and not to have one's 'territory' encroached upon. Brown and Levinson (1987) adapted Goffman's explication of face-threatening acts (FTAs) as performed through speech acts, constructing a detailed classification of the linguistic formulations (syntactic and lexical) which speakers draw on, in order to mitigate their FTAs. The effect of various mitigation strategies is a function of the relations of power and intimacy between speakers.

Goffman's positive and negative faces appear, rather as does Grice's CP, to have a basis in fundamental aspects of sociality. Politeness theory rests on a metaphorical basis, that of territory. Positive face is effectively a behavioural orientation to the self as desiring to be included in the same 'space' as other members of the group, and an orientation to others viewed as being included in the same group. Negative face is effectively an orientation to one's own autonomy and an orientation to others that respects their 'sovereignty', their right to freedom of action and to freedom from intrusion.

The notions of FTAs and of mitigation are also useful in understanding the practices of political talk – in particular euphemising strategies, forms of evasion, forms of solidarity and exclusion, and some devices of persuasion. The fact that politeness phenomena seem natural in everyday socialised interaction makes them to a degree unnoticeable in political exchanges. If a politician wishes to tell his or her electorate that taxes are to be raised, unemployment figures are up, inflation is spiralling, and the enemy is massing on the border, then these face-threatening acts (requesting sacrifices, issuing bad news, giving warnings) are verbalised in a strategic fashion, in order to lessen the affront. The politician has to achieve a balance between positive-face strategies and negative-face strategies. On the one hand it will be necessary to address positive face – appealing to patriotism, to pulling together, brotherhood, the cause of the proletariat, civilised values, and similar concepts that have as part of their frame some notion of the special characteristics of the self's group. It will follow that linguistic choices of particular kinds are made. A classic example is the repeated use of the first-person plural inclusive pronoun ('we' in English). On the other hand, such a politician will have to address negative-face risks – seeking to minimise the dangers to the freedom and security of both the collectivity and of the individuals that constitute it. This motivation will be matched by verbal behaviour of particular kinds – simply not referring to threatening referents, for example, or referring to them obliquely or by euphemism. There are problematic elements in this account, however. Being politic might be desirable in civil and private society; it is a matter of debate. It is a matter of much greater ethical debate whether being 'politic' is desirable in similar degree or at all in the public sphere. Why should one think that this is the case? One reply is that issues of power, though certainly not absent in the civil and private sphere, loom much larger in the public sphere.

The fine-tuning of language in use

When humans interact verbally, they do it with extreme rapidity and ease. The nature of communicative cooperation becomes clear. Participants in the interaction have to adjust to split-second timing in turn-taking and overlapping. They have to guess the other's mental representation – i.e., form a meta-representation. They have to check for consistency, social intent, possible deception, and other factors. The extraordinary detail and subtlety of this instinctive cooperative behaviour only shows up through careful analysis. For example, above we looked at the implicatures available in a real-life extract that we presented thus:

A: Mr X said that he should sack Mr Y.
B: well he's been saying that for a long time.
A: doesn't make him wrong.

In fact, the interaction itself was far more intricate. We can show some of the detail using notational conventions developed in the field of conversation analysis (see, for example, Schegloff 1972, 1979; Sacks, Schegloff and Jefferson 1974; Schegloff, Jefferson and Sacks 1977; Atkinson and Heritage 1984). What one finds is that interactants work together even in their disagreements, and on a micro level that normally escapes consciousness. The following is a transcription of the recording from which the edited versions shown above was abstracted:

A er he said that Mr Blair should recognize this as a very serious matter, he's
  said that | he *should ↑sack (.) Mr Vaz | *because of these allegations=
B | well he,* | yes*
A = against him.
B well he's been saying that for a long time=
   = .hh I mean he was | desperate*
A | <doesn't make* him ↑↓wrong↑

The transcription tries to include such fine details as hesitations (indicated above by (.)) and fillers (e.g., *er* . . . *hh* . . .), the beginning and end of overlapping talk (marked by vertical lines and asterisks), marked pitch changes and intensity (vertical arrows, italics), changes of tempo (e.g., increase in tempo is indicated by <), and 'latching' of pieces of talk (marked by =). Other conventions are listed in the Appendix. All such details are potentially significant for the interactants, and in later chapters we use these methods to analyse political micro-interaction.

The strategic use of language

Mainstream theories of speech acts, communicative cooperation, implicatures and related pragmatic phenomena do not make explicit connections with social and political categories. In the preceding section, however, we have repeatedly come up against these connections. If we ask what 'felicity conditions' are, for example, one obvious explanation comes in terms of social, political and judicial organisation. The concept of cooperation seems to require explication in terms of social intelligence. Even implicatures, which in many respects can be dealt with inside the domain of cognition, nonetheless seems to involve, at least for particularised implicature, a multiplicity of background knowledge that includes social and political values. It is instructive to consider a theoretical framework that reverses this perspective – a framework that takes the social interaction as its starting point and reaches out to linguistics and pragmatics to explain its concerns. We return therefore to Habermas's view of human communication, which was introduced in Chapter 2.[6]

Validity claims

The Habermasian epistemological framework holds that knowledge is not a neutral representation of an objective world 'out there', but is realised through what we are calling here language$_{l/u}$, determined by interests (Habermas 1971, 1973, 1979, 1981). This position provides a basis for seeing linguistic behaviour as a medium through which 'rationality' is realised. In Habermas's account rationality is not of the Cartesian or the Lockean or the Popperian kind, but of an intersubjective kind. Rationality is not a faculty of the mind, but an abstract goal of human coordination achieved through the exchange of utterances. Most interpretations of Habermas make the fundamental assumption that communication has a goal, and that this goal is a form of consensus based on understanding and agreement. As we have seen above in speculating on the evolutionary origins of the linguistic and the political, this is too one-sided. Language$_{l/u}$ is inherently ambivalent.

Rationality, then, in Habermas's account, depends on the postulate that humans possess 'communicative competence' ('universal pragmatics'), which involves validity claims. Habermas has argued that any utterer in any use of language is implicitly making, by the very act of uttering at all as a human in a social situation, four validity claims. The claims can be interpreted as follows:

1   The claim to 'understandability' (*Verständlichkeit*), i.e., that what the utterer says is intelligible. Habermas's point can be understood here as the utterer's assumption that (s)he and his or her interlocutor both speak language$_1$. This understanding needs some refinement, however, with respect to assumptions about dialects and registers of language$_1$, and also with respect to assumptions about mutually shared knowledge frames. Further, one could incorporate what Grice understands by 'manner': one is claiming not to be using language$_1$ obscurely, etc.

2   The claim to truth (*Wahrheit*), i.e., to asserting a propositional truth, or in terms used earlier to be truthfully asserting a representation of a state of affairs. This claim connects with Grice's maxim of quality, and could be expanded by inclusion of Grice's maxim of quantity. However, it appears to be concerned with the objective truth of assertions, independently of the utterer's beliefs, which is what the next claim is concerned with.

3   The claim to be telling the truth (*Wahrhaftigkeit*), i.e., the claim to be speaking sincerely, that is performing utterances that the speaker believes correspond to his or her intended meanings. This claim too connects with Grice's maxims of quality, and could be extended by the inclusion of quantity, in so far as it is concerned with an utterer's intention to deceive and with the condition of his or her beliefs.

4   The claim to 'rightness' (*Richtigkeit*), i.e., the claim to be normatively 'right' to utter what one is uttering, and as claiming the authority to be performing the speech act in hand. Grice does not appear to envisage this particular condition, but it is of considerable importance within the context of political language use. Specifically, it is linked with the relative power distribution between utterer and addressee.

The concept of validity claim is tied in with a threefold model of 'worlds': the social world and the objective world, together constituting the public sphere, and the subjective world, constituting the private sphere. In the course of social interaction validity claims are made implicitly, but if challenged may become explicit. What is important from the point of view of social theory and social criticism, is that rational truth, in Habermas's framework, can logically only emerge if the validity claims are freely challengeable and testable. That is to say, the abstract goal – we might characterise it as truth-for-humans – comes about only through what Habermas terms 'undistorted' communication.

In practice, Habermas observes, validity claims, which are implicit in all utterances, only ever come near to being realised in special circumstances (for example, in therapeutic discourse, he believes). In practice, most communication is distorted by the *interests* of participants, whether individuals or groups. Only in the hypothetical, or criterial, 'ideal speech situation', where interests and power do not constrain the free testing of the validity claims, can a consensual truth emerge. In particular, the ideal speech situation is unconstrained in the sense that 'a symmetrical distribution of the opportunities of choosing and practising speech acts exists for all participants' (Habermas 1971: 137; cf. Wodak 1996: 30). In such communicative action the goal is emancipatory. In social groups, however, particular interests and power relations will distort communication, it is supposed.

Like the maxims of the Gricean CP, the Habermasian validity claims of the universal pragmatics claim to be the necessary logical explanation for how human communication can work at all. However, there are differences. Grice's CP affords us an account of how communication is possible: it is possible only through a fundamental agreement to share meanings (information and other kinds of meaning), together with attendant 'machiavellian' consequences. The maxims are an account of how this takes place. There is some overlap conceptually with Habermas, particularly with respect to truth claims, sincerity claims, the quantity maxim and the quality maxim. Habermas does not include anything like the maxim of relation. This is partly because he does not explore in depth the hearer-based discourse-processing mechanisms that lead to implicature – relevance, however defined, is an important driver of implicatures.

Habermas's validity claims refer not to the underlying contractual or utilitarian conditions that render communication possible qua communication, and the selective evolution of language$_L$ explicable, but to the socio-political conditions under which different characteristics of language$_{I/u}$ manifest themselves. This is most clear in the case of the validity claim of 'rightness' (*Richtigkeit*), which has no counterpart in Grice. It focuses on, and politicises the social domain. The claim to 'rightness' partly means that the performing of speech acts are grounded in an implicit claim, on the part of the speaker, to inhabit a particular social or political role, and to possess a particular authority. Some such rights are widely distributed: up to a point, depending on one's material means, anyone can make a promise. But a very large number (one would guess, since no one has tried to count them) of politically and socially significant speech acts have their 'rightness' grounded by definition in the structure of legitimacy of the polity. Thus, a speech act such as giving orders in different organisational structures, sentencing a criminal, declaring war, refusing entry to a building or territory, calling a debating chamber to order, appointing judges, passing legislation . . . all such examples are possible in terms of 'rightness', though a more perspicuous term would be 'legitimacy'.

It seems to be implied in the theory of universal pragmatics that validity claims are understood by all normal socialised adult humans. If this is the case, such knowledge must provide the means by which systematically distorted communication can be produced to satisfy some interest. Conversely, it seems to be implied that humans can detect distorted communication. This does not mean, of course, that people will always bother to do so. Further, since that is the case, it seems also to be implied that the *illusion* of consensual (undistorted) understanding can exist. Habermas proposes that *self-reflection* constitutes a process whereby distortion by interests can be located and resolved. Wodak (1996: 32), who adopts a similar perspective, argues that discourse analysis (or language$_{l/u}$ analysis) is an instrument for exposing inequality and domination and for providing the means for more equitable and emancipatory discourse.

Strategies

If it is the case that validity claims are made in political language use, and that participants are able to challenge the validity of claims, then it should be possible to identify the means by which the claims are being overridden, whether obviously or non-obviously. Habermas speaks of the 'strategic' use of language when interests distort communication, that is, fall short of unconstrained communication or interlocution. It must be possible to characterise strategies by which utterers manage their interests. Such strategies are linguistically realised, but this is not to say that language$_L$ or language$_l$ incorporate resources uniquely dedicated to such functions. But they certainly do incorporate resources that may be so used, and some of these do recur again and again in critical analyses of talk and text. However, whether a given instance of the use of a language$_l$ is justifiably called strategic is a matter of social and political judgement, and it is possible to be excessively zealous in hunting down such details. Rather than work up from claims about the strategic potential of certain linguistic expressions in general, another approach is to postulate categories of 'strategic function' that linguistic expressions of various types may be (perceived to be) used for. Chilton and Schäffner (1997: 211–15) discuss four strategic functions, reduced here to three.

1   *Coercion*. Unlike the other functions this one is not purely linguistic, but dependent on the utterer's resources and power. Clear examples are speech acts backed by sanctions (legal and physical), such as commands, laws, edicts, etc. Less obvious forms of coerced behaviour consist of speech roles which people find difficult to evade or may not even notice, such as spontaneously giving answers to questions, responding to requests, etc., particularly if the questioners and requesters are perceived to have higher status or power. Political actors also often act coercively through language$_{l/u}$ in setting agendas, selecting topics in conversation, positioning the self and others in specific relationships, making assumptions about realities that hearers are obliged to at least temporarily accept in order to process the text or talk. Power can also be exercised through controlling others' use of language – that is, through various kinds and degrees of censorship and access control. The latter include the structure and control of public

media, the arena in which much political communication takes place. Another important language-related phenomenon that could be judged coercive is the strategic stimulation of affect. Although the precise details are under-researched, it is reasonable to hypothesise links between meaning structures produced via discourse and the emotional centres of the brain. Putting it simply, certain kinds of texts can stimulate certain hormones, and the effect may be automatic.

2   *Legitimisation* and *delegitimisation*. Political actors, whether individuals or groups, cannot act by physical force alone, except in the extreme case, where it is questionable that one is still in the realm of what is understood by 'politics'. The legitimisation function is closely linked to coercion, because it establishes the right to be obeyed, that is, 'legitimacy'. Why do people obey regimes that are very different in their policies? Reasons for being obeyed have to be communicated linguistically, whether by overt statement or by implication. The techniques used include arguments about voters' wants, general ideological principles, charismatic leadership projection, boasting about performance and positive self-presentation. *Delegitimisation* is the essential counterpart: others (foreigners, 'enemies within', institutional opposition, unofficial opposition) have to be presented negatively, and the techniques include the use of ideas of difference and boundaries, and speech acts of blaming, accusing, insulting, etc.[7]

3   *Representation and misrepresentation*. Political control involves the control of information, which is by definition a matter of discourse control. It may be quantitative or qualitative. Secrecy is the strategy of preventing people receiving information; it is the inverse of censorship, which is preventing people giving information. In another mode of representation/misrepresentation, information may be given, but be quantitatively inadequate to the needs or interests of hearers ('being economical with the truth', as British politicians put it). Qualitative misrepresentation is simply lying, in its most extreme manifestation, but includes various kinds of omissions, verbal evasion and denial. Euphemism has the cognitive effect of conceptually 'blurring' or 'defocusing' unwanted referents, be they objects or actions. Implicit meanings of various types also constitute a means of diverting attention from troublesome referents. Representing a reality is one of the obvious functions of discourse (language$_{1/u}$), and later chapters explore methods of analysing the process.

These three strategic functions are interconnected in practice. Representation and misrepresentation have a direct connection with the violation of Grice's maxims of quantity, quality and manner, and with Habermas's validity claims of truth and truthfulness. Misrepresentation strategies can clearly involve the coercive control of the physical channels of communication, as well as selection of the structure of language in use. Coercion strategies have a connection with Habermas's 'rightness' claim. Of course not *all* validity claims to rightness are coercive, so the idea of a strategic function called *coercion* is to enable us to identify those acts that are judged to be motivated by an intention to cause addressees to act in a way that otherwise they would not have chosen.

The strategies of *delegitimisation* (of the other) and *legitimisation* (of the self) may perhaps be conceptualised as lying at opposite ends of a scale. These end points may coincide with positive face (being an insider and legitimate) and negative face (being not only an outsider and thus not legitimate but also under attack). Delegitimisation can manifest itself in acts of negative other-presentation, acts of blaming, scape-goating, marginalising, excluding, attacking the moral character of some individual or group, attacking the communicative cooperation of the other, attacking the rationality and sanity of the other. The extreme is to deny the humanness of the other. At the other end of the spectrum legitimisation, usually oriented to the self, includes positive self-presentation, manifesting itself in acts of self-praise, self-apology, self-explanation, self-justification, self-identification as a source of authority, reason, vision and sanity, where the self is either an individual or the group with which an individual identifies or wishes to identify.

4   Representation

When humans interact verbally they may be simply signalling social roles, boundaries and bonds, as the last chapter suggested. But as we also saw, much of the interaction, whatever its social function, whatever its degree of truthfulness, deception or manipulation, has to do with communicating representations of the world. We now turn to the communication of 'meaning' in this sense.

Denotation and representation

In semantics, the branch of linguistics and philosophy that seeks to understand the nature of 'meaning', it is possible to approach 'meaning', whatever it is, as if it were entirely separate from context. Its sister sub-discipline, pragmatics, treats meaning as a function of context (speakers, hearers, speech situation, background knowledge). Linguists have long been debating the dividing line between semantics and pragmatics. What is clear to all sides in the debate is that the meanings of words, of sentences and of discourses are in the mind, not objectively given. The meaning of the word *democracy* is not waiting to be discovered in some objective realm; it is in the mind, or rather the interacting minds, of people in particular times and places. This formulation in itself poses a difficulty for those who wish to insist on a clear dividing line between semantics and pragmatics. For it appears that the meaning of the word *democracy* involves context; the meaning of the word cannot be plausibly entertained independently of context. True, one could choose to *stipulate* a meaning: for example, one might say that 'democracy is the system of election by majority voting' or is 'the dictatorship of the proletariat'. But in such cases one can ask: who says so, why and when? Of course *democracy* is an example of what Gallie called 'essentially contested concepts' (1956), and such concepts are essentially political concepts. However, *in practice* many, if not all, words require knowledge not only of some abstract context-independent meaning schema, but of immediate and not-so-immediate contexts of use.

One of the important ideas that has emerged from the philosophical and linguistic literature on meaning is the importance distinguishing between sense and reference. Meaning cannot simply be a matter of matching expressions to referents, that is, to things in the world. Consider for example: 'sovereignty is the cornerstone of the state system'. There is no actually existing entity 'sovereignty', but rather a collection of ideas and practices associated with it. Or again, consider: 'he believes in communism'. The fact that communism strictly speaking does not exist does not render the sentence devoid of meaning, unless one wishes to be polemical or to define 'meaning' very narrowly (in fact define it as narrowly referential). Consider also for example the two noun phrases: 'the Commander-in-Chief of the Armed Forces' and 'the President of the United States'. Even if one knows that these refer to the same person (the same referent), it does not seem plausible to say that they 'have the same meaning'.

In short, though it would be absurd to deny reference, reference is only part, though an essential part of the story. What is important for the study of language and politics is the way non-existent entities can be accepted as having meaning and the way in which *alternate* ways of referring to the *same* entity can have different meanings. This is to say that, in addition to referring, it is *sense* or representation in mind and in language-in-use that is crucial.[1]

Putting things very schematically, there are two broad approaches in semantics.[2] The first approach, generally called denotational or referential, is concerned with theorising links between linguistic symbols and entities 'out there' in an objective world, the approach we focused on in discussing reference above. From this perspective, nouns refer to entities, predicates denote sets of entities, sentences denote states of affairs and events. There is no doubt that if we are concerned with language and politics, we have to be concerned with truth and falsity in relation to a real world in which human interests and human suffering are real. If someone asserts, say, 'airforce x bombed civilian convoy y at time t', this has to be treated referentially in accordance with the understood meanings of the referring expressions (including the deictic expressions) and the predicates. Either the proposition is true or it is false with respect to objects, people and events. To adopt such a stance is an ethical as much as a linguistic–theoretical choice. It might be objected that if the agents referred to in this proposition did not *know* that the convoy was civilian, and that the verb implies *intention*, then the proposition is false or at least not verifiable. This is not an uncommon form of arguing in fact in political discourse, where agent responsibility is frequently at issue. In such cases, there is no obvious objective linguistic principle to reach for. We are in ethical territory again. Individuals have to decide whether such an objection is a case of what has traditionally been called 'casuistry', and whether the sentence as it stands is to be interpreted as representing a state of affairs in which x caused bombs to strike y.

However, things are not always so simple. What exists or what is real is not always agreed upon. What happens can be described in different ways, in ways that invoke not only different evaluations, for instance, but also different ontological perspectives. The same phenomenon, seen in gross, can, for example, be *represented*, simply through lexical and syntactic variation, as either an activity or a state:

> Sarah is working.
> Sarah is at work.

In the second sentence, the locative preposition is understood by English speakers partly as referring to a place and partly as referring to a state. Conversely, states may be represented as actions, as in:

> Karl is asleep.
> Karl is sleeping.

We thus contrast representational semantics with referential semantics. Let us reconsider the latter as follows. In a denotational semantic theory the 'matching' process which relates a logical form to a situation must correspond to the human ability to perform some such cognitive operation as judging truth. But such a theory does not answer, and does not pretend to anwer the question of what is true *absolutely*, out (as we say) there (as we say) in (as we say) reality. Individuals are matching logical forms, derived interpretively from the utterances produced by others, to their mental representation of reality derived via perception, and limited or coloured by their cognitive apparatus. Such mental representations are not arrived at individualistically, either. Collective, inter-subjective cross-checking via linguistic and other interaction among individuals contributes to whatever representations are entertained, and circulated, by individuals.

The examination of the political text and talk that are included in this book will in large part be an examination of possible mental representations stimulated by such text and talk. The investigation of how mental representations are built up during the process of communication requires looking into many different aspects of the linguistic structure, but there are two main avenues that we shall go down. One has to do with actors and processes in the worlds we construct – who does what to whom. The second has to do with this notion of 'world' itself, since the use of language in political discourse can be seen as a form of competition among political actors wishing to promote, to have accepted, their own particular 'world'.[3]

Cognitive approaches

Linguistic approaches to the processing of discourse – the interpreting of incoming language$_{l/u}$ by language users – have intersected since the 1970s with the broader discipline of cognitive science.[4] An application of cognitive approaches to political discourse is found in van Dijk's work (e.g., van Dijk 1990, 1993a, 2002; van Dijk and Kintsch 1983). The cognitive approach considers political discourse as necessarily a product of individual and collective mental processes. It seeks to show how knowledge of politics, political discourse and political ideologies involves storage in long-term memory (as personal or 'episodic' memory and social (or 'semantic') memory). Short-term memory deals 'online' with ongoing processes of discourse production and understanding, generating mental models of content and context. That is to say, representations are both stored and generated, those that are generated online being in part a function of long-term knowledge stored as social information about ideas, values and practices.

Frames

Long-term knowledge is frequently spoken of as stored 'schemata', or 'plans', 'scenarios', 'scenes', 'conceptual models', defined and distinguished by theorists in a variety of ways. In this book I shall principally use the term 'frame'. Frames can be defined as '"an area of experience" in a particular culture' (Werth 1999: 107). They are theoretical constructs, having some cognitive, ultimately, neural reality. In terms of their content, frames can be thought of as structures related to the conceptualisation of situation types and their expression in language$_{l/u}$. Situations involve 'slots' for entities (animate and inanimate, abstract and concrete, human and non-human), times, places, with relationships to one another, and having properties. The properties include cultural knowledge about such things as status, value, physical make-up. Certain properties specify prototypical roles in relation to other entities – for example, whether a participant entity is acting as an agent, on the receiving end of action, experiencing a sensation, and the like. For example, the meanings of the verbs *kill*, *murder*, *assassinate*, *execute* can be defined in terms of stored mental frames in which different types of actor fill the agent and the victim roles, the killing is legal or not legal, and other kinds of social and political background knowledge is involved.

Metaphor

Metaphor has long been recognised as important in political rhetoric. Only relatively recently has it been understood in cognitive terms (Lakoff 1987, 1993; Lakoff and Johnson 1980, 1999; Lakoff and Turner 1989; Johnson 1987; Turner 1991; Chilton and Lakoff 1995). The standard cognitive account stresses that metaphor is a part of human conceptualisation and not simply a linguistic expression that occurs especially frequently in oratory and literature. It is thought that metaphor works by mapping well understood source domains of experience onto more schematic ones. The source domains may be innate or acquired in development; they provide a source for conceptualisation. For example, vision and manual control provide a source for conceptualising conceptualisation itself: do you *see* what I mean? do you *grasp* it? Kinaesthetic experience, especially motion, bipedal gait and orientation, provides source frames for indirectly experienced concepts such as time, plans, purposes and policies. For example, the concept of control, rank and moral superiority appears, to go on the lexical evidence in many languages, to be conceptualised in terms of conceptual frames captured by terms like *over-under* and *high-low*. Political concepts involving leadership and political action conceptualised by movement or journey metaphors. This is why, for example, political discourse often includes systematic expressions like *coming to a crossroads*, *moving ahead towards a better future*, *over-coming obstacles on the way*, *not deviating from its plans*, and so forth. Social groups, and in particular sovereign states, involve the spatial source domain rooted in the experience of containment and boundary-setting. Social entities have 'a centre', 'insiders' and 'outsiders', people 'on the margins', etc. Such systematic lexical patterns appear to be grounded in essentially spatial experience. It could of course be the case that some social concepts are themselves basic and provide source domains. The linguistic evidence suggests that this would be true for 'family', which is mapped onto social entities that are not in the basic sense families, as well as onto concepts that do not involve humans at all.

It is important to be aware that metaphorical mappings can enter into quite complex bundles of meaning that involve other cognitive factors, in particular frame representations that are in effect stores of structured cultural knowledge such as knowledge about transport, the structure of houses, what illness is and what doctors do. A further important point about the cognitive theory of metaphor is that metaphorical mappings, which are usually unconscious, are used for reasoning, reasoning about target domains that are ill understood, vague or controversial. This is so because the source domains are intuitively understood and have holistic structure, so that if one part is accepted other parts follow. Such 'entailments' can be mapped onto the unstructured target domain, in order to derive inferences that would be otherwise not conceptually available, or vague in some way.

Consider a notorious example. Adolf Hitler, in *Mein Kampf* and in his other writings and speeches, uses the source domain of microbes and disease. Some of the things you know about microbes are that they get into the body without your seeing them and stay there, and that they are parasites and can cause disease. Some of the things you know about disease include the idea that causes of disease inside the body can be removed. Given these packets of knowledge, it only takes the mapping of the 'parasite' frame onto the 'Jew' frame for a whole array of inferences to be generated, almost spontaneously.[5]

Actors and events

One of the characteristics of human language is that it provides structures (often, but not only, sentences) that can be analysed into propositions, roughly in the logician's sense of the term. Propositions consist of 'arguments' (as they are technically and confusingly known) and a 'predicate'. Arguments prototypically appear as noun phrases, predicates as verbs (but also adjectives and prepositional phrases). To this core format, 'adjuncts' are often added, specifying such things as location, time and manner. This sort of reduction enables a discourse analyst to see very clearly what are the entities and the processes that the utterer is conjuring up in terms of who is doing what to whom, when, why, and so on.

Analysing the argument nominals in a text or stretch of talk provides the set of elements – the referents – that are posited in the utterer's discourse world. By 'discourse world' here I mean the mental space entertained by the utterer as 'real'. The referents indicated by the linguistic expressions, the nominal expressions, are participants in that world, whether physical entities or abstractions of various kinds. They are, to use Pinker's useful term, 'role-players' in that world (Pinker 1994: 107) or in another terminology, they have 'thematic (or *theta*) roles'.[6]

To do practical analyses of text and talk, a usable theoretical framework is needed. It is clear that the thematic roles of arguments cannot be neatly pigeonholed. Dowty (1991) proposes that all thematic roles can be understood as clusters of entailments about the predicate, and that traditional roles (*agent, source, patient, experiencer*, and so forth) are linked to one of two prototypical categories: prototypical agent and prototypical patient (P-Agent and P-Patient). It is possible that these prototypical categories are embedded in human cognition as a result of interaction with the physical environment. The entailment clusters seem to be significant for human activity, perhaps principally social interaction where issues of volition, sentience and causation are salient (Dowty 1991: 551, 572). Such social interactions could, for instance, include courts of law where questions of who caused what, whether wilfully or not, is at issue, and indeed political interaction where questions of responsibility, victimhood, intention, and the like are in play. The properties of Proto-Agent and Proto-Patient proposed by Dowty are:

Contributing Properties for the Prototypical Agent:
a. volitional involvement in the event or state
b. sentience (and/or perception)
c. causing an event or change of state in another participant
d. movement (relative to the position of another participant)
(e. exists independently of the event named by the verb)

Contributing Properties for the Prototypical Patient:
a.   undergoes change of state
b.   incremental theme
c.   causally affected by another participant
d.   stationary relative to movement of another participant
(e.   does not exist independently of the event, or not at all)

(Dowty 1991: 572)

Examples of P-Patients not existing independently of the verb-predicate would include: *the militia destroyed the village*; *John built a bridge*; *this situation constitutes a major dilemma for us*; *we need a new constitution*; *John is seeking a unicorn*. It also includes non-specific arguments: *he wants to buy a red car*, and the like. The distinction between P-Agents and P-Patients is one that we shall broadly adopt in our analyses (also Chilton 2000), but occasionally draw finer distinctions within the categories, such as *theme* (an argument changing location), goal (location towards which there is movement) and *cogniser* (an argument having conceptions or perceptions).

Discourse worlds

Discourse consists of coherent chains of propositions which establish a 'discourse' 'world', or 'discourse ontology' – in effect, the 'reality' that is entertained by the speaker, or meta-represented by speaker as being someone else's believed reality. There are various meaning ingredients that go into these discourse realities, but the essential one is the projection of 'who does what to whom, when and where'. In language use the speaker postulates discourse referents with different thematic roles. The roles are defined by the relations between the discourse referents. How do these abstract meaning schemata map onto language in use? The prototype is the clause, with (in English) its subject-verb-object structure. However, argument-predicate structure, along with their relations and roles, pops up in other forms – inside some noun phrases, in subordinate clauses in which some arguments might be implied, and in the semantic phe-nomenon of presupposition which is triggered by various syntactic and lexical structures. Presupposition is of interest because it frequently is 'existential' – i.e., it expresses the taken-for-granted existence of some referent. Overall discourse coherence is achieved, at least in part, by the recurrence of, and links between the different discourse referents of the discourse world.

Since the ontologies communicated by political speakers is of interest, we need a method for analysing their discourse. One device, which we shall use in a later chapter, is to 'filter' out the linguistic expressions that set up the recurring discourse referents and prompt for their thematic roles and relations. Here is an example, which lays the basis for some of the analysis we do in Chapter 9. It is the official transcript of the beginning of a speech given by President Clinton in 1999:

My fellow Americans, today our Armed Forces joined our NATO allies in air strikes against Serbian forces responsible for the brutality in Kosovo. We have acted with resolve for several reasons. We act to protect thousands of innocent people in Kosovo from a mounting military offensive. We act to prevent a wider war; to diffuse a powder keg at the heart of Europe that has exploded twice before in this century with catastrophic results. And we act to stand united with our allies for peace. By acting now we are upholding our values, protecting our interests and advancing the cause of peace.

We make sense of this effortlessly, with of course some variation depending on the time, place, interests and identity of hearers themselves. One of the things we are doing, potentially, is unpacking the sentences to make propositional representations, and we can display the potentiality in a simple way as represented by Table 4.1.

Table 4.1 Propositional representations

Argument 1 typically P-Agent, grammatical subject, typically a noun phrase	Predicate relation, action existence, etc., intransitive, transitive or ditransitive verb	Argument 2 typically P-Patient, grammatical object, typically a noun phrase	Other arguments e.g., noun, phrase or prepositional phrase	Adjunct/conjunct e.g., adverbs, participle phrases, conjunctions like 'and', 'if'
				today
Our Armed forces **agent (themes, i.e., thing moving)**	joined	our NATO allies **patient (location)**		in air strikes against Serbian forces responsible for the brutality in Kosovo
[US forces and NATO forces] **agent**	[made air strikes against]	[Serbian forces responsible for the brutality in Kosovo] **patient**		
[Serbian forces] **agent**	[are responsible for]	[the brutality in Kosovo] **patient**		
[brutality]	[exists]			[in Kosovo]

For the moment we are not concerned with meaning effects that have to do with social interaction (e.g., the use of 'we') but with the cognitive domain of participants, their roles and relations, i.e. with what exists and who does what. The dotted arrows in Table 4.1 take you to the 'unpackaged' propositional analysis (in square brackets) of noun phrases, embedded clauses and presuppositions. This example is a typical case of embedding of propositions within a prepositional phrase adjunct. The point of such packaging, and the effect, is that the bits of 'reality' so packaged are made less salient or more taken for granted as common ground for speaker and hearer.

Indexicality and the dimensions of deixis

Language-in-use, language$_{l/u}$, consists of utterances generated and interpreted in relation to the situation in which the utterer(s) and interpreter(s) are positioned. The term 'positioned' can be understood as a spatial metaphor conceptualising the speaker's and/or hearer's relationship to their interlocutor(s), to their physical location, to the point in time of the ongoing utterance, and to where they are in the ongoing discourse. 'Indexical expressions' or 'deictic expressions' are linguistic resources used to perform *deixis* – that is, to prompt the interpreter to relate the uttered indexical expression to various situational features.[7]

Space, time and society

Pronouns are one class of words that can perform deictic functions. For example, in political discourse the first person plural (*we, us, our*) can be used to induce interpreters to conceptualise group identity, coalitions, parties, and the like, either as insiders or as outsiders. Social indexicals arise from social structure and power relations, and not just from personal distance. Spatial indexicals relate to political or geopolitical space. Thus *here* may mean 'in parliament', 'in London', 'in the States', 'in England', 'in the UK', 'in Europe', 'in the West', 'in the northern hemisphere', etc. That is, *here* and its reflexes in *come/go*, *bring/take*, and the like, can require to be understood not simply in terms of a neutral physical location but in terms of some conventional frame.

Temporal deixis can have a political significance. It can require one to assume a particular historical periodisation – for example *nowadays, today*, or just *now* could require to be understood as 'after the revolution', 'after the fall of the Berlin Wall', 'after the election of New Labour', or some such. The concept of deictic centre (Verschueren 1999: 20) is sometimes used to denote the implied 'anchoring' point that utterers and interpreters construct or impose during verbal interaction. What is clear from political discourse analysis is that such anchoring depends on cognitive frames that embody conventional shared understandings about the structure of society, groups and relations with other societies.

While spatial, temporal and social deixis are usually distinguished from one another, it may be the case that space is in some way more fundamental. Bearing in mind the theory of metaphor outlined earlier, it is worth noticing that both time and social relationships seem, if one goes on the lexical evidence, to be conceptualised in terms of space, at least in part. Thus, as Lakoff and Johnson (1980) long since pointed out, time appears to be conceptualised either as an object moving towards the speaker ('the end of the war is coming') or as the speaker moving towards a time ('we are approaching the end of the war'). Similarly, social (and political) relationships are lexicalised, and conceptualised, in terms of space metaphors: for example, 'close allies', 'distant relations', 'rapprochement', are part of the vocabulary of politics (Lakoff and Johnson 1980; Johnson 1987; Lakoff 1987).

Spatial representations, including metaphorical ones, take on an important aspect in political discourse. If politics is about cooperation and conflict over allocation of resources, such resources are frequently of a spatial, that is, geographical or territorial, kind. This is obvious in the case of international politics, where borders, territorial sovereignty and access are often at issue. Politics can also be about the relations between social groups, viewed literally or metaphorically as spatially distinct entities. Political actors are, moreover, always situated with respect to a particular time, place and social group. Because of factors such as these, we shall treat spatial representation in discourse as particularly important in the study of political discourse. In addition to space, time and social distance, however, I am proposing that we add a third axis, which I will refer to loosely as 'modality'.

The modal axis: reality and morality

Texts enable hearers to generate cognitive structures in short and long-term memory, as it were backstage rather than upfront in the words themselves (Turner 1991: 206; Fauconnier 1985: xxii–xxiii). Among these structures are complexes of 'spaces', 'worlds' or 'sub-worlds', in the terminology of Fauconnier (1985) and Werth (1999). We can think of such structures as *discourse ontologies*. All forms of text and talk make assumptions about what *is* – what entities, locations, etc., exist and what are the relationships among them. People also make assumptions about the ontological *status* of these the entities in a repre-sented world (compare the brief discussion of 'source-tagging' and credibility in Chapter 2). For example, people's representations have entities that *may* exist, *might have* existed, *reportedly* exist, *definitely don't* exist, and so on. Entities and the relations among them may be represented as physically necessary, socially imposed or as morally imperative. There is a strong spatial element in this dimension also.

So, we are suggesting that in processing any discourse people 'position' other entities in their 'world' by 'positioning' these entities in relation to themselves

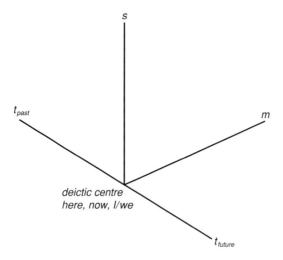

Figure 4.1 Dimensions of deixis

along (at least) three axes, space, time and modality. The deictic centre (the Self, that is, *I* or *we*) is the 'origin' of the three dimensions. Other entities (arguments of predicates) and processes (predicates) 'exist' relative to ontological spaces defined by their coordinates on the space (*s*), time (*t*) and modality (*m*) axes. This makes it possible to conceptualise the ongoing kaleidoscope of onto-logical configurations, activated by text, as in Figure 4.1.

On the space axis *s* we have spatial deictic expressions, e.g., pronouns. The speaker (Self, which may be *I* or a *we*-group) is at *here*. The entities indexed by second-person and third-person pronouns are 'situated' along *s*, some nearer to, some more remote from *self*. It is not that we can actually measure the 'distances' from Self; rather, the idea is that people tend to place people and things along a scale of remoteness from the self, using background assumptions and indexical cues. And this scale is only loosely related to geography: to English people Australia might seem 'closer' than Albania. At the remote end of *s* is Other. Participants that have roles in the discourse world as agents, patients, locations, etc., are located closer to or more remote from Self, whether or not the discourse indicates the location explicitly by way of some expressions such as 'near', 'close', 'remote', etc. As well as geographical distance this axis will locate entities that have metaphorical 'social' distance, again with or without explicit markers, such as 'near relations', 'close cooperation', 'remote connection', and the like.

On the *t* axis, the origin is the time of speaking, surrounded, so to speak, by an area that counts as 'now'. Because, as we noted above, time has a conceptualisation in terms of motion through space, relative distance to or from

Self, events, which carry a time of happening as part of their conceptualisation, can be located as 'near' or 'distant': 'the revolution is getting closer', 'the time for an agreement has arrived', 'we are a long way from achieving our goals'. Both past and future can be remote: e.g., 'way back in the remote past', 'a long way into the future'. For political discourse in general subjectively 'positioned' time periods can be of considerable importance – history, and which parts of it are 'close' to the 'us' is central to national ideologies and to justifying present and future policy.

With regard to the *m* axis a little more explanation is needed. The general idea is that Self is not only *here* and *now*, but also the origin of the epistemic *true* and the deontic *right*. The *m* axis seems to involve several strands. For instance, there are close connections between epistemic modality (having to do with degrees of certainty), deontic modality (having to do with permission and obligation) and negation. The first two, epistemic and deontic modality, are commonly thought of as scales, and are closely linked. But how are such abstract notions grounded? Talmy (1988) has argued that modal concepts, both epistemic and deontic, are grounded in intuitive force dynamics, that is, basic concepts about movement, pressure and obstacles. Following Talmy, Sweetser (1990) argues that epistemic modals (e.g., '*can* she have arrived already?') are meta-phorically derived from deontic modals (e.g., 'you *can* leave now') or ordinary 'dynamic' modals (e.g., 'she *can* fly'). The general idea is clear from polysem-ous expressions such as 'stopping' (forbidding) someone doing something, and 'letting' someone do something (allowing them to 'go ahead').

We are adding to this account, and focusing on, the fact that modality, like space and time and social relations seems to be also conceptualised in terms of remoteness. This approach is supported by evidence from polysemy. For epistemic 'remoteness' we find many expressions like 'not *remotely* possible', '*far from* the truth', '*approach* the truth', and so forth. The epistemic scale represents S's commitment to the truth of a proposition, ranging from confident prediction to near impossibility (Werth 1999: 314–15). It can be argued that at each end the scale should be extended to include 'true' (the modality of assertion), near to or co-located with Self, and 'untrue' or, better, 'falsity', at the remote end, that is, near to or co-located with Other. As many linguists have pointed out, negation is a function of discourse and takes its sense from its relation to propositions asserted elsewhere by the speaker (S). Since we are modelling situated discourse, the end points are speech acts: assertion and negation. A consequence of this approach is that conditional sentences, which involve both counterfactuality and irreality, can also be accounted for in terms of the remote part of the modality scale.

Deontic meaning, as Saeed (1997: 127) points out

> is tied in with all sorts of social knowledge: the speaker's belief systems about morality and legality; and her estimations of power and authority.

Particular instances of deontic meaning are obviously contingent on prevailing norms for the speaker and hearer. But this does not mean there are no general patterns. While the case is a bit more complex than for epistemic modality, deontic modality can also be theorised as a scale. Frawley (1992: 421–3) argues that the deontic scale has a proximity–remoteness structure, similar to that of epistemic modality. However, there is more conceptual complexity, because, as suggested above, social groups are conceptualised metaphorically on the basis of the image schemata *container* and *centre-periphery*. This is reflected in polysemous expressions such as 'he has gone *too far*', '*outside* the norms of convention', '*within* the bounds of decency', '*beyond* the pale'. Most telling are the concepts intuitively connected with 'insiders' and 'outsiders': insiders are those that 'stay close to' or 'stand by our standards'; outsiders are expected, or suspected, to do the opposite. That which is morally or legally 'wrong' is distanced from Self. The scale is directional, oriented toward the Self's authoritative 'position' with respect to Other. The end points are the speech acts of command ('you *must* do such and such') and prohibition ('you are *forbidden* to do such and such').

The polysemy of 'right' and 'wrong' supports the idea that epistemic and deontic scales are closely related: what is right is both truth-conditionally 'right' and legally or morally 'right', and correspondingly for 'wrong'. The scale *m* in the deictic space diagrams therefore stands for a composite scale, approximately as in Figure 4.2.

Figure 4.2 shows only modal verbs, but other linguistic expressions do the same kind of job. The underlying principles seem to be, in crude terms: Self is always right or in the right, the Other always wrong, or in the wrong. It is possible that a scale of this kind represents some universal conceptual pattern; what is certainly the case is that many instances of political discourse seem to build meanings that closely associate the Self with truth and righteousness, the Other with their opposite.

Returning to the model outlined in Figure 4.1 (see p. 58), what we are suggesting is that discourse is based on the expectation that anyone mentally processing it will locate arguments and predicates by reference to points on the

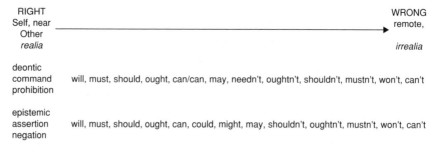

Figure 4.2 The rightness-wrongness scale

three axes *s*, *t* and *m*. In other words, they will have coordinates on *s*, *t* and *m*. The coordinates are established in the discourse as part of S's reality–space, the space that S expects H (hearer) to know and accept.

The coordinates are indexed in discourse by linguistic expressions ('space-builders' in Fauconnier's terminology, 'world-builders' in Werth's) of various types: tense, prepositional phrases, pronouns, modal expressions, and so forth, in conjunction with frame-based knowledge. Several propositions might cluster in the same 'space' – for example, the space of what did happen at some point in the past, of what ought to happen but has not yet, and so on. Some propositions involve arguments (prototypically agents and patients) that change their deictic coordinates (e.g., 'the President went to London', 'inflation increased in the 1970s', 'the truth slowly came out'). Further, there are links between the deictically indexed spaces. Anaphora (explicit and inferred), sequence and synchronicity are types of such relations, but more interesting are relations such as belief, hypothesis, purpose, intention, cause and conditionality. Analogy and metonymy are also types of intra-discursive relations between spaces. These relations may be inferred rather than explicit, as also may ontological spaces themselves.

As a stretch of discourse unfolds, the speaker and hearer establish mental representations, mental ontologies, in which certain entities are postulated explicitly or implicitly as existing. These entities may be manifest to the speaker and hearer in the physical setting in which they are interacting. Quite often, though, they are not. In political discourse, especially foreign policy discourse, the reality or realities referred to cannot possibly be actually present for speaker and hearer. The speaker thus has to do a lot of discursive work to enable, or induce the hearer to mentally establish a representation. This process requires that the point of intersection where Self is situated be taken for granted, at least for the purposes of the communicative exchange.

Inexplicit meaning

Meaning is not always expressed in explicit form, nor indeed is it always possible to do so. It is important to remember that meaning is not 'contained' in words, nor is it a thing to be discovered, or uncovered; rather meaning is constructed by human minds on the basis of language$_{l/u}$, using language$_L$, together with massive amounts of 'background' knowledge. However, there are evidently degrees of explicitness in the cues that language$_{l/u}$ provides for the hearer. Of course, it may be misleading to say 'language-in-use provides', since it is *people* who produce utterances, and they have some degree of choice in how exactly they prompt their hearers to construct the mental representations they would like them to construct. That is to say, speakers have a degree of choice in the wording and phrasing that prompts hearers to experience particular meanings.

Analysts of political language-in-use need to raise some of these meaning-packaging processes to consciousness.

Entailment

Entailment involves the fact that the semantic structure of languages includes, among many other things, truth relations between sentences that hold irrespective of whether those sentences are empirically verifiable or not. Thus, to cite a classic example, *the fanatic assassinated the president* entails *the president died*. The entailment relation implies that if an entailing sentence p is true, then an entailed sentence q is necessarily also true, and if q is false, then p is false. Entailments of this type are generated by lexical structure and by syntax. The sense of the word *assassinate* apparently 'includes' the sense *die* – a relationship similar to hyponymy, which in general is a source of entailment. An example of syntactic entailment would be the active and passive forms of a sentence.

While this standard account focuses on truth and logic, from the point of view of discourse analysis, some further observations are necessary. The existence of apparent lexical entailments may in some cases be a function of social or ideological beliefs. This is perhaps tantamount to saying that lexical structure itself should not be regarded as entirely independent of social and ideological beliefs, or to saying that lexical structure should not be regarded as analytically separate from discourse. For example, there may be certain speakers for whom the sentence *the surgeon entered the room* automatically implies *a man entered the room*. It is difficult to see that in terms of semantic relations, logic or the mental operation involved such an implication is different from entailment in the case of *assassinate–die*. What is interesting for political discourse is the automaticity of the relationship.

A second point about entailment in discourse concerns the strategic use that can be made of it. Consider, for example:

  (a) An Asian male was beaten up in the street.
  (b) A man was beaten up in the street.
  (c) Someone was beaten up in the street.

Here (a) entails (b) and (c). Though such examples tend to appear trivial, they can be significant in discursive interaction, because speakers may have reasons to prefer to give less rather than more information. For instance, in the above examples, a police officer may prefer, for one reason or another, not to focus on the racial identity of the victim. Even if the officer uses (b) or (c), he or she can still claim – privately or, if challenged, publicly – to be still telling the truth. Entailment *qua* truth relation guarantees this. Nonetheless, pragmatic issues cannot be avoided here. For the matter of *how much* information *should* be given is in any case a matter of social belief and expectation.

Presupposition

Presupposition, like entailment, can be viewed as a relationship between two sentences, in abstraction from any context of utterance. However, such a perspective breaks down as the phenomenon is examined more closely, and social knowledge has to be brought in to explain what is happening. From the logical point of view, presupposition is distinguished from entailment in the following way: a negated entailing sentence destroys the entailed sentence, whereas a negated presupposing sentence preserves its presupposition. For example, *the prime minister of Russia is visiting today* presupposes *there is a prime minister of Russia*. But the sentence, *the prime minister of Russia is not visiting today*, also presupposes *there is a prime minister of Russia*. For that matter, both the sentences *the king of France is bald* and *the king of France is not bald* presuppose the sentence *there is a king of France*. This sentence famously preoccupied Bertrand Russell and other logicians, because there is no king of France (not at the moment of speaking, anyway), so the presupposed proposition is false. This creates a problem for the truth-based logical approach.

Discourse analysis, especially if linked to a cognitive perspective, has ways of manoeuvring round this obstacle. Political discourse analysis perhaps has something special to add to the understanding of the phenomenon. One might say that Russell had a problem because he *knew* that there was no king of France, in 1905, when he published the seminal article that discussed this example. His historical knowledge of the world contradicted the presupposition of existence which proper names and definite reference in general carry. The interesting point is that one cannot stop the presupposition popping up, even though one knows that it is false — whence the sensation of cognitive discomfort. This way of looking at things is similar to, but not quite identical to Fauconnier's (1985) approach. A pragmatic perspective sheds further light. The problem arises only because the sentence is removed from the context of utterers and interpreters. An utterer who believed that there did exist a king of France (a latter-day French royalist, for example) might generate the sentence without contradiction, and a hearer with the same beliefs would also presumably have no problem. But their hearer, seeking to interpret the sentence, might not have such beliefs. This could mean either that the interpreter knows that France is at the time of speaking a republic and therefore cannot possibly have a king, or they may simply not know what the French constitution is (for example, if they are a child or uninformed for some other reason). In the first instance the sentence will be perceived as anomalous and may or may not be challenged; the speaker has presupposed a proposition that is not shared, is not in the common ground of the discourse. In the second case the existential proposition may be added to the interpreter's memory as a 'fact' of reality. Lewis (1979) calls this last phenomenon 'accommodation'. In either case, the presupposition pops up automatically, even though it may have to be discarded. There are many such examples of the defeasibility of presuppositions in the pragmatics literature. One can speculate that the automatic popping up of presuppositions is an evolutionary consequence of human communication. In small coherent speech-communities common ground can perhaps be safely assumed, and much information treated as 'old' and not in need of explicitation; this would be an advantage in circumstances where rapid processing would be an advantage.

In this and many other cases, presupposition can be seen as a way of strategically 'packaging' information. Some information (the existence of a referent or a proposition) can be treated as commonly known and accepted – that is, as 'old' information. If it is not known that it is known or accepted, it seems unreasonable to presuppose it. If the cooperative principle is operating, then the maxim of quantity should in some way govern whether a presuppositional strategy is used or not. If the speaker assumes some such information is not known and is cooperating efficiently, he or she will presumably package it lexically, syntactically and intonationally as 'new' information. The accommodation principle might be regarded as either a similarly advantageous processing feature or as an accidental consequence. In a political perspective, presupposition might be linked to what political scientists call consensus. Presupposition is at least one micro-mechanism in language use which contributes to the building of a consensual reality.

Presuppositions are not made explicit unless they are being challenged or rejected. The corollary of this is that presuppositions are used when they are not *expected* to be challenged or rejected. And there is a rider. It takes effort to retrieve, formulate and challenge a presupposition – the effort being both cognitive, and, since a face-threatening act is involved, also social. Speakers will therefore have the option of using presuppositions strategically to avoid challenge or rejection. Such avoidance has two advantages: it evades social threats and it may result in unconscious cognitive adjustments, to which the hearer adds propositions to representations of the world in memory – this being effectively what we mean by 'taking something for granted'.

Presumptions

The kinds of inexplicit meaning we have just discussed are those that appear most automatic or most tightly bound to the nature of linguistic systems. However, it will already be clear that presuppositions in particular are closely linked with interactive considerations and also with other forms of cognitive structure. For instance, presuppositions call up knowledge bases already held in long-term memory, as well as short-term memory of the ongoing speech context (van Dijk 2002).

Although in semantics and pragmatics the predominant understanding of presupposition refers to propositions, some authors (Fetzer 2002) use the term to include broader pragmatic principles. In particular, within speech act theory, for instance one might say that felicity conditions are 'presupposed', though not usually challenged. Within Grice's framework, one could say that the conversational maxims are 'presupposed', and, more fundamentally, the cooperative principle. Within Habermasian universal pragmatics, one could say that validity claims are always 'presupposed' every time an utterance is effected.

Behind this approach lies the idea that utterances are produced on the expectation that the anticipated hearers share some common ground with respect to the claims and conceptualisations. In terms of the Habermasian validity claims discussed in Chapter 3, the speakers whose texts we are examining can be thought of as claiming to: (a) be telling the objective truth; (b) be speaking truthfully, that is, not lying or distorting; (c) to be speaking in an intelligible language; and (d) speaking rightly. This latter claim we have taken to mean that the speaker is claiming to have the right, as established in some social framework of communication, to perform the speech acts that he or she is making. Because many of these 'claims' are implicit or presumed, I am going to refer here to presumptions, which combine the meaning of claim and implication.[8] We can understand what is going on in terms of coherence. The linguistic form of the utterances are 'coherent' only if certain presumptions are attributed to the speaker, presumptions which the speaker assumes are (or perhaps ought to be) accepted by the hearer. If one or more of the validity claims is fulfilled, we have a presumption. This point becomes important when we consider political discourse as a whole – we come to it with presumptions about its operation that are quite different from when we engage in, say, explaining to a friend how to operate a computer. And there are also different presumptions about the various sub-genres of political discourse, too, such that we have different presumptions about the way televised party political broadcasts operate from say the presumptions we bring to a lively political interview on the radio.

Part II

The domestic arena

5 Political interviews

In Chapters 3 and 4 we looked at ways of analysing the linguistic behaviour that we call political discourse. For the purpose of making sense of it, we artificially separated representation (the more obviously cognitive aspect) from interaction (the more obviously pragmatic). In this chapter we bring these two analytical perspectives together, in order to focus on a particular arena of modern political communication – the media.

In this chapter we look at the micro-structure of one particular genre that has come to rival the parliamentary institutions for making politicians accountable – the media interview. Such an example could be chosen from many different similar types in many different languages in many different contemporary societies. The case we have taken is from the British BBC: a radio interview on a well-known news programme, in which a prominent woman politician is being questioned vigorously in the run-up to the general elections of 2001. It is necessarily specific, but it represents a genre that is familiar around the globe. There are of course numerous cultural variations which readers will doubtless be aware of.

Radio interviews and electioneering

Here is a transcript of a radio interview that took place on BBC Radio 4 (the *Today* programme) two days before the UK general elections in June 2001. The interviewer is the well-known John Humphrys, and the interviewee is Margaret Beckett, Labour MP and Leader of the House of Commons. The point of the detailed transcript (see Appendix for conventions) below is that it shows up the micro-behaviour of these two speakers, locked in a very specific kind of human interaction.

1   JH   . . . ((preceding talk omitted)) there 're only *two* days to go now so what's

2   *worrying* the Labour Party. Margaret Beckett (.) <leader of the Commons in

3   the last parliament is on the line good morning to *you.*=

4   MB   =good morning.

5   JH   are you worried about *any*thing?

6   MB   yes I'm worried about people listening to Mr Hague, (.) and deciding not to

7   vote unless they're going to vote Conservative. (.) ((I)) think that would be er

8   *bad* for democracy and what's *more.* .hh er although at the moment er many

9   people in the media are saying oh well y'know might this be a good thing. /on

10   Friday. (.) ev'ryone who *doesn't* vote Labour (.) er or ev'ryone who *fails* to

11   vote will be taken as *ab*solute support for ev'rything Mr Hague is doing, or for

12   the way he's run this campaign and I think that would be an awfully bad thing.

13   JH   what (.) if we abstain from *voti*:ng, (.) on Thursday for all sorts of reasons

14   ↑some of which might be very ↑principled reasons. .hh /that would be taken as

15   support for William ↓↑Hague

16   MB   i' certainly *would.*

17   JH   ↑why?

18   MB   because it'd be taken as rejection (.) of the=

19   =↑govern↓ment│ and er ((..... inaudible . . .))*

20   JH   │and aren't we allowed to do that?*=

21   MB   =/ ↑oh ↓you're all ↑↓owed to do whatever you ↑↓like (.) but er you're asking me

22   what worries me:, (.) and *that's* what worries me: (.) \that we'll be told that you

23   know this is er a big surge. (.) /and you know er erm let's look at er what

24   happened in the United States, er huge continent, (.) millions and millions and

25   millions of people entitled to vote, er people obviously a lot of people deciding

26   that it *really* doesn't make much difference whether they vote or not and it the

27   thing turns on a *hand*ful of ↑votes │↓((*s, s, s, s*))*

28   JH   │ah: (.)   *but so they're actually entitled

29   to do that aren't they │because* many of them ↑↓↑sa:y (.) there's not a=

30   MB   │/oh yes *

31   JH   =lot of difference between any of them any longer, and that's hw wha' er

32   ex@@ctly er wha' many people are saying in ↑*this* country now │there's not=

33   MB   │> indeed =

34   JH   =a blind bi' of difference between ↑any of them *   │

35   MB   = they indeed they   did   (.) * no that's right that's ex*act*ly

36   what a lot of people said in America (.) and a lot of them said too the ideal the

37   thing to do was to vote for a third party give the major parties a shock, .hh

38   /and I wonder how satisfied they all are with the *out*come.

39   JH   (.) we:ll but nonetheless whether they're satisfied or not with the outcome it's

40   it's it's a democratic ex*pres*sion it ((sugg│ests th't)) *

41   MB   │((s s   don't *quarrel with that))

42   JH   ya. (.) <but I mean if you you ↑seem to be in a way you seem to be saying

43   well look they'll they'll be (.) really doing something ↑terrible they'll be

44   supp↑orting >William ↑Ha:gue (.hh) by not voting for us, (.hh) but they're

45   ↑*not* supporting William Hague by not voting ((for you)) we're a we're

46   absolutely entitled to say, (.hh) we're fed up with all of you \if that is our view

47   and we're not going to vote (.hh) /as a way of showing our ↑protest.

47 MB /yes. er I know. D'you know one of the things ((that)) \y er I mean you ask me
48   worry worried me most, it's people staying away that er worry me most
49   partly because of how it will be read and because I think I'm right in saying
50   that if .hh say one in four people who voted Labour (.) last time don't vote this
51   time we'll lose something like sixty .hh *very* good MPs and that will *certainly*
52   be taken .hh er as a very powerful signal but /the ↑other ↓thing that worries me
53   that's been running throughout this campaign .hh is the whole kind of thing
54   about .hh how *easy* it is to *do* everything. .hh I mean I've noticed that one of
55   ((the)) two of the people .hh who have (.) perfectly understandably and
56   perfectly fairly .hh been making strong protests about what is *still* .hh er th
57   concern about the state of our public services .hh have been saying also .hh er
58   an I'm not going to vote or I don't vote because there >isn't any point .hh /as if
59   *someho:w* it's terribly *easy* to turn things ↑↓round.
60 JH   cuz /that's|the impres*sion you gave us during the last cam|paign ((er fo fo))*=
61 MB |but that's* |oh come ↑↓on*
62 JH   =forty-eight hours to save the NH ↑S (.)| */it was all gonna ↑change
63 MB |oh*
64 MB   a l l look \John. (.) there isn't *single* person anywhere in Britain, .hh who
65   thought that what we were saying at the last election .hh was tha' if we were
66   elected the NHS would be (.) trans*formed* in twenty-four hours. =
67   =.h |/what   they   understood,*
68 JH   twen|ty- ↑four ↓hours ↑to ↓save* ↑the ↓N↑H↑S
69 MB   (.) \let's not be silly please
70 JH   I'm ↑*not* being silly | I'm being ↑↓hugely* ↑ser↓ious. When you say=
71 MB | \Yes you are.*
72 JH   =something like twenty-four hours to >*save* the NHS|the impression you=
73 MB |everybody who heard
74   that statement*
75 JH   =create* in the minds of the listener (.) is well if we vote Labour things
76   will change dram↑atically we are now four years in .hh and *many* people
77   believe \including many professionals with ↑in the NHS .hh that it is *worse*
78   now *worse* now .hh than it was four ↑years ago.
79 MB   no I don't remotely accept that. I mean if I think about erm (.) people *I* know in
80   the NHS (.) who were complaining to me before the election, .hh about the
81   size of the s the consultant teams they're working in in key ↑areas, .hh who
82   now have seen that position transformed who express as*tonish*ment to me:. .hh
83   that there are people who claim that it hasn't changed for the better. .hh /but
84   let's take a classic example this *week.* .hh there are people who have been
85   saying this week. .hh that the government is wrong to make the thee to to set
86   the ↑*targ*ets we ha:ve .hh to try an achieve to get more doctors into the health
87   service, .hh because they say there may not be enough people to train them.
88   .hh /now the people who *train doctors* .hh do not (.) get to the position where
89   they can train doctors in five ↑minutes,(.) they don't even get into that position
90   .hh in (.) four ↑↓↑years, .hh if there is a ↑*prob* ↓em (.) with (.) the (.) number of
91   people, the *adequacy* of the places and the staff to man those training places
92   .hh this is a problem we inherited. /and I do not believe (.) for (.) ↑one (.)
93   ↑*sec* ↓ond that there's *any*body in this country. .hh who thought that we were

```
94          saying that we could solve *all* the problems of the health service in=
95          =|((four)) minutes.* what they thought we=
96  JH        | alright     one,*
97  MB      =were saying was that we could make a star' (.) and I think that we s most
98          *cer*tainly *ha:ve* and a very good start.
99  JH      alright. one other story that has arisen this morning as you will know is sh is
100         that of Keith Vaz new er .hhh allegations against him. new evidence
101         uncovered by this programme, er what should ↓happen about that?
102 MB      what should happen about it is that those a allegations should be examined
103         through the (.) er proper channel:s that exist to (.) examine them. I thought that
104         Francis Maud's performance this morning was extraordinary. .hh he wants to
105         be the foreign secretary on Friday an he went straight from allegation to
106         penalty without touching ground in bet↑ween.
107 JH      well, he said that er mis | ter Blair should recognise this*
108 MB                               | <he said all sorts of extraordinary things that I'd be
109         cautious* about repeating I'd 've thought.
110 JH      er he said that Mr Blair should recognise this as a very serious matter, he s
111         said that | he *should ↑sack (.) Mr Vaz |      *because of these allegations=
112 MB                | well he,*                    | yes*
113 JH      = against him.
114 MB      well he's been saying that for a long time=
115         = .hh I mean he was| desperate*
116 JH                         |<doesn't make* him ↑↓wrong↑
117 MB      he was desperate to turn it into er a problem for the prime minister .hh the
118         problem for the prime minister (.) is (.) that we have an election now. where
119         there is ↑clear choice before the British people.=
120      |  =this is no' a referendum on the governm*ent.
121 JH   |  should you ignore the Vaz affair then?*
122 MB      /no it should be dealt with through the proper processes and with with (.) *deep*
123         respect to you ↓↑*John* .hh and fond as I am of you all the proper processes are
124         ↑↓*not*↑ through an interview on the *Today* programme of two minutes in the
125         morning. .hh there there are er (..) there're ↑people ↓whose ↑job it is ↓to ↑look
126         at these things and I ↓have ↑no ↑doubt at ↓all that they will be looked at .hh ↑if
127         Keith Vaz is returned as a member of parliament.
128 JH      \Margaret Beckett, many thanks.
```

Contexts

Rather than seeing political news interviews as sub-genres of the institution of
'news interviews' (Heritage and Greatbatch 1991), it makes more sense here
to view such interviews as a sub-genre of the institution 'political discourse'.
This means that we can expect such a sub-genre to incorporate contextual
references to the political institutions within which political actors operate, and
to recent political history. What is clear from looking at discourse that we
intuitively call 'political' is that participants are aware of social structures beyond

the local context of the current interaction. They have knowledge of those structures, of customs of discourse associated with, or constituting those structures, and of the past utterances of other speakers associated with those customs and structures.

In her first contextual reference, the interviewee requires her listeners to be aware that William Hague was the Conservative Party leader and main election competitor against Labour. Further, she assumes some knowledge of the content of Hague's recent utterances, for it is difficult to infer what Hague might have said from her formulation. In fact, Hague had been widely reported as warning potential and wavering Conservative Party voters that the Labour Party was about to win a landslide majority.[1] Only in the light of this can Beckett's opening remark (6–8) be made sense of: she can be understood as expecting listeners to infer, given a knowledge of the electoral process, that 'listening' to Mr Hague can mean either deciding to vote Conservative or deciding not to vote at all (thus reducing the Labour vote). Incidentally, the verb *listening* here has to be understood not simply in its basic sense which has to do with auditory attention-giving, but its extended sense of 'obeying', 'complying' or 'taking heed'.

The second contextual feature referred to (at 99–100 in the transcript below) requires that the listeners recognise and have in their memory store some details of the media reports associated with, Mr Keith Vaz. In fact, earlier in the year, Mr Vaz, who was a Labour MP (for Leicester East) and Minister for Europe, had been reported widely in the media because of alleged corruption. He faced eighteen allegations including allegations that he had solicited money and failed to declare links with businessmen. Although an investigation by the House of Commons Standards and Privileges Committee had cleared him of nine allegations, eight others remained in suspension. One charge had been upheld against Mr Vaz – his failure to reveal his links with a lawyer whom he had recommended for an honour in 1997.[2] Not only do the interviewer and interviewee take some representation of these facts for granted, the interviewer also evokes even more recent reportage – new allegations made public that very morning, according to which Vaz failed, during the most recent investigation into his affairs, to tell parliament about valuable properties owned by him in London. Contextual knowledge is crucial: Conversation analysis (CA) or similar type of analysis alone cannot explain either the 'point' of the exchange above concerning Vaz or the actual length and structure of the talk, with its interruptions, hesitations, repairs and fraught turn-taking.

The third contextual evocation (at 104) requires that listeners can identify Francis Maud, the Conservative MP for Horsham and shadow Foreign Secretary. Further, when Beckett says 'I thought that Francis Maud's performance this morning was extraordinary', hearers can infer only that Maud did (probably said) something that Beckett disapproves of relative to Mr Vaz. This may be sufficient for the utterance to make sense – but not much sense, and the uninformed hearer might feel (perhaps applying Grice's maxim of quantity) that the amount of sense is inadequate. She can, of course, assume that Humphrys (as a professional political journalist) will have heard Maud's utterances, but not that the generality of hearers has done so. Satisfactory interpretation of Beckett's allusion can only be constructed if the hearer knew that Maud had said inter alia that Mr Vaz had become 'a symbol of Labour sleaze and arrogance', and that 'Keith Vaz should be booted out of his ministerial office and Tony Blair must also withdraw his support for him as a Labour candidate'.[3] Again, the nature of the talk at the stage this reference is made can only be explained in terms of the contextual knowledge of the participants. One should perhaps here speak rather of 'intercontextual' or 'intertextual' knowledge.

Interactions

Interviews are structured by a question-and-answer format. However, quite apart from the fact that no one expects politicians to give 'straight' answers, things are not so simple.[4] Is it always the interviewer who asks the questions? Are they always 'neutral'? What functions do questions have, apart from requesting information?

The interviewer

Towards the end of the interview, after some rather turbulent disruptions of turn-taking, the question-answer pairs are more or less stabilised. At 99–101, the interviewer provides a preface followed by an explicit interrogative and at 100 the interviewer seems to begin a straightforward reply. There is in fact another turbulent episode, but the closure of the interview is executed by means of what appears to be a clean question-answer pair:

121 JH   should you ignore the Vaz affair then?*
122 MB   /no it should be dealt with through the proper processes.

However, closer inspection shows that the interviewer's question is in fact an interruption. Certainly, it has the form of an interrogative, but because it can be heard as a 'rhetorical question' it can function also as a comment on the interviewee's response:

117 MB   he was desperate to turn it into er a problem for the prime minister .hh the
118   problem for the prime minister (.) is (.) that we have an election now. where

119   there is ↑*clear* choice before the British people.=
120 | =this is no' a referendum on the governm*ent.
121 JH | should you ignore the Vaz affair then?*

There is a similar instance at 19–20, where the interviewer does not
wait for the conclusion of the interviewee's turn, and does not pose an
unequivocal question. Although the interviewer does indeed refrain from
'continuers' for considerable stretches of talk, he does nonetheless interrupt
before, and near to what appears to be the close of the interviewee's turn.
Such interruptions are frequent enough to be noticeable: 20, 27–8, 67, 95–6,
115–16, 119–20.

The interviewer does not, then, confine himself to posing questions, does not
wait until the indicated completion of an interviewer's turn, and does not even
perform an utterance that is unequivocally a question – something that also
makes one question whether he is adopting what Heritage and Greatbatch (1991)
call a 'neutralistic' stance.

The interviewee

Let us consider now whether the interviewee waits for the interviewer to
formulate a question, and how she deals with prefaces. It is worth noting first
of all that in the example just quoted, the interviewee treats the equivocal
utterance at 121 not as an objection, but as if it is a straight question at line 122
in keeping with the normative model, which it is to her advantage to do at
this point. The nature of the interviewer's 'questions' can have other consequences for the way in which interviewees feel free to handle them. Heritage
and Greatbatch (1991: 99) argue that '[the interviewee] has no rights to a turn
until a question is produced', and there is also 'a corollary expectation that
[the interviewer's] turns should properly consist of a question'. We can extend
this point somewhat. In our example we seem to have evidence that if the
interviewer's turn does not 'properly' consist of a question (e.g. it might be, or
also be, a critical comment, whether syntactically interrogative or declarative),
the interviewee may feel that she has a right not to wait for the end of the
interviewer's turn.

Interrupting and switching roles

Interviewers commonly 'preface' their questions with introductory remarks.
The prefaces that interviewers engage in are quite commonly, as Heritage and
Greatbatch rightly note, interrupted by interviewees. However, it is not always
clear when a preface, or part of a preface, is being interpreted as a question. For
example, at 29–30 in our transcript, the interviewer, who has interrupted the

end of the interviewee's answer at 28, is interrupted by a precisely timed 'oh yes'. This might be seen as a response to the interrogative syntax ('aren't they'). But this is another example of an equivocal utterance. The interviewer behaves as if he is using a tag question rhetorically to underscore a point rather than performing the speech act 'question'. The interviewee may or may not have been mistaken. Probably it was important for her to say an 'oh yes' (with a 'yes naturally!' kind of intonation), because what is at issue conceptually speaking is her adherence to a democratic entitlement – on which we have more to say below. But it is clear that as the interviewer's turn proceeds, with what is presumably a preface to an as yet unformulated question proper, the interviewee interrupts (at 32) before that question is reached. The reason for doing this seems to be the interviewee's desire to emphasise people's *saying*, and thereby implicate that what they say is in some way 'wrong' – again, we have more to say on this below.

This is not the only point at which this interviewee interrupts in order to re-establish her democratic credentials: a similar event occurs at 40, again during what is evidently a preface. In this episode (at 41–6), once the interruption is repaired (at the beginning of 41, with 'ya' and a hesitation), the interviewee waits for the completion of the turn. As it turns out, however, the interviewer never arrives at an explicit question! This is why, the interviewee, seizing the opportunity of a slight departure from the norm, simply says 'yes. er I know', which confirms a statement. This apparently also gives the interviewee the opportunity to formulate her *own* question, by reformulating the interviewer's initial interview-opening question: 'I mean you ask me what worries me . . .'. This develops into a long turn in which the interviewee is first able to address some of the previous issues raised and, more strategically, to shift the topic (at 52), while superficially remaining in the question frame: 'but the other thing that worries me . . .'. The striking thing here is that the interviewee has both challenged a preface and momentarily grabbed the right to put the 'questions', thereby setting the agenda.

What else does the interviewer do?

Does the interviewer engage in other kinds of speech act? How does he handle 'prefaces'? The interviewer in this example certainly uses prefaces in the form of statements, and these are often 'referred', i.e. involve the reporting of (alleged) utterances or beliefs of third parties assumed to be authoritative or legitimate opinion-holders (e.g. members of an electorate) in some frame of reference. However, two riders need to be added. First, it is not always obvious that statements are indeed prefaces to questions. Statements are often responded to by the interviewer. This could mean that there is a conventional expectation of a question, which is simply 'bypassed' if the question is somehow inferable from the preface. But in this case, can we talk of a preface–question structure at all? And does it not suggest that the interview institution is in fact changing its shape? Second, the prefaces, though they are often statements referenced to other voices, are not always such. For example, they may be objections, contradictions or even interpretable as insults.

This brings us to speech acts. In the example we have investigated, straight-forward questions do occur as direct speech acts (e.g. 5, 17, 121), but even these can be interpreted both by the interviewee and the hearing public as simultaneously implicating extra speech acts. Frequently, as we have seen, this is done by way of intonation. There are other interesting forms of indirectness that are ambiguous enough to modify potentially the supposed neutralistic role of the institutional interviewer. What are we to make of the following (the italics are added): 'if *we* abstain from voting' (13), 'aren't *we* allowed to do that' (20), '*we*'re absolutely entitled to say' (45), '*we*'re fed up with all of you' (45) and 'that's the impression you gave *us*' (60).

Now it is often made clear by Humphrys that this *we* has its referent inside the discourse world of persons he has referred to. Sometimes this is extremely clear by phrases that are in effect space-builders, often accompanied by prosodic features such as parenthetic intonation (lowering of register) and pausing: 'in the mind of the listener' (75), 'if that is our view' (45). But in some instances it is not entirely obvious that an utterance containing *we* (and thus potentially impli-cating the speaker's participation in an opinion, a departure from neutralism) is 'built into' someone else's mental space or utterance space. For instance, at 60, discussed above, the *us* in the interviewer's utterance could be processed online as referencing not the utterance space of the people referred to by Beckett (at 56), but to some group in which the speaker, the interviewer (the individual John Humphrys) includes himself. In certain cases there is not even any preced-ing text that could be regarded as building a space in which *we* can refer and is different from the discourse world of the speaker: this is the case for the examples from lines 13 and 20.

The question of 'neutralistic' stance

The radio and TV institutions in the UK, as elsewhere, are obliged through charters and licences to exercise impartiality and 'balance', and to refrain from the kind of editorial comment on public policy that would be found in politically aligned newspapers. This means that interviewers will, if they abide by these codes, refrain from explicit approval or disapproval of interviewee's statements, and from expression of personal opinion. Viewed from within this perspective, this impartiality doctrine has its limits. For instance, interviewers addressing 'extremist' political actors will express, directly or indirectly (the latter, as usual, largely by prosodic devices) their disapproval. For example, an interviewer

speaking to a British National Party spokesperson, or a member of an organisation judged to be a terrorist organisation, will challenge more frequently
and persistently and will use prosodic speech features that any member of the
speech community will understand to be disaffiliating or disparaging. The
same may apply to spokespersons from the left of the political spectrum,
including representatives of non-conventional (e.g. social movement) politics.
This kind of interviewer behaviour is probably to be understood in terms of
a *presumption*, in the sense of the term introduced in Chapter 4, that they
are speaking on behalf of the common values of the democratic polity within
which their news institution is sanctioned. Interviewers, then, are not so much
neutral as representative of an institution that is a representative of a political
consensus.

We have seen that in many instances the interviewer in our example does
maintain formal neutralism by building spaces in which statements refer and
predicate. But there is a further interesting feature surrounding the use of *we*. In
some of the examples we looked at above, the interviewer comes close to
identifying himself in his discourse world with a *we*-group that could conceivably
be identified by listeners with the electorate of which they all, including the
interviewer, are a part. It is not always clear that an interviewer's *we* is in this
consensual discourse world or, by indirect free discourse, represented as in the
belief space of some other person or persons.

A consequence of this is that the interviewer's role with respect to
legitimated political institutions is not entirely clear. It may be that what the
broadcast political interview is doing in its present stage of evolution is representing a clash between two institutions – the media and the political elites. Each
makes a claim to legitimacy. This theme runs through the data we have been
looking at. At the level of interaction, the use of overlaps and interruptions that
we have pinpointed are of a kind that suggest the neutralistic model in which
the interviewer and interviewee have clearly prescribed rights is not altogether
stable. The right to ask the questions, and the nature of those questions, is
not fully agreed upon by the participants. Indeed, from the evidence of the
interruptions and the kinds of speech acts involved, the participants seem to be
contesting the discourse roles, or negotiating them. This is corroborated on the
level of the 'content'.

For example, consider the interviewer's turn at 13, which implicates a
criticism concerning the rightness of the way his Labour government interlocutor
is interpreting voting behaviour. At 20, and again at 28 and 39 he responds,
and in some instances actually interrupts, to narrow this target further, making
assertions that implicate the claim that democratic entitlements are in some way
under attack. The interviewer here appears to be challenging the legitimacy of
the speaker in a rather fundamental way. A further perceived implication could
be that he is adopting the role of defender of democratic principles. Conversely,

the interviewee challenges the legitimacy of the broadcasting institution in the turn that constitutes her parting shot (skilled interviewees know how to tailor their remarks to the time available).

At 114 the interviewee has attempted to deflect a question concerning the alleged corruption of a Labour MP, by retaining the topic 'problem', but reformulating it:

117 [. . .] .hh the
118 problem for the prime minister (.) is (.) that we have an election now. where
119 there is ↑*clear* choice before the British people.= [. . .]

In a sense this is also a clash over who has the right to stipulate the questions – the 'problems' – that are discussible in news interviews. The interviewer's behaviour implicitly contests this appropriation of the topic-setting role, and he does so by interrupting at 120. This interruption functions on at least three significant levels simultaneously. First, it is in the form of a 'proper' question. Second, however, it is recognisable as a 'rhetorical' question (by virtue of its intonation contour and the tag 'then') that presupposes the answer 'no'. This is the expected answer also, and this is the third level, because it uses a deontic modal ('should') that evokes a presumed shared ethical frame or (at the least) a frame of political propriety:

120 | =this is no' a referendum on the governm*ent.
121 JH | should you ignore the Vaz affair then?*

And indeed Beckett does answer accordingly, remaining within the deontic frame that has been set up by 'should'. However, she immediately rejects the legitimacy of the interviewer and the broadcasting vehicle within which he is operating:

122 MB /no it should be dealt with through the proper processes and with with (.) *deep*
123   respect to you ↓↑*John* .hh and fond as I am of you all the proper processes are
124   ↑↓*not*↑ through an interview on the *Today* programme of two minutes in the
125   morning. .hh there there are er (..) there're ↑*people* ↓whose ↑job it is ↓to ↑look
126   at these things and I ↓have ↑*no* ↑doubt at ↓all that they will be looked at .hh ↑*if*
127   Keith Vaz is returned as a member of parliament.

In referential terms, the interviewee's response is extremely vague. It is pre-supposed (twice) in her utterance that there exist 'proper' processes for dealing with allegations of corruption. It is asserted that the 'proper' institution is not a broadcasting slot. It is also asserted by the interviewee that there exist 'people whose job it is' to investigate allegations of corruption, which may carry the implication that this 'job' is not a legitimate part of the role of interviewer. The referents of these terms are not explicitly indicated; the utterances serve primarily to define the limits of legitimate political interviewing. It is helpful to see what is going on not simply in formal terms but in terms of Habermas's validity claims (see Chapter 4 of this volume). What can be said is that there is a struggle over implicit validity claims – specifically the claim of rightness to particular speech acts and speech roles, roles which are in essence political roles. Further, however, this clash can be seen clearly in conceptual terms, i.e., at the level of 'content' of meaning. At several points, the turn-taking clashes coincide with language evidently intended to claim or challenge *legitimacy* of a specific speech act combined with a specific referential object.

Propositions and presumptions

Contexts are important as we saw earlier, because they can be seen as knowledge that define the 'worlds' which speakers presume in their discourse.

What is presumed?

Presumptions involve two dimensions. First, a speaker may presume shared knowledge frames (facts, individual political actors, time schedules, institutions, and the like). Second, the speaker may presume that such frames are not only known (stored in long-term memory) but also *accepted* as normal and legitimate. In short, presumptions are not only about what is true but also about what is right. Presumptions can be linked to belief systems of various kinds – to formalised ideologies, to implicit ideologies, to consensus as to a political constitution and (as we shall see in a later chapter) to religious beliefs. It may of course turn out that the presumptions of one speaker may be contested by another. This is what makes political discourse idiosyncratic, essentially dynamic and of particular importance for an understanding of a political culture as a whole. Let us consider just one part of the transcribed interview in these terms (see Table 5.1). The part in question revolves around the understanding of fundamental issues in parliamentary democracies: voting and political inferences based upon voting behaviour.

It is striking that the beginning of this exchange hinges on words ('Commons', 'party', 'Labour', 'Conservative', 'parliament', 'democracy') that presume a large amount of political knowledge concerning the political institutions, party system and electoral processes. Once this presumptive set of frames is activated, successive talk is presumed coherent. Political discourse in any political culture requires that participants in political discourse have mental representations of this type. But more interesting is the fact that after the framework is established, the exchange proceeds to areas where there is potential for disagreement or uncertainty.

Table 5.1 Presumed knowledge in a political interview

Interview: Humphrys–Beckett, 3 June 2001	Presumed knowledge
. . . what's *worrying* **the Labour Party** . . . leader of **the Commons** in **the last parliament . . .** . . . people listening to **Mr Hague** and deciding not to vote unless they're going to vote **Conservative** . . .	UK party system. UK parliamentary constitution, duration of parliaments, recent political history. Mr Hague is leader of Conservative Party. Labour and Conservative are opposed. Political speeches and their effects.
. . . . . . that would be **bad for democracy** . . . ev'ryone who *does*n't vote Labour (.) er or ev'ryone who *fails* to vote will **be taken as** *ab*solute support for ev'rything Mr Hague is doing . . . and I think that would be an awfully **bad thing** . . . it'd **be taken as** rejection (.) of **the** ↑govern↓**ment** . . . JH aren't **we allowed** to do that? MB ↓you're **all**↑↓*owed* to do whatever you ↑↓like	Democracy exists in UK and is positively valued. Voting, abstention and elections. Political inferencing from voting behaviour. Identity and role of 'the government'. Consensus on freedom of voting, non-voting and rejection of government.
. . . in the United States . . . millions and millions and millions of people **entitled** to vote . . . a lot of people deciding that it *really* doesn't make much difference whether they vote or not and it the thing turns on a *hand*ful of ↑*votes*↓ . . . JH but so they're actually **entitled to do that** aren't they	Not voting has negative consequences *versus* right not to vote.
in America . . . a lot of them said too the ideal the thing to do was to vote for **a third party** give **the major parties** a shock,	There are major and minor parties; a two-party system. Implied that voting for third party has negative consequences.
JH it's it's a **democratic ex***pression* it ((suggests th't)) MB ((s s *quarrel with that))	Consensus on right not to vote.
JH we're a we're **absolutely entitled to say, (.hh) we're fed up with all of you** \if that is our view and we're not going to vote (.hh) /**as a way of showing our** ↑*pro*test. MB. /Yes. er I know . . .	Non-voting indicates protest.

Political reasoning

As we have noted, Beckett's first reply depends on a context in which Hague can be understood as having urged voters either to vote Conservative, or, in order to prevent a Labour landslide victory, not to vote at all. In other words, Beckett has to set up a discourse world in which people have this understanding. Then, on that premise, she has to claim that there are consequences. Argumentation based on conditional propositions – if A happens, then B will happen – is extremely important for politicians, since one of their roles is to claim knowledge about cause and effect. Conditionals, in natural discourse, as distinct from propositional logic, are closely linked conceptually with causation. Consider the passage (6–12), reproduced below, in which Beckett argues in this way about the effects of not voting:

```
6  MB   yes I'm worried about people listening to Mr Hague, (.) and deciding not to
7        vote unless they're going to vote Conservative. (.) ((I)) think that would be er
8        bad for democracy and what's more. .hh er although at the moment er many
9        people in the media are saying oh well y'know might this be a good thing. /on
10       Friday. (.) ev'ryone who doesn't vote Labour (.) er or ev'ryone who fails to
11       vote will be taken as absolute support for ev'rything Mr Hague is doing, or for
12       the way he's run this campaign and I think that would be an awfully bad thing.
13 JH    what (.) if we abstain from voti:ng, (.) on Thursday for all sorts of reasons
14       ↑some of which might be very ↑principled reasons. .hh /that would be taken as
15       support for William ↓↑Hague
16 MB    i' certainly would.
17 JH    ↑why?
18 MB    because it'd be taken as rejection (.) of the=
19       =↑govern↓ment│ and er (( . . . . . inaudible . . . ))*
20 JH              │ and aren't we allowed to do that?*=
```

Using the filter method outlined in Chapter 4, we can see that she is entertaining the following set of propositions, some embedded inside one another as shown in Table 5.2.

Table 5.2 leaves out most of the interactive elements, but it is worth noticing in passing the way in which the two participants cooperate in communicating an apparently seamless logical sequence. Several interesting features become clear. The analysis demonstrates the different layers of discourse world that the recursive properties of language make possible – the different spaces built by the expressions 'worry that', 'think that', 'decide that', the conditional form 'would', and so forth. Some of these are forms of meta-representation: Beckett's use of language claims to be representing other people's representations (in particular, via the expression 'be taken as'). Another obvious feature is that within and across these discourse worlds quasi-logical and quasi-causal relations are set up: sometimes this is made explicit through connectives such as 'if', 'unless', 'why' and 'because'.

Table 5.2 Embedding of propositions in interview talk

Argument 1 typically P-Agent, grammatical subject, typically a noun phrase	Predicate relation, action, existence, etc., intransitive, transitive or ditransitive verb.	Argument 2 typically P-Patient, grammatical object, typically a noun phrase	Adjunct/Conjunct e.g., adverbs, participle phrases, conjunctions like 'and', 'if'.
[Beckett] I	am worried about	P1	
(a) P1 people	listen to	Mr Hague	and P2
P2 [people]	decide	P3	
P3 [people]	not vote		unless P4
P4 [people]	vote	Conservative	
(b) I	think	P5	
P5 that (= P1–P4)	would be bad for	democracy	
(c) people in the media	are saying	P6	
P6 this (= P1–P4)	might be a good thing		

Table 5.2 (continued)

Argument 1 typically P-Agent, grammatical subject, typically a noun phrase	Predicate relation, action, existence, etc., intransitive, transitive or ditransitive verb.	Argument 2 typically P-Patient, grammatical object, typically a noun phrase	Adjunct/Conjunct e.g., adverbs, participle phrases, conjunctions like 'and', 'if'
(d) P7 [people who] P8 [people who]	not vote fail to vote	Labour	on Friday, or
P9 ← P8	will be taken as	absolute support for everything Mr Hague is doing	
			and
I	think	- - - - P10	
P10 that (= P9)	would be an awfully bad thing		
(e) [Humphrys]			If P11, [then] P12
P11 we	abstain from voting		on Thursday, for all sorts of reasons
P12 that (= P11)	would be taken as	support for Mr Hague?	
[Beckett]			
P13 it (= P11)	certainly would		
[Humphrys]			why?
[Beckett]			because P14
P14 it (= P11)	'd be taken as	- - - - P15	
P15 [people]	reject	the government	
[Humphrys]			and
P16 [we]	aren't allowed to do	that (= P15)?	

Political discourse, looked at in terms of representation, seems intrinsically to involve the ability to engage in reasoning about future effects and their causes, and in particular to 'read the minds' of other people, specifically the people involved in political processes – here, the voters. Reading the mind of political opponents and supporters is related to the linguistic and cognitive ability to meta-represent.[5] Finally, deontic judgements are also an essential component: the whole purpose of the political reasoning process is to make claims about what is and what is not, might be or might not be, 'a bad thing' or 'a good thing'.

However, it is also clear that this kind of political reasoning depends heavily on presumptions. The logical progression from one proposition to the next is not evident from the content of the individual propositions alone: there must be some bridging premises or abductions, which we are calling presumptions. Let us look more closely at the way the discourse unfolds, in terms of the propositions isolated in Table 5.2, and the links between them. In Beckett's 'worry' world there are at least five sub-worlds (a), (b), (c), (d) and (e):

(a) 'I am worried that':
P1: Hague might cause P2–P4
P2–P4: people will decide between voting Conservative or not voting at all.
Inference from P2–P4: if they do not vote at all, they are not voting Labour.

Understanding P1 to P4 and drawing the inference requires at least the presumptions listed in Table 5.1 concerning the two-party system and the potential effects of political speeches. Of course, the British party system is not, strictly speaking a two-party one, and what is politically significant is that the political reasoning that is engaged in here appears to presume that it is. One should also note that the voting system itself is a binary one (as distinct from, say, a proportional voting system), which itself imposes a particular kind of political inferencing.

(b) *Deontic inference* made by speaker in her 'worry' world: P5 not voting is bad for democracy.

Understanding this, and its connection to the preceding propositions, requires presumptive knowledge about the existence of what is meant by the term *democracy*, that it exists in the UK and that it is possible to harm it. Since the speaker does not spell out why the scenario she describes is bad, hearers have to deduce for themselves that not voting is (or might be thought to be) bad for democracy, and they probably do this on the basis of a stored understanding that democracy is defined by voting. Here they will have to infer, specifically, that it is defined by the obligation to vote rather than by the right to vote.

(c) In the media people's discourse world:
Deontic proposition, P6: not voting might be good thing.

Probably this is interpreted by hearers as 'a good thing' for democracy. Again, hearers are left to figure out, on the basis of presumed knowledge about elections, democracy and parities, how not voting could be construed by someone as beneficial.

(d) In the media people's discourse world:
P7: people not vote Labour
P8: people not vote at all
Attributed inference, P9: people support Hague.

The speaker apparently drops the idea of uttering 'if P7 then P9'. Perhaps this is because, given the presumptive knowledge about two-party systems, if you don't vote Labour this pragmatically implies voting Conservative, which produces the quasi-tautology 'if X votes Conservative then X supports Hague'. Here, too, one can see that many contingent presumptions are needed to conclude that we do indeed have a tautology. The upshot is that Beckett corrects herself and communicates P9 instead. All these 'backstage' cogitations are taking place in the discourse world set up by the space-builder 'be taken as', which may be assumed to be the media people's discourse world. Again, the way 'be taken as' is interpreted, because it lacks an agent, depends on a large amount of presumed knowledge.

So, Beckett claims P9 – that if people do not vote at all they are supporting Hague. In formal terms, if it is false that they vote, it could nonetheless be true that they support Hague, and there is no inference at all concerning either their support or their rejection of Labour. In fact, this is the point that the interviewer makes at (13–15). But, in general, political reasoning works in other ways. The interviewee seems to be driven by the presumed binary structure of the party and voting system, though not necessarily in ways we expect. Consider the schematic structure of P9: 'if X does not vote at all then X supports Hague'. At first glance, one might think that if X does not vote for Hague then X either does *not* support Hague or is indifferent. So why would Hague ask people not to vote? And how can Beckett claim that not voting for him constitutes 'absolute support for everything Mr Hague is doing'?

First, Hague's (reported) utterances have to be understood within the presumptive frame of two-value party logic, where the default assumption is that if X does not vote for Y, then X will vote for Z. Thus the reported Hague is asking people not to vote for Labour, presumably focusing on wavering voters who *might* vote Labour and on people in general who make the either-one-party-or-the-other assumption their default.

Second, there is actually another useful inference pattern available in political logic:

if X is not for Y, then X is against Y; if X is not for Y, then X is for Z.

This is an argument used by politicians specifically in processes of coalition-building, including the international context of alliance-making. Hague's reported position is consistent with this notion. For Beckett, whose interests as a Labour Party politician are threatened, it becomes salient. When the interviewer actually challenges her reasoning processes, asking her for the reason why not voting implies support for Hague (or could be so taken), Beckett does in fact produce precisely the two-valued argument:

it'd be taken as rejection of the government,

which, in propositional terms, includes something like the following schematic sequence of inferences:

(e) *Assumptions*
if X is not for Y, then X is against Y
if X is not for Y, then X is for Z
P8, P11: X does not vote (for anybody)
P12: X votes for Z
P15: X rejects Y.

That is to say, if people do not vote for the government they are (taken as being) against the government. The interviewer exploits the superficial *logical* incoherence (how can not voting for someone mean supporting that person? In any case, couldn't people have lots of reasons for abstaining?). The interviewee is forced to make the either-for-us-or-against-us argument explicit.

Matters are not, in the heat of debate, all that clear-cut. In principle one would expect that the truth value of propositions within a discourse-world space would be limited to that space: i.e., X takes p to imply q ought to be true for X but not for the speaker herself. However, one wonders if there is not some leakage, or conceptual blurring of the boundaries between belief worlds. The proposition P9 is asserted by media people (or perhaps people in general), and it is their asserting it that is 'an awfully bad thing'. This seems to be conveyed by the expression 'be taken as'. But is that the only interpretation a hearer might entertain? Is Beckett saying she herself believes not voting equals support for Hague? Or only that certain people will 'take it' that way? Or is it the same thing for her? Maybe we just cannot tell, because the passive construction ('be taken as') has left out the agent, so hearers are left to fill it in, and the candidates are not just 'people in the media' but also people in the electorate at large. Or conceivably, 'we the government' – which would explain her coming out with P14 and P15 at lines 18–19 of the transcript.

Finally, in this sequence of the interview, a shift of focus is brought about by the interviewer, when he interrupts:

> it'd be taken as rejection of the government
> and aren't we allowed to do that?

It is pertinent here to recall Grice's cooperative principle and the conversational maxims. As is the case throughout, the *communicative* assumption of the participants is that they are cooperating. When one proposition or turn follows another, therefore, it is expected that the new proposition be relevant, that is, that it can be coherently *related* to what has preceded. Now, when Humphrys makes the above interjection, the interviewee and the listening public have to infer a connection. How do they do this? Humphrys uses the pro-verb *do*, showing that the noun phrase 'rejection of the government' has been analysed into a proposition, with 'we' (and all its attendant ambiguities) inferred as agent (see Table 5.2).

The most important detail, however, is the appearance of an overt deontic expression, *be allowed*. The deontic space has been already opened up by Beckett's talk of 'bad' and 'good'. Humphrys's choice of word narrows the deontic conceptualisation down to the field of permissions and rights. His choice of phrasing and intonation implicate two further propositions, roughly:

> P16': you are saying that we are not allowed to P15
> P16": it is not true, or not acceptable, to make this assertion.

The relevance of his implications is given by presumptions, specifically the frame of beliefs about democracy, which crucially includes the proposition that we *are* allowed, have the right, to reject a government. Note that Humphrys' implicated propositions are now not in an embedded discourse space (where something is 'taken as' being something by certain people, or 'worried about' by Beckett), but in the reality space of interviewer, interviewee and listeners. That this is the case is shown in Beckett's next turn, where she relocates the proposition in the embedded meta-represented discourse world:

> but you're asking me what worries me, and *that*'s what worries me: that we'll be told that . . . (21–2).

At the interactive level

We can ask what is Humphrys *doing*? He has led his interviewee into what is a logical dilemma within the presumptive frame of political values. She has said that non-voting is bad for democracy. Now she is saying that non-voting equals rejecting the current government, so she appears to be also saying that rejecting the current government is bad for democracy. However, given the frame-work of political presumptions that have been evoked, and which provide the conceptual bedrock for this discourse, it is everyone's democratic right (in the UK, for instance) to 'reject the government'. So, having once invoked democratic conceptions, Beckett can now appear to be contradicting them, or made to appear that she is. Such manoeuvres are probably intrinsic to the system of discursive logic that underpins political argumentation within democratic discourse communities.

As a politician who can only act within, and must legitimise herself within, this discursive system, Beckett has no choice but to give way on this fundamental matter. Her embarrassment at being caught in the dilemma is reflected in the wide pitch variation at 21, together with the interjection 'oh' (affecting surprise perhaps that she should be suspected of undemocratic tendencies of thought), perceptible overstatement ('allowed to do *whatever you like*') and the rebuilding of an embedded discourse that we have already noted. What will Beckett's next move be?

She cannot entirely leave the topic for fear of being seen as evasive. So she drops the 'rejection of the government' explanation and reformulates. Again, however, Humphrys will attempt to construct a logical contradiction, given the premises of the political conceptual system. Beckett introduces another common form of argumentation – analogy, specifically with the voting patterns in the recent US presidential elections. This manoeuvre actually extends over 23–38, punctuated by objections from the interviewer. Ignoring the interruptions (28–35), we see Beckett trying to put the following analogical argument:

(a) people believed that the there was no difference between the parties
(b) people therefore did not vote at all
(c) people therefore voted for third parties
(d) this produced narrow margins in votes cast for the two parties

She claims also, indirectly, by implicature at 38, that people are not satisfied with the consequences of their own beliefs. There is an implied warning: that non-voting and voting for a third party yields results that contradict the desires of those non-voters and third-party voters. There is, of course, as with any analogical argument, a further claim, namely, that the analogy itself is a valid mapping from one domain to the other. In fact the validity of comparing US presidential and British parliamentary elections is not challenged by the interviewer. What *is* challenged is propositions (a) and (b) above – not the factual truth claim, but the presumption that there is something 'wrong' about people doing what the propositions predicate of them (that they are epistemically wrong and deontically wrong). In political terms, it is the democratic right not to vote that the interviewer is raising. In response to Beckett's claim at 26–7 that people do not vote because they believe that voting makes no difference, and in response to Beckett's inexplicit but inferable disapproval of this belief, Humphrys interrupts to assert that 'they are actually entitled to do that'. Beckett cannot, any more than before, challenge this democratic premise, and she doesn't. Nor does she challenge Humphrys's explanation (at 29–34) as to the particular grounds upon which they are so entitled, namely, the lack of apparent difference between major parties. In general, then, not only do presumptions about political ideas, practices and values enable the building of coherent discourse to take place, but those very presumptions themselves can be brought into focus by the verbal action of journalists. A particular type of language-using social role thus comes into being.

The nature of broadcast political interviews

Are political interviews on radio (and in other media) instances of institutions of the polity? They are not generally treated as part of constitutional arrangements in the same sense that assemblies, parliaments, senates, presidencies, and the like are, whether constitutions are written or not. It is true that constitutions may limit or legitimise certain kinds of government control of media. But in the example analysed we have a very clearly structured communicational institution that is believed by participants in it to be a part of the political process. It seems logical and realistic to treat such media institutions as political institutions, managed by normative rules and presumptive patterns of behaviour and belief. The evidence is apparent in the content of interviews of this type, since the right of interviewers and of the media in general to act in certain ways becomes a topic of discussion and actually woven into the ongoing verbal interaction.

Another striking characteristic of the exchanges we have dissected is that many propositions are in a meta-represented modality; in other words, they are processed in a space that is not that asserted as holding true in the current reality of the current speaker, but in some future, possible, alleged, feared, etc., reality. In line with this, there are many main verbs of propositional attitude and utterance – *say that*, *worry that*, and the like. Political argumentation in the public sphere seems in large part to involve claims and counter-claims on the basis of 'rightness': this has clear linguistic and discoursal reflexes. Equally important is the fact that argumentation that bears on this area of conceptualisation is frequently meta-linguistic, in the sense that participants raise for inspection the meanings ('impression', 'what seems to be said', etc.) the possible interpretations of public utterances. The management of public utterances, the assumptions and implications attributable to them is crucial. The inspection and challenge of public utterances thus becomes an expected discourse topic, a focus of interest and argument.

6   Parliamentary language

We have examined political questions and answers in the media context and we shall now look at questions and answers in parliament. The main concern of this chapter is to explore the characteristics of this particular genre of democratic discourse, with the aim of extending our understanding of what sort of verbal behaviour is in play and how it works.[1] The emphasis is on the micro-structure of the language viewed primarily as politically significant interaction among individuals.

Institutional rules

Most if not all parliamentary assemblies enable representatives to pose questions and receive replies, though the institutionalised procedures and discursive devices vary. In the British parliament, the putting of questions has been acknowledged since the late seventeenth or early eighteenth century to be an important sub-genre of parliamentary discourse. As an institution, question time has been formally recognised since 1869. The specific institution of Prime Minister's Question Time is characteristic of the British parliament and constitution, but dates only from 1961. Canada is another example, but few constitutions institutionalise the presence of the head of government in the main legislative assembly in this way. An examination of the discursive processes is therefore of intrinsic political interest. Constitutionalists, historians and standard textbooks seek to characterise the function of parliamentary questions. The British parliamentarians' rule book declares that questions have two functions: 'to obtain information or to press for action', adducing a parliamentary debate of the 1893–4 session for the information part (Erskine May 1989: 287; also Clerks in the Table Office 1979: 7). But most political commentators say that questions are also 'weapons in the party battle', and maintain that asking for information is now an unimportant function, while pressing for action can on occasion lead to practical outcomes (Adonis 1993: 132, 136–8).

Turn-taking rules

In the formal sense, 'asking a question' in the British House of Commons is the culmination of a lengthy discourse process, involving several channels, speakers and writers. Members have to give notice of questions to officials (The Clerks in the Table Office) at least two days in advance (and not more than ten sitting days). Which of the questions are asked, and in which order, is decided by the 'shuffle', nowadays a computerised randomising of the numbers assigned to each question. Questions are published on the morning following tabling and at this point officials from the relevant ministerial departments extract their questions and prepare answers, together with background briefing, for their ministers to accept or amend. The official briefings also aim to anticipate the non-tabled, non-scripted 'supplementary' questions. These questions arise in several ways during question time. In general a member is called by the Speaker, and the member puts his or her question, referring to it by number, after which point the questioner, and other members, are invited to put follow-on questions. In the case of prime minister's questions there is a standard device, peculiar to the British parliament, which enables members to put general and possibly surprise questions to the head of government.

In principle, all ministers may be questioned only about matters within their responsibilities. Since the prime minister's responsibilities are very specific, members put a ritual question, which is followed up by a 'supplementary' question that has not been tabled in advance. In practice, prime ministers will actually be prepared for such questions by their officials, but the subsequent verbal interaction may be spontaneous. There are three types of ritual, or 'open' questions intended to avoid transfers to other ministers and to catch the prime minister unprepared (Clerks in the Table Office 1979: 11–13; Irwin *et al.* 1993). One example of this is to ask if the prime minister will pay a visit overseas or to a town in the questioner's constituency. The supplementary question then has to be constructed to retain some, often tangential relevance to the town or country referred to. In the second type the speaker asks about the prime minister's planned meetings with some person or body – a means of introducing some degree of topical relevance. The third type, utilised by the MP Paul Marsden in the extract analysed below, is to ask the prime minister to list his engagements for the day. Such questions are regarded by commentators as totally 'transfer-proof' and generally permit the questioner to put a supplementary question on virtually any topic.

There thus exists an institutionalised turn-taking system regulating the question–answer interactions in the House, a system that has changed from time to time over the past two or three centuries. The current system for oral-answer questions, substantially unchanged since 1906, can be summarised as follows:

(a) indicate wish to obtain an oral answer by sending written question to clerks' office (supervised by Speaker of the House);
(b) clerks monitor content and form against rules and conventions;
(c) questions selected and ordered by random process;
(d) questions printed and published;
(e) in the debating chamber the Speaker calls the name of the questioner in the randomly decided order;
(f) Speaker stands and gives number of the question;
(g) minister replies;
(h) Speaker calls for supplementary question;
(i) questioner puts supplementary question;
(j) minister replies.

Only one supplementary question is automatically allowed, but members may indicate the wish to ask further supplementary questions by standing and 'catching the Speaker's eye', at what conversation analysts would normally call a 'transition relevance place'. Leaders of the opposition in particular have special turn-taking privileges: in the example analysed below, William Hague puts three questions in sequence. Overlaid on this institutionalised system is the verbal interaction within the actual speech event of question time. To be sure, there are overt rules at this level: the Speaker (president or chair in other assemblies) alone may select the next speaker, and interruptions are not officially allowed. However, there is, as will be seen from the micro-analyses below a further level – a level at which parallel interactions occur, interactions which have little to do with question–answer routines in the ordinary sense, but which are politically potent and arguably constitute the main function of question time.

Regulating the practice

There are several mechanisms by which the genre is regulated. One method consists of the prescriptive rule books such as Erskine May and the handbooks that derive from it. Then there are at least three kinds of discursive practice that constrain how the genre is played out. First, the clerks in the Table Office, who receive the draft questions, will control the form and content, requesting changes in accordance with rules and practice. Second, there are Hansard's supposedly verbatim transcription, which in fact 'corrects' the form of interrogatives (and other features) to produce an idealised model of the session that is supposed to have taken place. Third, there are discourse practices within the discourse itself – practices by means of which the Speaker of the House and the MPs themselves correct utterances that are not acceptable in the genre.

Erskine May's rules control the channel of communication, the form and the content of questions. Questions requiring an oral response in the chamber have

first to be put in writing and the ministers responding will give their oral reply
from a written brief. Rules governing the form of questions and their content
are detailed and numerous and not clearly distinguished from rules about content. Among the discourse-related specifications are the following:

> The purpose of a question is to obtain information or press for action; it
> should not be framed primarily so as to convey information, or so as to
> suggest its own answer or convey a particular point of view, and it should
> not be in effect a short speech.

In pragmatic terms these requirements seem to be designed to control the use
of declaratives and the possibility of presupposition, implicatures and invited
inference. There is more detail, using traditional terminology, in a subsequent
paragraph headed 'Argument and disorderly expressions':

> Questions which seek an expression of an opinion, or which contain arguments,
> expressions of opinion, inference or imputations, unnecessary epithets, or
> rhetorical, controversial, ironical or offensive expressions are not in order.
> (Erskine May 1989: 287)

As will be seen, the existence of these rules does not prevent their being broken.
The question remains as to what is the nature and function of the parliamentary
discourse that involves institutionalised question-asking.

What happens in parliamentary question time

What utterers may be doing in practice at question time, and indeed what is
the nature of this institutionalised genre, can only be gleaned by close analysis
of the interaction itself. We have noted that Hansard 'corrects' the utterances
of members of parliament. Such correction is a form of discursive 'repair' – the
mechanism present in all talk whereby speakers and hearers correct mistakes
and hitches in ongoing discourse. (Schegloff *et al.* 1977; Levinson 1983: 339ff.).
Examination of repairs in parliamentary questions can provide insight into how
'questions' may be judged to be functioning in the political culture.

Repairs: initiation, bonding and bounding

In this context, repairs are much more than corrections of mishearings or mis-
understandings, and more than the idealised controls of Hansard's editing. It is
useful to extend the idea of conversational repair to include cases where some
socially agreed rules of a genre are infringed. Such repairs are simultaneously
constructions of the idealised genre norms. The fact that they occur is evidence

that speakers are aware of infringements. If we analyse these complicated interactions in detail, we can get further insight into the ways in which talk constitutes
politics in parliamentary settings. The following transcript displays the ways
in which the utterances of members of parliament are normalised 'online'. By
inspecting it more closely we can also hazard some guesses as to the underlying
functions.[2]

House of Commons, 7 July 1999: Bob Laxton (L)

L (can) I say to my er right honourable (.) friend just how welcome er was
the announcement that he made this morning of the (.) six hundred and
fifty million pounds worth (.) of PFI er investment and contracts within
the national health service. (.) /and can I say that for (.) er the *a*rea an
the locality that I partly represent \er Derby south and Derby city in
particular. (.) the one hundred and seventy-seven million pounds worth
of investment (.) er which will bring together (.) acute services. (.)
possibly on one site that will enhance and improve health care within
southern Derbyshire. (.) is gonna be vitally important. (...) /but I think
in addition to that. (.) in addition to that.

M   ((xxxxxxx

M =xxxxxxxxxxxxxxxxxxxxxxxxxxxxxxxxxxxxxxxxxxxxxxxxxxxxxxxxxxxxxx=
S   or or *o*rder (.) the house is getting very impatient because the
honourable gentleman is not putting a question (.) an I say to
the house this is the first time this honourable member has had
an opportunity to put a question to the prime minister and the
house should be tolerant (.) (but) do put your question now
please.

M =xxxxxxxxxxxxxxxxxxxxxxxxxxxxxxxxxxxxxxxxxxxxxxxxxxxxxxxxxxx*
L   thank you madam. (.) thank you madam speaker. (.) would my
right honourable friend agree with me (. . .) {gestures}* that
in particular for the very first time in the city of Derby. there
will be the creation of a community hospital on one of the
existing sites (.) a much needed and what will be a much valued
(.) facility.=

M =((HEAR HEAR xxxxxxxxxxxxxxxxxxxxxxxxxxxxxxxxxxxxxxxxxxxxxx))*
P   Madam Speaker I do agree (.) I agree with my
honourable friend (.) he is right (.) er he is right he's
entirely right and in Derby particularly what will
happen is that there will not only be a community*
hospital but at the same time as a result of the new
contract that's been announced today we will also
get all the acute services for the people of Derby on
the one site so people aren't going to have to go to

different places to get acute service care. And again
our experience with this PFI is that it does deliver
the contracts on cost and on time and of course
these were all hospitals that were promised under
the previous government and never actually started
or delivered.=

M =((HEAR HEARxxx))

To begin with, Laxton, who is a new MP, puts 'questions' that are, pragmatically speaking, statements: approximately, 'the announcement was welcome'.
His only interrogative comes as a politeness form that prefaces the statement:
'can I say to . . .'. However, the MPs remain silent until he raises his pitch level,
and says 'but I think in addition that'. The falling intonation at the end of
this segment gives the cue for interruption by the opposition MPs. We can
infer that their pretext is not just the previous length and non-canonical form
of the utterance, but also the use of an explicit opinion marker ('I think') and
the discourse marker explicitly indicating further extension of the turn. At this
point Laxton's gestures (in general, gestures in parliamentary discourse are
probably of fundamental importance) underscore his infringement of the well-
known rule about the length of turns. As he utters 'in addition', and as he
repeats the phrase, he moves his left hand in three horizontal jerks across his
chest (iconic of linear lengthening). Something happens at this point: Laxton
stops speaking, bows slightly and nods, as he sees Madam Speaker beginning
to stand up (standing and sitting are crucial gestures in the parliamentary proceedings). The Speaker's words, however, may imply either that the putting
of the question is taking too long or that the *form* of the question is not acceptable. What is significant is Laxton's reflexive recognition (through the gesture
and falling silent) simultaneously of the authority of the Speaker and of his
transgression.

The Speaker of the House does not intervene until the MPs have interrupted
the current speaker, and done so for a significant length of time at significant
volume. The Speaker constitutionally has the power to preserve orderly conduct, but she is not simply reprimanding a disallowed overlap. In this example,
the Speaker appears to be imposing two kinds of order. She is controlling the
MPs' interruption of the current speaker, but she is also controlling the syntactic
form and pragmatic force of the current turn-holder's utterances. In effect she
is commenting meta-discursively on the MPs' verbal behaviour, offering an
interpretation of the motives for their interruption. The Speaker thus does not
correct Laxton directly, but only in response to vocalisations from MPs.[3] The
Speaker alone is entitled to use non-questions – in this instance assertions ('I
say . . .' and the explanatory 'because . . .'), and directives ('the house should . . .'
and the imperative form 'put your question now please'). One effect of the

Speaker's words may be to trigger construal and construction of what is going on as a kind of initiatory test for the novice member.

After the Speaker's ruling, Laxton has himself to interrupt the MPs, with formulaic thanks to the Speaker. This time he changes both syntax and wording in order to approximate to what is Hansard's preferred form, the frequently used 'would my right honourable friend agree with me'.[4] What happens at this point is significant because it resolves the hitch, and does much more besides. Again, gesture is crucial. After Laxton has uttered the required formula, he pauses, and then raises his forefinger in an upwards pointing gesture, moving it forwards twice. The gesture conventionally demands attention, and in this culture indicates something like 'I have scored a point'. Its general function here is that of a discourse marker, giving cognitive salience to the words just uttered and, importantly, indicating the utterer's own awareness and control. The timing of the numerous participants in this group performance is precise and significant. As Laxton is ending his reformulation ('would my right honourable friend agree with me'), MPs' laughter (though not indicated in the transcript) is audible. After completion of the gestures, MPs' interruptions cease, leaving Laxton to speak the non-formulaic part of his 'question'.

'Questions' as initiations

In fact, this is still not a question in the strict sense. Indeed, it is scarcely a request for information, nor is it a request for action. So what has been going on in the previous exchanges? It is necessary to take the sequence of exchanges as a whole, and in particular to consider Laxton's 'questions' in relation to the prime minister's 'answers'. Since questions and answers in the idealised sense of this genre are either requests for information or requests for action, let us consider whether this is the case. Laxton's first two sentences can be interpreted as expressing certain explicit propositions, together with a variety of presupposed propositions, and one or two adjuncts:

> (a) the announcement of £650m PFI investment is welcome
>   the prime minister made the announcement this morning
> (b) (preposed adjunct (beneficiary): for Derby
>   I represent Derby
>   the £77m investment is going to be vitally important
>   the £77m investment will bring together acute services
>   these services will possibly be on one site
>   several sites currently exist
>   ?bringing acute services together will improve health care in Derbyshire
>   health care in Derbyshire is inadequate

The antecedent of 'that' in 'that will enhance and improve health care within southern Derbyshire' is unclear: hearers might model it online as either the bringing together on one site or the investment in general. The last listed presupposition is triggered by the change-of-state verb *improve*. After the Speaker's intervention, Laxton now requests, in the conventional lexical and syntactic form, his leader's agreement with another assertion, an assertion that partially overlaps referentially and propositionally with his preceding attempts:

> (c) (pre-posed adjuncts: time, location) for the first time in Derby
>   a community hospital will be created
>   this hospital will be on one site
>   several sites currently exist
>   such a hospital is needed
>   such a hospital will be valued

In none of these three sets is any new propositional substance introduced, except perhaps for the politically significant concept of 'community hospital' introduced in (c). One significant change from the cognitive point of view may be subtle shifts in 'salience' (Verschueren 1999: 173–200), suggested above by indentation. In his final formulation (c), Laxton seems to be literally asking for the leader to agree with four propositions marked both by syntax, by intonation contour, pauses and by order of meaning constituents.

Interestingly, Blair responds to the order of salience. First, he responds to the request that he agree with the utterer: indeed, he repeats the word *agree* twice, and the phrase 'he's right' three times. It is also important that these words are spoken simultaneously with the chorus of approval ('hear hear') from Labour MPs. Laxton has expressed approval of the leader's policies, he has managed to do so in the approved format, and he has elicited approval from his peers and from his leader. This part of the exchange seems to be tantamount to acknowledgement that he is, in virtue of his performance, initiated into the parliamentary discourse community. This activity can scarcely be described as seeking information or seeking action. It could be described as a form of bonding behaviour among members, an act of bonding that is simultaneously an act of bounding. In addition, Laxton may be seeking to obtain a public commitment of some kind from the government; of course, he is also advertising himself to his constituents through the television transmission.

The prime ministerial answer

Thus far there is little to suggest that information was sought through the 'question', other than the expression of agreement; nor was 'action', except in the sense of the act of agreeing. Blair repeats one of Laxton's pre-posed adjuncts, the next two propositions, and in the same order as Laxton, thus demonstrating his agreement. But he does more besides. Laxton's propositions are refocused. Blair manages, in a way that Laxton does not, to give equal salience to the first two propositions (there will be a new hospital, the hospital will be on one site), by using 'what will happen is that', and 'not only . . . but at the same time'. Further, however, he works less salient propositions into his utterances by way of adjuncts and presuppositions. In particular he introduces causal links and consequential links. The pragmatic relevance of the causal link ('as a result of the new contract that's been announced this morning') is probably to claim credit for the government. The relevance of the consequence clause ('so that people aren't going to have to . . .') seems to be to lay claim to the advantages of large single-site hospitals.

What Blair is doing is not giving 'information' as one might ordinarily understand the term, but performing verbal acts whose pragmatic function has to be understood in relation to competing political parties. The main job of the whole exchange, may in fact be 'bonding' as well as 'bounding', the ongoing construction of sameness and difference between parties. The evidence for this frequently comes from paralinguistic behaviour – the latching of supportive vocalisations,[5] the use of smiling by Blair as he does his 'agreeing', the use of laughter to acknowledge Laxton's self-recognition. Laughter can of course serve the opposite function, as will be seen. Synchronisation is also central to this type of bonding behaviour; it is iconic of togetherness. The discourse of several individuals and groups in the communication space is 'orchestrated' spontaneously – that is, several voices, mutually monitoring one another, begin, finish and overlap, rise and fall in pitch and loudness, with remarkable timing.

The 'question', then, cannot be understood simply as a request for action or information. Once normalised, Laxton's question literally asks whether the leader agrees, as do a significant number of same-party questions. But even if the request is merely for the action of agreeing, the speaker and his hearers in all probability anticipate a positive answer. Returning to the discussion of the cooperative principle discussed in Chapter 3, one can ask what this implies for the maxim of relevance. Clearly, the MPs accept his formulation as relevant. What they therefore accept is a locally applicable relevance criterion: they accept and expect a form of verbal behaviour that has several simultaneous and interlinked political functions – being initiated into question-time discourse and parliamentary discourse in general (one might call it 'westminsterese'), seeking the leader's approbation, grooming the leader, bonding with fellow party members, advertising oneself to constituents who might be viewing, and contributing to the discursive construction of party boundaries. These are acknowledged activities, thus 'relevant', but can apparently only be executed if the speaker abides by the rules of the genre, principally the collective fiction that a 'question' is being put. They can be understood as ritual acts of conformity with the tacit rules and practices of the House, and also as a demonstration of the ability to *perform* interactively with other MPs and with the Speaker. An ability to demonstrate mastery of language may be an important and even an expected element of political behaviour, though not a necessary one, since examples of inarticulate leaders are not impossible to find.

Clash of leaders and more repairs

The Laxton–Blair exchange illustrates, among other things, that the 'question' can be part of the testing of a novice member. What about seasoned leaders? In the same parliamentary session, an apparently simple slip of the tongue can be seen to be deeply embedded in the testing of leaders. The following extract, is again ostensibly a question–answer sequence. It occurs at the beginning of the session, which is opened by an experienced Labour MP, Paul Marsden.

Marsden has tabled the ritual question about the prime minister's engagements, to which the prime minister reads the ritual reply from his folder. Marsden is then called again to speak. His 'supplementary question' leads to a verbal duel between prime minister and opposition leader. By the rules of the genre, any member may rise to his or her feet to signal the desire to put a question following another speaker. The Speaker of the House will give or withhold permission; by convention, opposition members, and in particular the leader of the opposition are given priority. In this episode William Hague, the opposition leader, challenges the prime minister's response to Marsden. (The numerals relate to gestures, which are noted at the end of the extract.)

House of Commons, 7 July 1999: Paul Marsden (Ma), Prime Minister (P) and Opposition Leader (O)

Ma {looking down right towards P} I thank my right honourable friend for that er reply. And can I ask im that in light of yesterday's launch of the er new white paper on *health* which aims to save some three *hundred* thousand *lives*, (.) over the next *years*, (.) er er can I ask im er whether h er he thinks he will agree with me that this will benefit *everyone*. but in par*ti*cularly, (.) those on low incomes (.) and those from socially disadvantaged backgrounds, er those same people, who {the Tories}₁ wrote off er | er when they were in office erm* er with their two-tier | NHS system=

M | ((HEARHEARXXXXXXXXX))*

M =((HEAR HEAR))=

P = {rises looking at folder} (w'l) Madam Speaker, (.) we have targets both to reduce the death rate from cancer, (.) and the death rate from heart disease. if I can just deal with (.) *cancer*. (.) we are also, (.) going to put some sixty million pounds, directly into services for the three most *common* cancers, (.) {looks up} we're then putting another *hun*dred and fifty million pounds, into providing state-of-the-art e*quip*ment for (.) cancer, (.) and there are going to be an *ex*tra four hundred cancer, (.) specialists, (.) and increased spending, (.) on cancer drugs. /All of this of course will take time, (.) but it *will* end up (.) with a *vast*ly improved service for people suffering from this disease.=

M   =((hear hearxxx))

S | Mr William Hague=

M   =((HEAR HEAR hear hear))=

O   =Why didn't e just mention in the answer e just gave, that the waiting list to see a consultant has *doubled* in this country since he beca:me prime /minister.(.) is e gonna keep on blaming other people for that or are {*he* and his ministers}₂ going to take responsibility (.) for this miserable /*fail*ure.=

M   =((HEARHEAR|XXxxxxxxxxxxxxxxxxxxxxxxxxxxxxxxxx*))

P |{glances at S} (yuh) Madam Speaker, (.)*
waiting lists are actually {*down*}₃ as a result (.)|of this government's policies,
                                                      |/WAITING LISTS ARE
                                                      |{DO:WN,}₃ (.) AND IT
                                                      |IS {*THIS* GOVERN-
                                                      |MENT}₄*=

M |((HEARHEARxxxxxxxxx))*

P   =THAT ARE PUTTING AN EXTRA {*TWENTY-ONE BILLION POUNDS*
INTO THE *HEALTH*}₅| SERVICE (..)* *OPPOSED*, BY THE CONSERVATIVE
                    |/PARTY. =

M |((XXXXXX))*

M   =((XXXX|XXXX))

S | Mr Hague.=

O   ={glancing at S} Well Madam Speaker it's a good job that there isn't a waiting list for a straight answer or we'd be here|for a very (.) > very long
                                                                                |time indeed.<the fact is*=

M |((XXXXXXXXXXXX))*

O   =the number of consultants is down, the number of complaints is up, the waiting list promise has been broken, the waiting list to get *on* the waiting list has been doubled, | the junior* doctors've

M |((YESXX))*

O   =been betrayed, <the head of the MBA said in his speech on Monday, >|(1.5){GESTURE}₆ (1.5)

M |((HAHAHAXXXXXX=
=X|XXXXXXXXXXXXXXXXXXXXXXXXXXXXXXXX|XXXXXXXXXXXXXXX*))

O |>/the BM\A: . (4.0) /<the head of the=
                                          |
S |=or or order ORDER ORDER
                                          (.) ORDER (how)*=

O => >the head of the \BM\A:: | *said in his* *speech*/ *on*\ *Mon*/*day*:,< (.)* glad
everybody's listening, =

M | ((HURRAYxxxxxxxxxxxxxx*xxxxx))*

O =listen to the next bit as well. (.) | he* said congratulations Mr Blair:
morale has never been=

M | ((XXX))*

O = >so low.< (.) now (.) will he now will he now give the house the figure.
(.) will he give the house the figure >the ACtual: figure.< the actual *figure*
for the number of people waiting to see a consultant.

P (. . .) Madam Speaker, (.) the waiting lists, (.) are, > sixty-two thousand
below the level that we inherited.< they are sixty (.) two thousand. (.)
the figure now is just over one million that is sixty-two thousand (.) be*low*
the level we inherited, (.) average (.) waiting times {< I am giving
the figures. >}₇ average waiting times (.) >are now (,) *shorter*, < and in
relation to junior doctors' (.) *hours*, when we came to office, there were
six thousand five hundred junior doctors, (.) working {more than fifty-
six hours a week, <that's an *un*acceptable figure,>}₈ /it is now, (.) four
thousand=

Gestures

[1] From 'er those same . . .' switches gaze towards Tory bench opposite before pointing with index finger
towards opposition bench.

[2] RH index moves away from body at chest height horizontally towards opposite front bench.

[3] Downwards head movement; slaps side of dispatch box on second 'down'.

[4] RH index moves towards own chest.

[5] Jabs with RH index at folder on dispatch box on stressed syllables.

[6] Shakes head to left and downwards to acknowledge error, simultaneously smiling.

[7] Looks up from folder to interrupter.

[8] Looks up at opposition, frowning; nods head on 'fifty' and on 'un'.

What is at issue is again the real function of the 'questions' posed and
'answers' given. Marsden's question, although in a form that Hansard eventually
normalises, is essentially of the conventional agreement-seeking type and passes
unchallenged. The syntactic presentation is not very dissimilar from Laxton's:
an adjunct is pre-posed and several presuppositions are carried by embedded
clauses:

(pre-posed adjunct) in the light of yesterday's launch of the new white
paper on
      health
      the white paper was launched yesterday
      the white paper aims to save some hundred thousand lives . . .
this will benefit everyone
this will particularly benefit those on low incomes

this will particularly benefit those from socially disadvantaged backgrounds
the Tories wrote these people off
the Tories had a two-tier NHS system when they were in office

Despite being incorporated by way of a relative clause the last two propositions are given salience in several ways. The extraction of 'those same people' is
interactively probably less important that the pauses and the accusatory pointing
gesture accompanied by a shift of gaze that frames 'the Tories'. Not only does
this work to elicit supportive vocalisation from Labour members, synchronised
with the clause 'when they were in office', but a further presumably strategic
pause permits the turn-final phrase 'with their two-tier NHS system' to elicit
a latched response. Effectively, the current speaker has selected the next speaker
– the supporting MPs – in a kind of turn-taking system that runs parallel to and
meshes with the overarching official turn-taking system managed by the Speaker.
It is further worth noting that Marsden's verbal actions work successfully and
are apparently taken as fully relevant, despite the rather vaguely general nature
of the core proposition in his question and despite the high likelihood that
the prime minister is going to agree that his policies will 'benefit everyone'.
The actual interrogative, though too idiosyncratic for Hansard, also seems to be
acceptable to the assembled MPs.

The prime minister does not assert agreement, as he did in the Laxton
episode. Marsden is not a novice, and the utterance exchange is not this time
being constructed as an initiation. There may of course be other motivations for
the lack of endorsement of Marsden's propositions. Some observers would note,
for instance, that the MP's presuppositions regarding the national health service
are of a rather 'old Labour' socialist character: conceivably Blair chooses not to
endorse this conceptual framework. In any event, the response is minimally
linked to the question, and is hedged with the words 'well, Madam Speaker', we
have targets . . .'. At the end of his turn Blair's utterance implicates criticism of
the opposition, given the presumption of adversarial interaction in the context.
The leader of the opposition takes his cue.

Hague presumes mutual knowledge about an opinion expressed at that time
in the public sphere – the opinion that waiting time for access to the health
service was unacceptably long. The two interrogatives ('why didn't he just
mention . . . ?' and 'is he going to keep on blaming . . . ?') correspond to two
aspects of the preceding exchange. The first interrogative uses the overspecific
content of Blair's utterances to imply that the prime minister is evading the
waiting-list issue. This move can be understood in the light of the Gricean
quantity maxim. The second interrogative works primarily by presupposition:
'keep on' presupposes *is doing currently*, while the interrogative 'are they going
to?' presupposes *is not doing currently*. But of equal importance are the paralinguistic
features. Hague's performance is characterised by high energy – the use of hand

gesture and wide rising–falling intonation contours, which have a general tendency to mean 'challenge'.[6] These features coincide with the use of the pronoun 'he' instead of the conventional respect form ('prime minister'), the non-aspiration of this pronoun, and the casual phonetic assimilation in 'gonna' – features which can variously be interpreted as marking Hague's regional Yorkshire origin, his masculinity, his populist appeal, or perhaps honesty. All this prompts latched vocal support from the Tory members. In order to save face, Blair must interrupt without too much delay.

So the prime minister rises to his feet and this implicit appeal to Madam Speaker is sufficient to end the vocalisations and establish a new turn in which a response to Hague is expected. Hague could scarcely be expecting answers that abide by the maxims of relevance and quantity, in some absolute sense. In terms of local expectations, the response is of course 'relevant'. Blair simply asserts that they have decreased; he also asserts, though this assertion is not linked directly to the preceding one, that the government has increased spending, opposed by the Conservatives. The prosodic features and accompanying gestures are an intrinsic part of the performance – as the reader will see from the transcript.

What can be clearly seen is that Blair responds to Hague by stimulating vocalised support, and he does this by pausing after 'as a result', by increased physical gesture and by increased volume. The point seems to be to establish strong demarcation between the parties on an emotive public issue: claiming to further the health of the people is an important ethical claim with serious consequences. Blair seats himself without further elaboration of what is meant by his assertion that the lists are 'down', a gesture that enables Hague to accuse Blair again of evasion and to introduce reference to further expressions of critical opinion in the public sphere, the dissatisfaction about junior doctors' working conditions. Both the waiting lists and the junior doctors are thus turned into active topics and, again, Blair must respond at some point. But he is momentarily spared by a slip of the opposition leader's tongue:

O =been betrayed, <the head of the MBA said in his speech on Monday,>
    (1.5){GESTURE} (1.5)
M ((HAHAHAXXXXXX . . .

He was expected to say 'BMA' and must repair his slip. In ordinary conversation the repair system involves a combination of: (a) choice of *initiation* of repair either by self (the current speaker) or by other; and (b) *actual* verbal repair either by self or by other. Such repairs can take place at several opportunities in the sequencing of conversational turns, and evidence suggests that there are distinctly ranked preferences (Schegloff *et al.* 1977; Levinson 1983: 339ff.). But what happens in the case of the Hague's slip?

Hague has started to adduce a quotation from an authority, the head of the British Medical Association. To discursively mark this as quotation his tempo increases. Perhaps because of this, he produces 'MBA' (Master of Business Administration) instead of 'BMA'. Now the first- and most preferred opportunity for self-repair would be during this first speaking turn, but there is no evidence that Hague is aware of his error. Hague does not reach the end of his turn, which would be the next (and second-most preferred) opportunity for self-repair. In fact he does not initiate repair. The MPs register the slip, but do not wait for the end of the turn ('transition place'), which would be the third opportunity for repair, but interrupt. The interruption occurs not immediately after 'MBA', but fairly precisely at an interruption opportunity after a tone group. Perhaps also time is needed for processing and group coordination. As far as can be ascertained from the broadcast version, the interrupters do not actually do the correction by uttering 'you mean BMA' or some such. Predominantly they laugh. Hague then corrects himself. This sequence corresponds to the classic account in so far as it is an example of other-initiated self-repair. However, it differs in that turn-taking is not observed: the MPs interrupt, albeit in synchrony with the speaker's rhythm and (in the intonational sense) phrasing. One cannot really, therefore, regard the other repair here as being a 'next-turn repair initiator', since the turn is interrupted. Interruptive other-initiation of repair can be regarded as dispreferred, non-cooperative and face-threatening.

In the context of parliamentary discourse and of this episode in particular a number of implications spring to mind. Hague's self-repair is almost the least preferred strategy – he only just saves himself from having others do the actual repair. This is probably insufficient, and for this reason he adopts several linguistic strategies to redress the balance. Hague is apparently made aware of his slip by laughter, which, as a human signalling behaviour, can indicate either bonding or rejection. The Conservative members cannot be seen smiling or laughing. It takes Hague a relatively long time to recall the error. In general, imperfections of this type are not stored in memory, unless they have some significance (Verschueren 1999: 41). This one has, as is indicated by the intensity of the Labour MPs' mirth; it is probable that a meaningless reversal of sounds would have been ignored. In this instance hearers can easily interpret Hague's mistake as motivated, even ideologically motivated, since it could appear that the conceptual domain 'business' has somehow leaked into and dominated the conceptual domain 'medical care', and the Conservative Party traditionally is the party of business. This may account for the amount of time and energy that goes into this particular interruption.

A great deal of time and energy, relatively speaking, also goes into Hague's management of this interruption. His self-repair is not only late but has been initiated by a derisive interruption. This seems to mean that not only does Hague have to repair the error in the narrow technical sense by uttering the correct form, but he has to repair the damage done to his 'face'. He could of course, simply make the correction and proceed, but he does a great deal more than this. As is common when such discourse crises occur, a cluster of communicative devices come into play. Perhaps significantly, Hague responds first of all by gestures, gestures that acknowledge that his mind has now recalled and recognised the slip, and by grins that may signal some form of sharing that mitigates the adversarial effect of the interruption. Unlike the case of Laxton, however, there is no element of submission, but rather some signal of what intuitively sounds like weary condescension. He demonstrates initiative and control by himself interrupting the continuing noise made by members. The prosodic features of his 'the BMA' – rallentando vowel-lengthening, step drop in pitch – have a broadly conventional meaning in English that is difficult to characterise technically but involves something like 'yes I know and it's not very interesting'.[7]

However, this does not silence the MPs and Hague has to do more work. It takes him about four seconds to begin to repeat the full phrase 'the head of the BMA', but this coincides with Madam Speaker's intervention, which itself deploys relative high vocal force. Hague is now able to repeat the corrected sentence, and he does so deploying the same prosodic features as earlier, where stylised 'sing-song' contours signal repetition and bored attitude. Increased volume has to cover the opposition's mocking cheers, but conclusion of the tone group now coincides with the end of this interruption, creating space for a further utterance that cannot be explained as strictly necessary to the repair or to the question he is supposed to be putting:

glad everybody's listening . . . listen to the next bit as well

At one level, we all know what is going on here, but let's try to take it apart. First, the wording and the normally not permitted imperative ('listen to the next bit') may be interpreted as teacher–pupil style, continuing what may sound like classroom prosody in the earlier segments. What is more, the semantic and pragmatic content (listening and the imperative form) has to do precisely with the requirement of attention and control. Odd as it may seem, this is an indirect way of reasserting face and status. Second, as already noted, and notwithstanding notable examples to the contrary, leadership in human societies is generally associated with superior eloquence, mastery of language. Perhaps mastery of language iconically represents control in general. Evidence of this is the fact that it *matters* that Hague has momentarily lost verbal control, and that he puts much effort into reasserting his rhetorical powers.

Moreover, he succeeds in returning to his 'question'. This in itself is important, for two reasons. First, he has not yet put a question – has indeed spent a lot of time making assertions – and strictly speaking he still needs to put a question to legitimise his speaking at all. Second, it is quite likely that the Labour interruption could be interpreted as an attempt to cover Blair's relatively weak answer with regard to waiting lists and junior doctors' conditions, and to 'shout down' a difficult question. Frequently, speakers do claim that adversaries' interruptions are attempts to do just that.[8] Hague does not in fact take this option, at least not overtly. But he does assert his right to put his question. Awareness that Labour members may have been trying to divert him from doing this is perhaps reflected in the formulation and delivery of the question.

To appreciate the importance of these repair-management episodes, one has only to consider the consequences if either Laxton or Hague had failed to resolve the discourse crisis. Suppose Laxton had simply sat down in embarrassment not grasping why the MPs were interrupting; suppose Hague's short-term memory recall had failed him, or if he had failed to find an acceptably self-assertive rejoinder that was also cooperative at some level with the broader discourse of the House of Commons. In the case of Hague, his discourse management enables him to proceed to press the government concerning health service waiting lists, and he is able to do so, under the conventions of the House, by completing what is his second question and going onto a third.

Form and performance

In the production of parliamentary discourse, form is important, but performance is crucial. In analysing Hansard's normalisation of syntactic form, it emerges that certain syntactic forms are preferred because they align prototypically (though not always pragmatically) with the canonical questioning acts (requesting information and requesting action) which Erskine May and other authorities assert to be the function of parliamentary questions. The genre thus has an 'ideal form' which plays a role in the real-life verbal behaviour of the House, in guiding speakers' production, in providing the criteria by which the Speaker can assert control and, what is more important, in providing the opportunity for speakers to manipulate and provoke interaction. These exploited opportunities themselves have a predictable form.

The close examination of repairs when different kinds of malfunction – transgressing the ideal-form rules, making forbidden reference (e.g., to the royal family) in questions, physical and psychological malfunctions (slips of the tongue, etc.) – can reveal a layer of verbal activity that parallels the supposedly primary level of information-seeking. Repairs provide opportunities for performing numerous discourse acts which have very little to do with 'questions'. In addition to repairs, there are routine interruptions in the form of standardised calls of approval ('hear, hear', 'yes, yes') or objections ('order, order', 'no, no'). These take many forms, and depend heavily on paralinguistic channels. They require further investigation, but what is clear is that they are regular, they are coordinated, and they fulfil political functions. Comparing the cognitive content of parliamentary 'questions' with their interactive components suggests that the latter are predominant.

Speculating about functions is just that: speculation. But if one asks what sort of group behaviour is going on in the House of Commons, in such examples as we have analysed, it is difficult to resist noting the following. The Members of Parliament accept some aspects at least of the 'ideal form' as a framework for exploitation. New members have to show that they understand this and can master it. Leaders of both sides of the House (and the spatial metaphor of opposition is crucial to the conduct of political discourse) have especially to demonstrate their mastery of the discourse. Leaders are rhetorically tried and tested at the Dispatch Box. Such behaviours can be seen as forms of bonding – with the institutionalised discourse practices of Parliament on the one hand and on the other with the political party. They can also be seen as forms of bounding – the constant construction of boundaries between the political parties. It is true that, simultaneously, individual MPs are seeking to coerce ministers into revealing information or showing weakness (for instance by 'open' questions, the use of presuppositions, the manipulation of interruptive vocalisation). And of course there is an ongoing discursive effort to establish versions of reality, different accounts of the political universe at the cognitive level. But such activity frequently appears to be subordinate to the bonding/bounding function. In a general sense, none of this would come as a surprise to many a political journalist. What a linguistic and discourse-analytic account can achieve is a detailed description of the political behaviour in question, and show how verbal and political behaviour are enmeshed.

7   Foreigners

In this chapter, in contrast with the last two, we are not focusing on particular institutions of political talk, but on a certain set of topics and ways of talking about them. The two examples we shall look at are separated partly by time – a political speech given in 1968 and another given thirty-two years later. And they are markedly separated in terms of the social actors and milieu. What both texts have in common is that they refer to, and express attitudes towards the category 'foreigners'. This category is not fixed and objective, but constituted in discourse by these very types of text and talk.[1] As far as our method of analysis is concerned, while the minutiae of interaction still tell us a great deal about political micro-behaviour, we shall concentrate on strategic functions, in the sense discussed in Chapter 3.

'Rivers of Blood'

The first example is a speech given by Enoch Powell, a maverick Conservative politician, in Birmingham, England, in April 1968.[2] This was about five years after Martin Luther King gave his 'I have a dream' speech. Powell, a classicist by training, brought himself notoriety by quoting Virgil in his peroration:

> As I look ahead, I am filled with foreboding. Like the Roman, I seem to see 'the River Tiber foaming with much blood'.[3]

Among other things this piece of rhetoric involved an indirect-meaning strategy. Without the taking of responsibility that explicitness requires, the speaker appears to be making available the inference that interracial conflict will occur in Britain as a result of excessive immigration. Subsequently, Powell was expelled from the shadow cabinet by the Conservative leader Edward Heath.

Legitimisation and coercion strategies

An important first step is to describe the pragmatic units of the text. What speech acts are performed in which sections? What appears to be the practical purpose of saying such and such in the context of the speech? Table 7.1 illustrates one way in which the analysis might be done for a portion of the 'Rivers of Blood' speech. The headings in the table attach strategies to sections of the text, in the sequence in which they occur, together with some illustrative text. The category labels are arrived at simply by asking: 'what is the speaker doing here in saying this?'. Naturally, labelling stretches of language as serving strategic functions is an interpretative act on the part of the hearer and analyst. Any candidate for being interpreted as strategic is a stretch of language – i.e., a symbolic construct made of words and syntactic structures. I focus primarily on lexical signals, which are marked in bold type, bypassing a detailed description of syntax, to focus on a pragmatic interpretation.[4]

Legitimising

A relatively informal analysis like this can highlight possible inferences that the hearer may draw or assumptions that the hearer may make, though not of course all of those that are possible. What also emerges is that the non-explicit meanings, as well as, or possibly even more than the explicit ones, have functions that in the context of political communication can be seen as legitimising or emotionally coercive. It is also possible, using this kind of display, to see different *types* of legitimising and emotive function. Thus in this text at least there seem to be two basic kinds of legitimising. The first type is essentially epistemic. It has to do

Table 7.1 Interpreted strategies in Powell's 'Rivers of Blood' speech

Legitimising/delegitimising strategy	*Emotive effect*
The **supreme function of statesmanship**	
speaker is a supreme statesman	
is to provide against preventable **evils**. In seeking to do so, it encounters obstacles which are deeply rooted in human nature. One is that by	**fear of unspecified dangers**
the very order of things, such **evils** are not demonstrable until they have occurred . . .	**fear of unspecified dangers**
whence the besetting temptation of all politics to concern itself with the immediate present at the expense of the future. Above all, **people are disposed to mistake**	
speaker does not make mistakes	

Table 7.1 (continued)

Legitimising/delegitimising strategy	Emotive effect
predicting troubles for causing troubles and even for desiring troubles: 'If only,' **they love to think**, 'if only people wouldn't talk about it, it probably wouldn't happen'. Perhaps **this habit goes back to the primitive belief** that the word	desire to be 'not primitive'

> *I do not have this habit, and am not primitive*

| and the thing, the name and the object, are identical. At all events, the discussion of **future grave** but, with effort now, avoidable **evils** is the most unpopular and at the same time **the most necessary** occupation for the politician. **Those who knowingly shirk** it deserve, and not infrequently receive, | fear of future
fear of unspecified dangers |

> *I do not shirk moral duties*

| **the curses of those who come after.** | fear of blame, shame, |
| A week or two ago I fell into conversation with a constituent, a middle-aged, **quite ordinary working man** | loyalty to group, paternalism |

> *therefore from a reliable source*

| employed in one of our nationalised industries. After a sentence or two about the weather, he suddenly said: 'If I had the money to go, I wouldn't stay in this country'. [. . .] '**I have three children**, all of them been through grammar school and two of them married now, with family. I shan't be satisfied till I have seen them all settled overseas. In this country in fifteen or twenty years' time the **black man will have the whip hand over the white man**'. | protective feelings for family

fear of domination |

> *this is not speaker's assertion; it's from a reliable source*

| I can already hear the chorus of execration. How dare I say such a horrible thing? [. . .] The answer is that **I do not have the right not to** do so. Here is **a decent, ordinary fellow Englishman**, who in broad daylight in my | loyalty to group |

> *therefore from a reliable source*

Table 7.1 (continued)

Legitimising/delegitimising strategy	*Emotive effect*

own town says to me, his Member of Parliament,
that his country will not be worth living in for
his children. **I simply do not have the right
to shrug my shoulders and think about
something else**.

> there exist moral rights and duties that I observe

What he is saying, thousands and hundreds of
thousands are saying and thinking

> therefore from a reliable source

– not throughout Great Britain, perhaps, but in
the areas that are already undergoing the total
transformation to which there   **fear of change**

> England is being totally transformed

is no parallel in a thousand years of English
history.

In fifteen or twenty years, on present trends,
there will be in this country $3\frac{1}{2}$ million
Commonwealth immigrants and their
descendants. **That is not my figure.
That is the official figure given to
Parliament by the spokesman of the
Registrar General's Office**.

> therefore from a reliable source

There is no comparable **official figure** for the
year 2000; but it **must** be in the region of five
to seven million . . . Whole areas, areas, towns
and parts of towns across England towns across
England will be **occupied** by sections of the   **fear of domination, invasion**
immigrant and immigrant-descended population.
As time goes on, the proportion of this
total . . . **will rapidly increase**. Already by   **fear of numerical
1985 the native-born would constitute **the   domination**
majority**. It is this fact above all which creates
the **extreme urgency** of action now, of just   **fear of imminent threat**
that kind of action

> there is a need for immediate action

which is hardest for politicians to take, action
where the difficulties lie in the present but **the
evils** to be prevented or   **fear of unspecified dangers**

Table 7.1 (continued)

Legitimising/delegitimising strategy	Emotive effect
there exist unspecified dangers	

minimised lie several parliaments ahead.
The **natural and rational** first question with a
nation confronted

I am rational, and natural, and these qualities are good	

by such a prospect is to ask: 'How can its
dimensions be reduced?' . . . the significance and
consequences of an an **alien element** introduced   **fear of outsiders**
into a country or population . . . The answers to
the **simple and rational question** are equally

simplicity and rationality are good; rationality is simple	

simple and rational: by stopping, or virtually
stopping, further **inflow**, and by promoting the   **protective container schema**
maximum **outflow**. Both answers are part of the
official policy of the Conservative Party

therefore I am uttering official Conservative policy	

It almost passes belief that at this **moment 20**   **fear of numerical**
or 30 additional immigrant children are   **domination**
arriving from overseas in Wolverhampton
alone every week – and that means fifteen
or twenty additional families of a decade
or two hence.

these numbers are large, large numbers are dangerous	

Those whom the gods wish to **destroy**, they   **fear of destruction**
first make **mad**.

this is a classical quotation, therefore trustworthy	

We must be **mad**, literally **mad**, as a nation to   **fear of madness**
be permitting the annual **inflow** of some 50,000
dependants . . . It is like watching a nation busily
engaged in **heaping up its own funeral pyre**.   **fear of death, fire, madness**
So **insane** are we,

permitting immigration is committing suicide	

that we actually permit unmarried persons to
immigrate for the purpose of founding a family
with spouses and fiancés whom they have never
seen.

Table 7.1 (continued)

Legitimising/delegitimising strategy	Emotive effect

the action referred to is insane	

Let no one suppose that the **flow** of dependants will automatically tail off. On the contrary, even at the present admission rate of only 5,000 a year by voucher, there is sufficient for a further 25,000 dependants per annum *ad infinitum*, without taking into account the **huge reservoir** of existing relations in this country . . . In these circumstances nothing will suffice but that the total **inflow** for settlement should be reduced at once to negligible proportions, If all immigration ended tomorrow . . . the prospective size of this element in the population would still leave the basic character of **the national danger** unaffected . . . years or so. Hence **the urgency** of implementing now the second element of the Conservative Party's policy . . . If such a policy were adopted and pursued with the determination which the gravity of the alternative justifies, the resultant **outflow** could appreciably alter the prospects for the future.

It can be no part of any policy that existing **families** should be kept divided; but . . . we **ought** to be prepared to arrange for them to be reunited in their countries of origin.

repatriation reunites families, therefore it is a moral duty	

[. . .] The third element of the Conservative Party's policy is that all who are in this country as citizens **should be equal before the law and that there shall be no discrimination or difference made between them by public authority**.

my statements are compatible with moral and democratic norms	

As Mr Heath has put it we will have no 'first-class citizens' and 'second-class citizens'. This does not mean that the immigrant and his descendants should be elevated into a privileged or special class or **that the citizen should be denied his right** to

there exist citizens with rights which might be denied	

continued activation of container and fluid schema

continued activation of container and fluid schema

protective feelings for family

evoke righteousness emotions

Table 7.1 (continued)

Legitimising/delegitimising strategy	Emotive effect
discriminate in the management of his own affairs between one fellow citizen and another,	
citizens have a right to discriminate	
or that he should be **subjected to inquisition** as to his reasons and motive for behaving in one lawful manner rather than another.	fear of domination
currently citizens might be subjected to inquisition	
There could be no grosser **misconception of the realities** than is	
there are realities some people do not understand; I do understand these realities	
entertained by those who vociferously demand legislation as they call it 'against discrimination', whether they be leader writers of the same kidney and sometimes on the same newspapers which year after year in the 1930s **tried to blind** this country to **the rising peril** which confronted it,	memory of fear of Nazi threat in 1930s; anger at people who conceal threats
increased immigration is equivalent to Nazi threat of invasion; anti-discrimination legislation is equivalent to appeasement	
or archbishops who live in palaces, faring delicately with the bedclothes pulled right up over their heads. They have got it **exactly and diametrically wrong**.	satisfaction: being 'right' (epistemically and morally)
I have got it exactly right	
The discrimination and the deprivation, the sense of alarm and of resentment, lies not with the immigrant population but with those among whom they have come and are still coming.	fear of domination
there exists discrimination against the white British population	
This is why to enact legislation of the kind before Parliament at this moment is to **risk throwing a match onto gunpowder**. The kindest thing that can be said about those who propose and support it is that **they know not what they do**.	fear of fire and distruction

evoke righteousness (biblical allusion) |

with the speaker's claim to have better knowledge, recognition of the 'real' facts. Related to this claim is the claim to be more 'rational', more 'objective', even more advanced in his mode of thought than rivals or adversaries. Epistemic claims are frequently also backed up by lists, statistics and sources that the speaker presumes the hearer will accept as authoritative.

The second type is deontic.[5] The speaker claims, explicitly or implicitly, to be not only 'right' in a cognitive sense, but 'right' in a moral sense. There is an important overlap in this domain with *feelings* as well as 'factual' representations. The speaker will seek to ground his or her position in moral *feelings* or intuitions that no one will challenge. The analysis suggests that certain intuitive, emotionally linked mental schemas are being evoked. Certain emotions that can be reasonably regarded as in some way basic are evidently stimulated – most obviously fear, anger, sense of security, protectiveness, loyalty. We can be even more precise. The fear is linked to fear of invasion (including the historical memories of the Second World War that the speaker can presume some of his hearers will have) and fear of domination. The protectiveness is towards one's family. The sense of security is related to one's geographical territory, the loyalty towards those with whom affinity can be established or assumed. Underlying this there seems to be some general schema of self *versus* other, or that which is close *versus* that which is distant. There is good reason to think that these emotions are ones that have evolved in human brains for reasons of survival – but any functional component can be recruited in particular circumstances for particular ends. It is perhaps significant that the self–other schema involves a covertly metaphorical mode of expression that is derived from representations of physical space. This is apparent if one takes seriously the recurring use of three related lexical sets: those to do with spatial containment, those to do with movement in and out of a containing space, and those that conceptualise moving bodies (here immigrants and emigrants) as a fluid, whence the recurrent vocabulary of 'inflow' and 'outflow'.[6]

The legitimising strategies used by Powell can, then, be easily picked out. The most important one seems to be the establishing of moral authority and common moral ground; it leaves available the inference that political opponents are not moral. Quite prominently the speaker asserts his own superior rationality, leaving open the inference that opponents are irrational. The various legitimising strategies that we can interpretatively isolate here correspond roughly to Habermas's 'rightness' validity claim discussed in Chapter 3. Closely linked is the claim to be telling the truth – Powell makes a series of assertions which he backs up with devices that seem to be strategically chosen to ground their truth claims, i.e., give them 'credibility'. One way of simultaneously claiming to be truthful and legitimising oneself in a wider political sense is to claim an *authority* as the source of an assertion. Powell's authorities are worthy of note: at one extreme he cites Virgil, at the other what he calls the 'ordinary' working man and the 'decent' Englishman. Another method, which simultaneously invokes rightness and truth, by laying claim to rationality (more epistemic) and reasonableness (more deontic), is to adopt quasi-conversational patterns that are also quasi-disputation patterns, such as question-answer pairs. The speaker is claiming morality, rationality and veracity as guarantees of his authority to make assertions about immigration and the behaviour of immigrants.

Coercing

Identifying coercive strategies is heavily dependent on interpretation. An entire oration might in some sense be judged 'coercive' on the grounds that it uses rhetorical mechanisms that seek to persuade. Even the strategy of legitimising/ delegitimising, together with the 'rightness' validity claim, can be seen as part of coercion. However, this does not prevent picking out particular stretches of speech that seems strategically designed *predominantly* to coerce.

We can distinguish two kinds of coercion in the analysis, one forcing emotional responses, the other cognitive responses. With respect to the first kind, if we are claiming that a certain use of language is coercive, this can be done by considering speech acts, and more particularly, the *perlocutionary* effects of speech acts (Austin 1962), difficult to specify though they are. Thus one possible effect that some of Powell's utterances may have is the inducement of fear by making truth claims, in the form of predictions, about causal effects – for example, predicting that uncontrolled immigration will cause damaging events. In terms of speech acts, Powell is issuing warnings; in terms of contextualised political language use, he is using a coercive strategy in so far as he is (conceivably) causing fear of contingent events and actors involved in them.

Emotive coercion, we may speculate, can occur when certain vocabulary or certain propositions receive mental representations that are in some way linked (neurologically, in fact) to emotion centres of the brain (the limbic system). For instance, some kind of fearful response may be stimulated by such terms as 'urgency', 'national danger' and 'evil', terms which are dispersed through the text. It is also conceivable that affect is stimulated by the cognitive schema mentioned earlier, and indicated in Table 7.1 – namely, the spatial containment schema which grounds the conceptualisation of one's country as a closed container that can be sealed or penetrated. It seems reasonable to refer to coercion here, or more precisely emotive coercion, because emotional effects that certain uses of language might induce are not necessarily under the control of the hearers affected, and because the speaker can in many instances be reasonably assumed to know that certain emotional effects are possible or probable.

The second kind of coercion is propositional rather than emotive, and involves the different forms of implied meaning (indicated in the shaded boxes in Table 7.1). What we are looking at is propositions that hearers are somehow induced to entertain in the course of processing current discourse. Because of the minimal communicative cooperative principle, hearers expect language$_{1/u}$ to be coherent and apply local maxims appropriate to the context and genre. For example, in reading or hearing Powell, one cannot do otherwise than make certain moment-ary online assumptions or accept certain implications – for example, that there exists such a thing as 'a primitive belief that the word and the thing, the name and the object, are identical'.

The mechanisms of 'forced inferences' include presupposition, implicature and presumptions, as outlined in Chapters 3 and 4. Two things need to be emphasised. One is that many of these implied propositions derive from what we have termed presumptions and are highly variable – that is, they may not occur for all hearers. The second thing to emphasise is that if implied proposi-tions are automatically processed in working memory, this does not necessarily mean that they are stored in long-term memory as true, i.e., as part of the hearer's own representation of reality. What long-term cognitive effect they have remains an open question; maybe they have none. But from a pragmatic point of view it is clear that such propositions are not easily challenged in explicit dialogue, even when hearers might find them inconsistent with their own representations of reality or find the truth claim faulty.

Legitimising vocabulary and emotively coercive vocabulary often seem to go hand in hand. A term such as *evil*, for example, quite plausibly has affective associations that are somehow very close to the moral conceptualisations that the word is also linked to. Is there more than meets the eye in this apparent tendency for self-legitimisation and emotivity to be associated? Possibly. It could be, for example, that feeling oneself to be 'in the right' is not just a cognition of a state of affairs; the cognition itself might be linked into emotional pathways of the brain. The emotions involved could, perhaps, be connected to protection of the family, protection of the group, protection of territory, fear of aggression, fear of loss of control. In the text we have analysed they certainly seem to be linked in this fashion. Legitimisation and emotivity can also be pragmatically linked in reporting the alleged, and presumptively authoritative quotations of others. In the case of Powell's claimed quotation from the 'decent, ordinary fellow Englishman', the cognitive representation might be linked with affective valuation. Attribution to a source also makes it possible to frighten and simul-taneously legitimise by making predictions, such as 'the black man will have the whip hand', while simultaneously evading personal responsibility for the assertion. The process of self-legitimisation and the accompanying evocation of emotions are dependent upon a particular representation of the world.

Representations: Who is the victim?

In Table 7.2, which is based on a portion of the text of Powell's speech, we turn to the representational dimension of language use, the construction of reality by

Table 7.2 Propositional structure in a portion of Powell's 'Rivers of Blood' speech

Argument 1	Predicate	Argument 2	Other arguments	Adjunct/conjunct
entry to this country	was	admission to privileges and opportunities eagerly sought	to the immigrant	
[the immigrant AGENT	entered		this country GOAL]	
[somebody AGENT	admitted	the immigrant THEME]	to privileges and opportunities GOAL]	
[the immigrant AGENT	sought	privileges and opportunities GOAL]		
the impact upon the existing population	was	very different		
[immigrants entering the country AGENT	impacted upon	the existing population PATIENT		in a different way]
				For reasons they could not comprehend and in pursuance of a decision ... on which they were never consulted
they [=existing population] COGNISER	found	themselves made strangers in their own country.		
[they COGNISER	could not comprehend	reasons]		
[someone AGENT	was pursuing	a decision]		
[someone AGENT	did not consult	the existing population]		
[someone AGENT	made	the existing population PATIENT	strangers in their own country]	

They
COGNISER
found
their wives unable to obtain
hospital beds in childbirth

[their wives
AGENT (blocked)
were unable to
obtain
wives of the existing
population obtain hospital
beds in childbirth]
hospital beds   in childbirth]

[the immigrants
AGENT
caused
wives of the existing
population obtain hospital
beds in childbirth]

(they)
found
their children unable to obtain
school places

[their children
AGENT (blocked)
were unable to
obtain
school places]

[the immigrants
AGENT
caused
(children of existing
population be unable to
obtain school places)]

making truth claims about particular configurations of categories and events. Which participant entities (here they are human groups) are postulated in Powell's social ontology? And what sort of relations are taken to exist among them? The participants considered here are actors referred to as 'immigrants' and 'strangers' and the domestic population, the latter being designated by various referring expressions. The part of Powell's speech we are looking at in Table 7.2 is the following:

> But while, to the immigrant entry to this country was admission to privileges and opportunities eagerly sought, the impact upon the existing population was very different. For reasons which they could not comprehend, and in pursuance of a decision by default, on which they were never consulted, they found themselves made strangers in their own country. They found their wives unable to obtain hospital beds in childbirth, their children unable to obtain school places, their homes and neighbourhoods changed beyond recognition, their plans and prospects for the future defeated; at work they found that employers hesitated to apply to the immigrant worker the standards of discipline and competence required of the native-born worker; they began to hear, as time went by, more and more voices which told them that they were now the unwanted.

One of the striking characteristics of the text becomes plain – that actions, effects and recipients are not always expressed overtly, but are bundled up inside noun phrases (NPs). In some cases the predicate is clear, while the arguments may be very much a matter of guesswork – guesswork that hearers nonetheless engage in, while the speaker's expression remains inexplicit. In other cases, whole events or actions may be bundled up into single NPs, so that events themselves may be treated as agents that cause effects. There may be a large number of such 'hidden' – but implied and inferred – propositions. Not all of them are indicated in Table 7.2. But what is important is the universe of actors, actions, receivers of actions, places, etc., in which some of the implied meanings are very deeply 'embedded'. That is to say, if hearers do indeed make mental representations that involve such meanings, then it is on the basis of minimal cues, which, incidentally, the speaker could disavow on the grounds that 'he never *actually said* that'. For example, the analysis includes as a possible implied proposition: 'immigrants prevent wives of existing population obtain hospital beds' and 'wives of existing population want hospital beds'. It seems likely that some such representation is involved in the process of making sense of, or seeing the 'point' of, what the speaker is saying, although those exact words are not uttered.

There is also the non-specified Agent of passive constructions that is glossed in italics in Table 7.2 as *someone*. An intended referent can only be inferred, by the hearer, by way of contextual knowledge and background knowledge about contemporary politics. Consider, for instance, the sequence of passive constructions, which does the job of making 'they' the grammatical 'topic' of the sentence and the text, and at the same time making them the Patient of an unspecified Agent's action:

they were never consulted
someone never consulted them,

themselves made strangers
someone made them strangers

their homes and neighbourhoods changed
someone changed their homes and neighbourhoods

their plans and prospects defeated
someone defeated their plans and prospects

standards and competence and discipline required of the native-born worker
someone required standards of discipline and competence of the native-born worker

they were the unwanted
someone did not want them.

Who it was who failed to consult the ordinary member of the 'existing population', or made them strangers in their own land, did not want them, and so forth, is left to the hearer's imagination – that is to say, his or her ability to make an appropriate inference on the basis of whatever background knowledge they have of the political world. It is plausible to suppose that they would come to the conclusion that the agents of change, of neglect, etc., are either the politicians criticised by Powell or the immigrants themselves.

Table 7.2 shows the recurrent appearance of particular referents as an argument in the propositions encoded into Powell's sentences: *they* or *them*, standing for *the existing population*, i.e., the majority white population of Britain, and *the immigrant*. What we are interested in here is what 'role' they play in the world that Powell's speech is evoking, and this can be gleaned from the semantic role in the linguistic expressions. In fact, whether the lexical exponents of 'existing population' are grammatical subjects or grammatical objects, or only indirectly implied as an argument, their semantic roles is predominantly that of a proto-Patient (see Chapter 4) – that is, they are on the receiving end of actions, perceptions and feelings. For example, they passively 'find' that things have happened to them. In contrast immigrants 'seek' an objective – i.e., are active agents of searching. The 'existing population' appears in potentially agentive

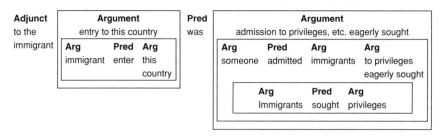

Figure 7.1 Presupposed propositions

semantic roles but the associated agentive predicate is negated: conceptually speaking, agency is blocked. There is, as we have seen, an indirect implication that it is immigrants who are doing the blocking, or 'prevent' them realising certain goals.

Even within NPs, the same participant structures are found. It is worth looking more closely as an example at a portion of the sentence analysed in the first line of Table 7.2:

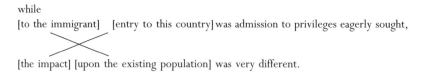

One obvious feature is Powell's classical chiasmus – the criss-cross parallelism between prepositional phrases and noun phrases in the two parts of the sentence, as shown above. More important, the words *entry*, *admission* and *impact* are grammatically nouns, but conceptually they rest on quite complex action schemas and spatial schemas. Propositional structures are nested by presupposition inside argument structures (Figure 7.1).

Most deeply embedded, and most difficult to isolate and challenge online, is the presupposition, 'immigrants sought privileges', which is a truth assertion. Semantically, the predicates access the conceptual schemas of movement and contained spaces – entering and letting in. So we have adversative surface syntax, double nesting of propositions and semantic symmetry too! The concentration of effects may iconically represent the antagonism that is being conceptualised, largely through the basic inside-outside structure of the cognitive schema container (see the discussion of metaphor and schemas in Chapter 4).

'D'ya remember that Enoch Powell?'

It has been proposed that xenophobic discourse by elite speakers enters a network of communicative interchanges, involving the media and chains of face-to-face interaction that spread into the everyday talk of non-elite networks in a community (van Dijk 1993b; Reisigl and Wodak 2001; Wodak 2002). The precise mechanisms whereby such communication of concepts takes place is not known in detail. Although sociolinguists have been aware for a long time of the importance of social networks in language change (Millroy 1987), and although such networks are clearly significant for the spread of ideas and values as well as phonological and morpho-syntactic changes, the task of investigating the network of communication leading to the spread of concepts and norms on a national scale (the nation being the relevant political speech community for the issue at hand) would be enormous. The media would interlock with the networks of school, neighbourhood and subcultures of numerous kinds. We have to cut that particular story short. On a microscopic scale the sections below examine xenophobic talk among young British white males, unemployed and probably involved in crime. What is the connection between an elaborate speech by a prominent politician given to his constituents nearly thirty years previously and a sordid conversation among three disaffected young men in a London bedsit?

The context and the text

On 22 April 1993, a gang of white men murdered a young black man at a bus stop in London. Police investigations were prolonged, and allegedly hampered by racist attitudes. Three of the prime suspects were put on trial in 1996 in a private prosecution, which failed for lack of evidence. All three were acquitted, which means under English law that they can never be tried again. There were allegations of 'structural racism' in the police force, but the point here is to examine the language use of the young males suspected of the murder.

The following transcript was produced at the Stephen Lawrence Inquiry in 1997.[8] Its source was a police surveillance video that had been installed in the house of the suspects, here labelled A, B and C. The extract from their conversation reproduced below was recorded on 3 December 1994.[9]

1   C No—
    B Win and all that I think it was Cameroon, a fucking nigger country
    A Who was saying that
    B Fucking our presenter English presenter saying Oh yeah we want
5   Cameroon to win this, why the fuck should he want niggers to win it
       when they're playing something fucking like Italy or something like a
       European fucking team—
    A It makes you sick dunnit
    B Gets on ya nerves—
10 A You rubber lipped cunt [laughs]

[*A picks up knife from window ledge, sticks knife into arm of chair.*]

A   I reckon every nigger should be chopped up mate and they should be
     left with (nothing but) fucking stumps

B   D'ya remember that Enoch Powell—that geezer he knew straight
15   away he went over to Africa and all that right—

A   Is that what happened

B   Yeah he, he knew it was a slum, he knew it was a shit hole and he
     came back here saying they're uncivilised and all that and then they
     started coming over here and he knew, he knew straight away he was
20   saying no I don't want them here no fucking niggers they'll ruin the
     gaff and he was right they fucking have ruined it

A   Is he still alive

B   I seen him on a programme the other day—

A   What was he saying

25 B   He wasn't saying nothing about niggers and all that he was just saying
     about—something else

A   I wanna write him a letter Enoch Powell mate you are the greatest, you
     are the don of dons get back into parliament mate and show these cock
     suckers
30   what it's all about, all these flash arrogant, big mouthed, shouting their
     mouths off, flash dirty rapists, grass cunts

B   Yeah fucking rapists and everything

A   supergrass thing mate only took off since niggers come into the
     country it's niggers that's all it is

35 B   --

A   fucking corey suckers they are

A   black corey sucking cunts

The contrast with the Powell speech needs no comment. But there are
specific differences that are linguistically relevant. First, while Powell's speech
was a monologue directed at a relatively diverse group of listeners, the men's
conversation is a cooperative, turn-taking conversation. Second, this fact alone
means that the salient strategic functions will be different. Powell could be
expected to be intending to persuade at least some of his hearers and overhearers
to adopt a particular representation of reality and particular value judgements
concerning that representation. The conversation of the six young men, on
the other hand, is apparently produced by a self-supporting group of like-
minded individuals, and one might not expect there to be a need for either
coercive persuasion or for legitimisation. As we shall see, however, if the text is
examined by filtering it through the methodological grid provided by the notions
of legitimisation, coercion and representation, it is possible to obtain some
insights into this type of discourse.[10]

Self-legitimisation in the group

Enoch Powell, as we have seen, presumes certain moral axioms, which include rationality, protection of the weak and the rights of the in-group (British subjects). Turning to the world of A, B and C, does it make sense to speak of self-legitimising presumptions resting on moral axioms? They would doubtless find it laughable to be talked about in these terms, but let us proceed to look more closely at the way this sample unfolds.

First of all, it is possible that the group interaction here has precisely the function of legitimising the members in terms of the values and identity of that group. That is to say, in this group, the speaker is 'right' to say what he says because it produces group cohesion, because it simultaneously produces and corroborates the group's defining values and representations.

B kicks off a conversational sequence (1–13) by reporting to the group what a commentator has said on a TV showing of a recent football match (2). The report requires a response, which A supplies (3) in the form of a question, initiating a question–answer pair. It appears, however, despite A's straightforward interrogative syntax, that this is not simply a request for information. B (at 4–7) certainly provides the information ('our presenter') but also treats A's question as a request for more detail. What B then does is extend the reportage in the form of direct speech ('we want Cameroon to win this') overlaid with commentary. This comes with various details whose function seems to be to steer, in effect to modalise the value interpretation of the reported statement. First, there is the irony marker 'oh yeah'.[11] Second there is a 'rhetorical question' of a type that presumes the answer 'no'. The workings of this type of utterance can be explained in terms of the co-operative principle. The question is relevant because the interlocutors' presumptions lead to the answer 'no'. The interlocutors are in fact, as will become even clearer, cooperating hard to achieve a kind of group consensus and solidarity. Third, there is the use of the intensifier 'fucking'. The frequent use of this word is indexical – in general in British English at the relevant period it indexes membership of a specific male culture. But it simultaneously has a semantic contrasting function – for example, 'fucking our' foregrounds in-group identity, as does 'fucking like Italy' and 'European fucking team'. (The term is thus not exclusively pejorative.)

B's response to the question first-pair part thus provides information but can also be interpreted as a form self-display, which can be further understood as seeking common ground (or oriented to his positive face wants). There is perhaps insufficient detail in the transcript to be sure of what is going on in the next turn, but it appears that A gives a confirmatory response to the approval-seeking display that has just been offered: 'It makes you sick dunnit', where the tag does two jobs. On the one hand, it constitutes an acceptance of B's display, and on the other it appears as a first part in a new adjacency pair. Thus B responds with a semantically more or less synonymous response: 'Gets on ya nerves'.

What happens next (10–13) can be seen as the product of this mutual verbal stimulation. A enacts a stabbing, with a direct address form ('you') oriented to an imaginary black victim. The obscene description categorises the imagined victim as black, and simultaneously indexes A as a member of a male racist sub-culture. The commentary (13) is directed to B (addressed as 'mate') and the group, presumably. I am suggesting that the extreme violence of the action and the accompanying language are in part generated by the internal dynamics of the group and its needs. However, this is far from being the only aspect of the self-legitimising process.

Self-legitimisation: constructing an authority figure

Assuming that there is no break after line 13, B makes a shift in the conversational topic, albeit one that satisfies the principle of relevance by being embedded in a background knowledge frame – namely, the opinions of Enoch Powell concerning black people, the topic of the previous stretch of talk. Possibly this turn occurs at this point in the conversational flow precisely because of A's violent role-play: it is a way of legitimising the scenario that their preceding talk has concocted. That is to say, there is a group need to justify A's stabbing and mutilation of an imaginary black person (13–14). Hence the interlocutors construct a narrative sequence (14–21) initiated by the conventional opening 'd'ya remember . . .'. The sequence is sustained by A's questions. Throughout the extract A appears to adopt a questioner role, which is possibly that of a *faux naïf* stimulating the other interlocutors to make explicit their representations, values and group identity.

One might wonder whether this kind of discourse, produced by these kinds of actors, would put much effort into justifying, legitimising or providing evidence. In fact the text shows that a considerable amount of their verbalisation seems to have the function of legitimising their assertions. The character of this self-legitimising is rather specific, and heavily dependent on invoking a presumed figure of authority.

Whereas Powell seeks authority by telling stories about the 'ordinary' man and woman, the youths in the extract use Enoch Powell himself as legitimisation of their violent imaginings. It is not simply that the name of Powell is associated for this group with elite authority. It is of course likely that their knowledge of Powell and his politics is vague in the extreme. But the linguistic details of the recounting also seem to be seeking to establish the rightness of Powell's validity claims, at least as the youths report those claims to one another. The most telling detail is the repetition of 'he knew'. As we shall see, Powell has an agentive role of 'cogniser'. Objective knowledge on the part of Powell is also implicitly claimed (via various cultural frames concerned with direct experience, such as 'seeing with one's own eyes' and the like) by reporting that 'he went over to Africa and all that'.[12] The remainder of the dialogue in the extract up to line 30 can also be seen as functioning as part of this self-constructing legitimisation. Speaker A initiates two further adjacency pairs (22 and 24). What is the point of these particular exchanges? Given the preceding exchanges, it is possible to regard 22–3 as a means of further legitimisation. The speakers appear to be seeking to establish the reality of the Powell authority figure, his TV appearance being probably taken as legitimising *ipso facto*. The second question-answer pair (24–5) is interesting because it again shows A's interest (as at 3), in who is making what sort of utterances. Without further data, it is not clear what function this particular exchange has, though it is likely that A is being interpreted by his interlocutors as stimulating explicit racist utterances. This makes B's response (25–6) puzzling out of context. The most likely under-standing is that he simply is unable to give what A is seeking. The consequence seems to be that A takes this to conclude the narration sequence (what Powell said on TV) and to require some form of coda. Interestingly, this takes the form of another use of 'you' by A, this time not pointing to black people (as at 10), but to their supposed opponent, Powell himself. Speaker A engages indeed in another piece of play-acting with an imaginary other. Having already enacted the mutilation of black people, he now enacts a 'letter' to Enoch Powell. The eulogistic meanings of the one counterbalance the destructive meanings of the other: 'you are the greatest you are the don of dons'. The extremity of the violence is counterbalanced by the hyperbolic legitimisation.

Hitherto, A has done little but stimulate explicitation by means of interrogatives. In this turn he is now engaging in his own species of verbal virtuosity. He produces (30) a lengthy noun-phrase description that appears to pick out politicians who do not chime with the group's xenophobia. As we have seen throughout, there is a kind of antiphonal pattern (verse and response, so to speak), and someone is required to corroborate verbally A's display – a role somewhat limply taken on by B (32), whose performing of this turn seems to enable A's new verbal display (33–7) directed at black people in general.

Representation: victims, aggressors and being right

It is worth noting that the abuse directed at opponents and used to categorise them descriptively does itself presume some sort of value system, a system that involves a negative pole linked to violence and forms of sexual behaviour ('rapists'), and perhaps aligned with a polarity based on the conceptual oppositions such as *taboo-non-taboo*, *dirty-clean* and *purity-danger*. Such polarities enter into the formation of social categories, as argued by Douglas (1970). Legitimising oneself or one's group requires representing the world in such a way that one's own 'position' in it, that is, one's rightness in relation to others, is consistent with such a representation or follows from it. Thus, if dirt and cleanliness provide a cognitive schema and contribute to the construction of an ordered universe, such a schema can be viewed both as functioning as representation and legitimisation. An underlying schema for sexuality will provide the same resource. In our sample of dialogue, political opponents and black people appear to be represented as sexually threatening, partly because they are represented as engaging in sexual practices that the group presumably regards as tabooed. A stereotype according to which black people are sexually threatening to white people also seems to be in play and may explain the nature of the lexical choices. We shall not pursue the lexical semantics here, however. Instead we will apply the same technique as we did for Powell's speech (Table 7.2), which enables us to make some comparisons with respect to 'who does what to whom' in the world of these interlocutors.[13]

Compared with the Powell text, propositions are relatively explicit. The speakers do not wrap up their assertions inside NPs, nor do they leave them to be inferred. Table 7.3 helps us to see clearly which kinds of argument fill which kinds of role in this (admittedly restricted) extract. Consider first the Agents – those role-players that perform some intentional material action, as specified by the semantics of their predicate. We find words referring (directly or associatively) to black people in Proto-Agent role: *Cameroon*, *niggers*, *they*. Which kinds of arguments fill the Patient role of such predicates? In the first occurrence ('Cameroon win this') of such a verb, the Patient is 'this', standing for 'this football game', and has very little to tell us. The second one ('they're playing, etc.') has a referent categorised 'European' as its Patient role-player, but the verb *play* does not justify any generalisations. However, the next three tell their own story:

> they started coming over here
> they'll ruin the gaff [place]
> they have ruined it

These propositions are conceptually in line with what we have seen for the Enoch Powell speech, and perhaps not surprisingly they are linked with Powell himself in the youths' conversation. There is a striking progression in the way the propositions are grounded. Initially they are presented under Powell's verb of 'saying' and are prima facie therefore not endorsed by the speaker. But the endorsement, the assimilation of someone else's reality into the reality of the speaker, is accomplished in 'he was right they have ruined it' and made quite explicit. The speaker is tagging the source of his meta-representation, and that source has already been carefully set up as a source of legitimising authority. In two of the propositions that we have isolated, although the Agents (in both cases the word 'it') are not identified with black people, they do refer to previous

Table 7.3 Propositional structure in a portion of xenophobic talk (Lawrence Inquiry transcript)

Argument 1	Predicate	Argument 2	Other arguments	Adjunct/conjunct
	win and all that			
I	think	it was Cameroon, a fucking nigger country		
[Cameroon AGENT	won]			
[Cameroon	is	a fucking nigger country]		
who	was saying	that?		
fucking our presenter English presenter	saying	saying Oh yeah we want Cameroon to win this,		oh yeah
[we	want	Cameroon to win this]		
[Cameroon AGENT	win	this]		
				why the fuck
[he]	should [he] want	niggers to win it		when, etc.
[niggers AGENT	win	it]		
they (Cameroon) AGENT	're playing	something fucking like Italy or something like a European fucking team		
It AGENT	makes	you PATIENT	sick	dunnit

Table 7.3 (continued)

Argument 1	Predicate	Argument 2	Other arguments	Adjunct/conjunct
[it] AGENT	gets	on ya nerves PATIENT		
I COGNISER	reckon	reckon every nigger should be chopped up		mate and
they (niggers)	should be left	with nothing but fucking stumps		
[someone] AGENT	**should leave** PATIENT	**niggers**	**with nothing but stumps]**	
[ya]	d'[ya] remember	that Enoch Powell		
that geezer, he (Powell) COGNISER	knew			straight away
he AGENT	went	over to Africa and all that GOAL		right
[that]	is . . .	what happened		
[something	**happened]**			
he (Powell) COGNISER	knew	it was a slum		
[Africa	**is**	**a slum]**		
He (Powell) COGNISER	knew	it was a shit hole		
[Africa	**is**	**a shit hole]**		and

He **AGENT**	came	back here **GOAL**	and then
[he]	saying	they're uncivilised and all that	
[?Africans] **AGENT**	are	uncivilised]	
they (Africans) **AGENT**	started coming	over here **GOAL**	and
he (Powell) **COGNISER**	knew		
He **COGNISER**	knew	straight away	
he	was saying	I don't want them here no fucking niggers	
[I (Powell)]	don't want	them . . . no fucking niggers **here]**	
they (niggers) **AGENT**	'll ruin	the gaff **PATIENT**	and
he (Powell)	was	right	
they (niggers) **AGENT**	fucking have ruined	it (the gaff) **PATIENT**	

propositions in which black people are projected as being unjustifiably favoured, and the Patients are the present interlocutors themselves, represented via the verb's semantics as being caused to be physically afflicted: 'make sick', 'get on the nerves of'. In passing, it is also worth noting the clear-cut spatial deixis in the conceptualisation that the discourse constructs, through the use of *here*, *back here*, *go—come*.

So far the world looks like the one that Powell projects – whites are victimised by blacks. But there is a serious difference. In two focal propositions black people are vividly projected as the recipients of violent material actions, namely, 'chop up' and 'leave with nothing but stumps'. The passive construction allows the speaker to make no overt reference to an agent – although, as we have seen, the speaker accompanies the words with a gesture that does identify both imaginary actor and imaginary victim. Here it is worth adding that the verbs are modified by a deontic modal 'should'. Among other means of legitimisation this speaker uses a meaning that conventionally invokes moral rightness. This may tell us something about verbal references to material violence: in social groups such acts have to be legitimised (however abhorrent they are for external observers) in some way, even if only minimally by means of the use of a deontic modal.

Conceivably, the more potentially abhorrent the referent action can be seen to be, in relation to some standard known to the group addressed, the more verbal legitimisation has to be applied. At least, such appears to be the case for the episode we are scrutinising, as we have already seen. Analysing the propositional structure in the form of Table 7.3 makes it very clear that the most frequent predicate, for this conversational episode, is not in fact semantically a material action at all, but certain kinds of psychological process. Predominantly these are, perhaps surprisingly on the face of it, epistemic. The repeated verb *know*, as well as the proposition 'he was right' can be treated as evidential modifiers, expressing absolute certainty on the scale of epistemic modality. The word *right* is especially interesting, since it is deontic as well as epistemic. The mental space projected by the 'space builder' *know* (see Chapter 4), Powell's mental space, is transparent, or coincides, given the semantics of the space builder, with the reality of the speaker. Specifically, the discourse of the interlocutors seems oriented towards grounding the assertion that black people have damaged white (by implication) people and have damaged the place they inhabit, and towards establishing the ground by constructing an authority figure. Moreover, the violence against black people represented propositionally in A's talk, lies within a deontic space built by *should*. In this space black people are represented as being justifiably mutilated. It is possible that this projected space is further legitimised by the carefully invoked authority figure, but Powell's discourse does not project violence in this fashion. At this point one leaves the domain of description. It is the critical interpreter's responsibility to evaluate discourse of the kind we have been investigating and relevance of Powell's public oration and its mediation.

Part III

The global arena

8   Distant places

Thus far we have concentrated on political discourse within the domestic arena, taking the UK as our example. We have also looked at how the 'foreign' world beyond the border might look to insiders, whether elites or not. We now turn to the world in which sovereign states interact with one another. This global arena involves types of interaction that are ever increasing in kind and complexity, to the point where state sovereignty, in the view of some thinkers, is diminishing (e.g., Camilleri and Falk 1992; Walker 1988). The increased flow of information, of people, money and goods – all of these dimensions are reflected in, or are constituted by, enormous changes in language and discourse. It is impossible to deal with all dimensions, so Part III of the book looks at the most salient aspect of globalisation in the late twentieth- and early twenty-first century – the spread of wars, terrorism and military interventions. In this domain, too, one has to be selective. We therefore concentrate on the world's post-cold-war superpower, the United States of America in its relations with the rest of the world.

In this chapter and in the two that follow our approach to international political discourse in this new context will focus on the nature of conceptual representations, and in particular the conceptualising of geopolitical space. In addition, we shall find that the language of self-legitimisation stands out – a not surprising fact, since the new environment at the turn of the twenty-first century called for new actions that had to be explained to multiple audiences. Most difficult to pin down, and perhaps most important, are the changing presumptions and establishing of new contexts.[1]

Space, time and modality

Within American political culture, European entanglements always cause alarm bells to ring. On 24 March 1999 the American president gave a long and complex address to the nation, intended to justify American involvement in a military action in a far-away place, among a far-away people, of whom the American electorate knew little. In investigating this speech, we shall make use of the idea that space, geography and territory somehow enter deeply into the use of language in general and into the political use of language in particular. As we saw in Chapter 4, we can think of discourse – language in use – as a process in which readers/hearers set up discourse worlds ('conceptual domains' or 'ontological spaces'), which carry a deictic 'signature' for space, time and modality, and relationships among them. Discourse consists of a set of coherent propositions, with their interrelated arguments and predicates, distributed across these spaces. Even apparently simple discourse involves 'movement' between spaces: these can be thought of as functions characterised as 'belief', 'hypothetical', 'dream', also epistemic functions like cause and consequence, and deontic ones like reason and purpose. As we have seen in earlier chapters, many propositions are not overtly verbalised but communicated by, for instance, presupposition, implicature or presumptions. Different discourse types have different kinds of predications, spaces and relations between spaces.

What kind of propositions, spaces and interspace relations make up the kind of text type that we recognise as *justification* (or legitimisation, as we have called it previously) in particular? More specifically, what is the discourse make-up of the justification of war? Even more specifically, of course, we are considering how the president of the United States justified military intervention in a particular set of historical circumstances, though we are assuming that features of the discourse will be representative of a class or type of such texts.

An American president's coordinates

The first two sentences of President Clinton's text set up some of the main elements of the speech. A 'president's address to the nation' depends on a set of expectations about the way language will be used, whatever the topics raised, but we shall focus here on that aspect of this particular address that has to do with the representation of the world beyond the familiar domestic world of the American audience:

   (1) My fellow Americans, today our Armed Forces joined our NATO allies in air strikes against Serbian forces responsible for the brutality in Kosovo.
   (2) We have acted with resolve for several reasons.

Sentences (1) and (2) establish the entities in the discourse reality, the relations between them and their relation to the point of utterance. The linguistic expressions that index these entities are:

I (*my*), Americans, armed forces, NATO allies, Serbia, Serbian forces, Kosovo.

Presumed knowledge (frames, and scripts) seems to be activated, for example:

warfare scripts, geographical frames, moral frames containing antithetical value orientations (*responsibility*, *brutality*, *resolve*, *reasons*).

Geographical frames are also evoked. These might be poorly specified for some hearers, and providing more detailed content turns out to be an important feature of the speech. Such specification also emerges not simply as objective geographical knowledge, but as deictically organised *geopolitical* knowledge. Sentence (2) seems to induce a conflation of the *I* concept and *our armed forces* concept into a *we* concept. Discourse expectations, based on frame knowledge of text types, and social knowledge of the process of justification in general, induce the expectation that 'reasons' will be stated in the succeeding portions of discourse.

There is a further important aspect, one that is closely tied to the 'geo' frames mentioned above, namely the deictic structuring of the opening utterances in terms of the three-dimensional discourse space discussed in Chapter 4. The opening words, 'My fellow Americans', simply establish an extra-textual relationship between speaker and hearers such that the hearers are postulated as present in the same (political) space and as proximate to the speaker. The space builders here that might prompt a hearer in this direction are: 'my', 'fellow' and 'Americans'. Not all the lexical selections are imposed by the linguistic system: 'my' at least could be absent. The deictic centre is constructed as a relation between speaker and hearers inside a political entity, and personal proximity seems to be a possible inference. Establishing spatial conceptions of this type is, as we shall see, important in the text as a whole.

If we analyse the clauses, verbal nouns ('strikes'), presupposition ('the') of sentence (1) alone, the propositions listed below appear to be prompted. Each one is deictically coordinated with respect to the deictic centre. Inside the brackets are arguments, and the predicate is outside. On the right are the expressions that trigger the building of separate mental spaces (or 'discourse worlds'), as well as an indication of the cognitive frames that seem to be drawn into play, and which correspond to what we have earlier called 'presumptions', i.e., structured knowledge of institutions, values and the like that the speaker takes for granted.

(a) joined (our armed forces, our NATO allies) *space builders*: our, our, today, -ed *cognitive frames*: America, armed forces, alliances

(b) air strikes (our armed forces and NATO, Serbian forces)

space builders: zero anaphors (the grammatical subject of 'joined' is also the Agent in 'air strikes')

cognitive frames: warfare

(c) responsible (Serbian forces, brutality in Kosovo)

space builders: preposition *in*,

cognitive frames: geographical and political knowledge

(d) exists (brutality in Kosovo)

space builders: the, in

cognitive frames: geographical knowledge, moral categories.

Figure 8.1 represents the deictically specified reality spaces that are dependent upon the deictically specified reality space of the speaker (S), in sentence (1). The ellipses in the diagram impressionistically represent mental spaces triggered by space builders (typically prepositional expressions, adverbials or predicates, as suggested above), and are marked *a*, *b*, *c* and *d*, corresponding to the propositions listed above. Within the spaces are entities called up by referring expressions and their anaphors. The 'locations' with respect to the three dimensions are assumed to be largely determined by knowledge and value frames. For example, in the frame assumed by the speaker in this case, 'my fellow Americans', are closest to S, 'NATO allies' are closer than 'Kosovo' and 'Kosovo' is closer than 'Serbian armed forces'. The positions indicated on the axes are scalar and relative and not meant to be quantifiable. It is important to note that italicised *Kosovo* is not supposed to denote some real-world geographical place, but the concept *Kosovo* in some mutually expected conceptual frame. Entities are located with respect to their three coordinates, and indicated 'X'. Straight arrows represent predicates, impressionistically, as processes in space and/or time. Arrowed arcs represent predicates that set up reality spaces. Links between spaces that exist if hearers make certain kinds of inference (using cooperative coherence principles and frames, for example) are indicated by broken-arrowed arcs, without attempting to indicate the detailed nature of the inference.

In terms of *m*, the value for sentences (1) and (2) seems to be 'proximate' – that is, actions referred to are asserted as true (and right) without modification. In terms of *t*, they are asserted to have taken place within the mutually understood time zone denoted by 'today'. As for *s*, the situation is a little more complex. The propositions contained within the first sentence are syntactically linked (prepositions, zero anaphora), creating conceptual links. The deictic centre is linked by pronominal anaphora. '[T]he brutality in Kosovo' may be interpreted as a separate ongoing space, if the hearers have contextual knowledge. There are two spaces: one in which proximate forces join more distant but still relatively proximate allies and joint attacks against distant entities. The first of these is extended along the *s* dimension – an important feature of the

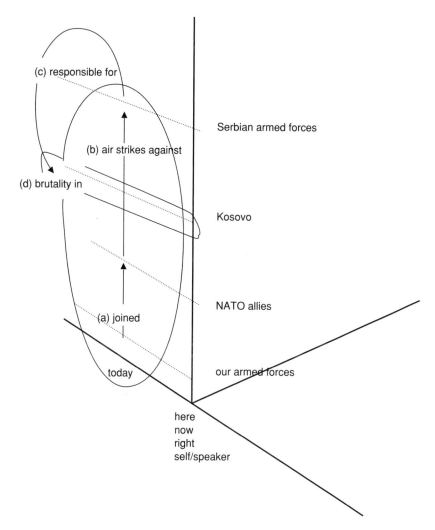

Figure 8.1 Deictically specified reality spaces

entire text, and one of the key features that Clinton has to justify. The second space is a distant geopolitical area. What is the relation between the two spaces? The syntax of the linguistic expressions (mostly an inferred anaphoric chain) links one of the arguments in the first space to a predication in the second space – this link is lexically provided by 'responsible for', which we can understand as a part of the conceptual relation *causation* or *agency*. Attributing causation and/or agency is an important element in justification discourse. But the word *responsible* is interestingly polysemic – the president has 'a responsibility' to 'deal with problems such as this', while the Serbs bear 'responsibility' for, or 'are responsible for', the brutality. So causation (or agency) and moral motivation are semantically related.

Thus in the first two sentences the conceptual structures evoked are precisely those, which, given the context, require justification. Spaces defined in this way – i.e., coordinated deictically – constitute much of what we experience as cohesion and coherence in a text, and particularly in political texts in the international relations context.

Space and time, history and geography

At several points in the text, the speaker appears to put considerable effort into specifying points on the spatial axis, and equally into 'locating' events in a historical time–narrative. A good example occurs in the following (25–35):

(25) Ending this tragedy is a moral imperative.

(26) It is also important to America's national interest.

(27) Take a look at this map.

(28) Kosovo is a small place, but it sits on a major fault line between Europe, Asia and the Middle East, at the meeting place of Islam and both the Western and Orthodox branches of Christianity.

(29) To the south are our allies, Greece and Turkey; to the north, our new democratic allies in Central Europe.

(30) And all around Kosovo there are other small countries, struggling with their own economic and political challenges – countries that could be overwhelmed by a large, new wave of refugees from Kosovo.

(31) All the ingredients for a major war are there: ancient grievances, struggling democracies, and in the center of it all a dictator in Serbia who has done nothing since the Cold War ended but start new wars and pour gasoline on the flames of ethnic and religious division.

(32) Sarajevo, the capital of neighboring Bosnia, is where World War I began.

(33) World War II and the Holocaust engulfed this region.

(34) In both wars Europe was slow to recognize the dangers, and the United States waited even longer to enter the conflicts.

(35) Just imagine if leaders back then had acted wisely and early enough, how many lives could have been saved, how many Americans would not have had to die.

(36) We learned some of the same lessons in Bosnia just a few years ago.

(37) The world did not act early enough to stop that war, either.

(38) And let's not forget what happened – innocent people herded into concentration camps, children gunned down by snipers on their way to school, soccer fields and parks turned into cemeteries; a quarter of

a million people killed, not because of anything they have done, but because of who they were.

(39)   Two million Bosnians became refugees.

(40)   This was genocide in the heart of Europe – not in 1945, but in 1995.

(41)   Not in some grainy newsreel from our parents' and grandparents' time, but in our own time, testing our humanity and our resolve.

The sentences (25–6) seem to have a particular job to do – namely, to situate their assertions on the deontic part of the m scale. Since (by anaphora with the preceding discourse) the assertion refers to entities (US or US and allies and events in Kosovo), the deictic region affected is extended along s; and since S presents the process 'ending this tragedy' without tense markers, the reality space is not extended along t. (See Figure 8.2, where the numbers refer to the sentences.) I have assumed that the entities on s which are involved in the reality spaces are scaled at relative distances from S and his hearers. Again, these relative distances are not meant in this graph to be measurable in miles or kilometres – they are simply an indication of what one might call geopolitical distance.

At the intersection point (the origin) of the three axes, is 'this map' (the president is seen pointing to a visual aid). What is important is that the map itself is not, or does not represent, an objective reality, though it may be taken to do so by viewers. It has scant meaning without the verbal accompaniment. What it does is set up a reality space that is specified by the verbal commentary. Further, it is important to note that hearers must, in order to interpret the text as cooperatively coherent, infer that (27) and the following sentences – the ones about where Kosovo is and what it is like – are intended to motivate either (26), that national interests are at stake, or both (26) and the assertion that action is a moral imperative (25). Sentences (28–30) can be regarded as building a 'map representation' space. This is a conventional pragmatic function, by which cartographic images are taken to represent objective reality spaces (cf. Fauconnier 1985: 3–34). 'This map' in the studio (or 'in' the viewers' living room) represents a conceptual space that is mutually understood as remote ('there' in (31)), but which the map presented 'here' and 'now' brings into conceptual and perceptual closeness. In the process of specifying the map's conceptual projection space, the hearer is prompted, by the modal 'could' in (30'),

(30')   countries that could be overwhelmed by a large new wave of refugees from Kosovo,

to set up a space located at the *possibility* end of m, and perhaps in the *near future* zone of t. This is not part of the televised map picture; it is part of the

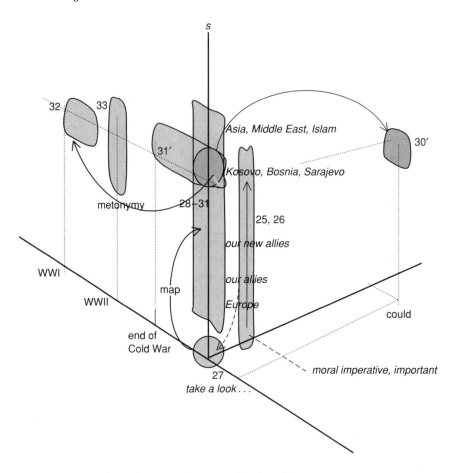

Figure 8.2 Events located on spatial, temporal and modal axes

conceptual 'picture' conjured up by the discourse. This space shift is conceptually crucial for the transition to (31), which is in the form of a generalised likelihood of 'major war' and thus threat to American interests.

There are other complexities in sentence (31), in particular an embedded narration along *t* (31′):

(31′)   . . . who has done nothing since the Cold War ended but start new wars and pour gasoline on the flames of ethnic and religious divisions.

The relevant coordinate on *s* is evoked vaguely by 'there' and 'in the centre of it all' in (31). Though syntactically embedded, (31′) is in a sequentially focal position, both in terms of sentence intonation patterns, and in terms of its discursive role as a concluding move in this sub-unit of the speech. It also involves metaphorical processing, which we discuss below.

In this complex space-time-modality discourse, the historical space is extended, as it were, backwards, metonymically, by way of reference to the spatial location *Sarajevo* (32). Kosovo is linked to Sarajevo ('the capital of neighboring Bosnia'). Sarajevo is linked metonymically to World War I and World War I to World War II and the Holocaust. The links can be said to be metonymic because the relation between Kosovo, the Sarajevo and World War I is one of conceptual 'contiguity' in a historical–knowledge frame. 'Sarajevo' here is used to evoke the whole World War I frame. And the expression 'this region' (33) is used in the same metonymic fashion to evoke the World War II and Holocaust frames. Once in play in the activated context of the discourse, these discursively linked frames are used as the basis for two sets of generalisations: (31) relating to the geographical space conceptualised 'around' Kosovo, and (34–5) relating to the flashback historical space conceptualised in connection with Sarajevo.

These generalisations in turn form the basis of (36) and its elaboration in (37–41). The chain of argumentation is surprisingly long and intricate: Kosovo→ Bosnia→Sarajevo→World War I→World War II→back to Bosnia→analogy between Bosnia (and by inference the other wars mentioned) with Kosovo. How does this work in detail?

Metaphor and remote events

Both (31) and (85) involve metaphor. This is not coincidental. In both cases metaphor seems to be deployed strategically as part of an embedded piece of argumentation about the 'closeness' of the danger and the urgency for America to act militarily. Both metaphors, moreover, use *fire* as their source domain and project this structured knowledge frame onto the target frame *conflict*, yielding a number of metaphorical entailments.

The linguistic cues that seem to require some form of metaphorical interpretation (31) are the emboldened ones below:

(31)   All the **ingredients** for a major war are there: ancient grievances, struggling democracies, and (31′) **in the centre** of it all a dictator in Serbia (31″) who has done nothing since the Cold War ended but start new wars and **pour gasoline on the flames of ethnic and religious division**.

The word 'ingredients' could be regarded as a conventionalised lexical item with associated meaning. Alternatively, it might be from a *cooking* frame, and the sense of the discourse might be generated from a metaphorical inference based on a metaphor *producing an artefact is cooking*, where the underlying concept is some form of causation, or 'causing-to-come-into-existence'.[2] The 'ingredients' are 'struggling democracies', etc., and the unmentioned but entailed 'cook' or causative agent is 'a dictator'. This latter phrase is a definite description that the hearer can identify, by inference, with the referent of 'Milosevic'. This particular way of maintaining the reference probably also enables the hearer, by prompting frame knowledge of political concepts, to advance the argument that the Balkans are dangerous and bad. Anyone processing the text, therefore, may at some level of cognition infer that the dictator is likely to cause a major war. This inference is partly triggered by the preposition 'for'. As Figure 8.3 suggests, the space that this potentially sets up is a space that is represented as some sort of modal possibility and as positioned in the unspecified though not too remote future.

The prepositional phrase 'in the centre of it all' can be considered from two perspectives. On the one hand, it can be treated as a deictic space builder that sets up a geographical location for 'a dictator', where 'it all' has (along with 'there') the locations mentioned in sentences (28–30) as its antecedent. On the other hand, 'in the centre of it all' does, it might be argued, mean a bit more than that. What may be happening to a text interpreter here is that their discourse processing is accessing the *centre-periphery* schema. It has been claimed that this image schema is important for a number of systematic (meta-phorical) concepts that are lexically encoded (Lakoff 1987; Lakoff and Johnson 1980; Johnson 1987). In some contexts the centre-periphery scheme will be mapped onto self and other. However, in this context the centre is related to other's space. To speak of the other's centre is generally to indicate the other's principal causal agency (for example: 'he was at the centre of the conspiracy'). Further, this notion is linked in the discourse to the following composite spatial concept:

> movement outward from a centre of a contained space in a threatening fashion for those (including self) who are outside the space.

It is sometimes the case that a stretch of text, such as a speech, involves recurrent conceptual schemata. The fire metaphor (the knowledge frame includes the knowledge that fires spread out from a centre) is also coherent with that kind of spatial schema. The metaphorical mapping from fire as source domain to violence and conflict as target domain is of course to some degree conventional-ised. The point, however, is that metaphors are conceptually dynamic: if a mapping from fire to conflict is introduced into working memory, then what is entailed in one's knowledge about the nature and behaviour of fire also seems to be entailed in the target domain, in this case conflict. Thus if fire can be

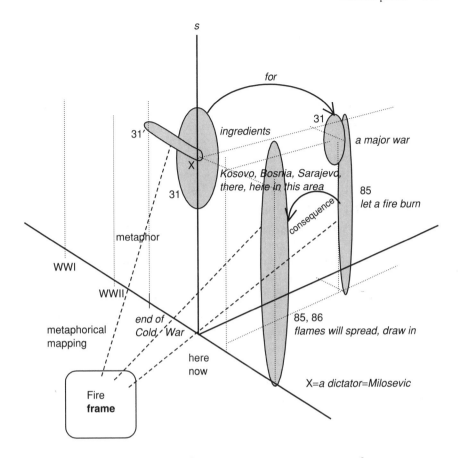

Figure 8.3 Metaphor supporting inferences concerning events remote from centre

increased by someone actively adding fuel, so *mutatis mutandis* can conflict; if fire is liable to spread, so is conflict; and so forth. The receiver of the text is obliged to make inferences when confronted with 'gasoline' and 'flames', and thus to access the concept of fire and the frame associated with it, a cognitive discourse process that presumably also makes the further entailments inferentially available.

In sentences (78–86) Clinton returns to the visual map image:

(78)   We must also remember that this is a conflict with no natural national boundaries.

(79)   Let me ask you to look again at a map.

(80)   The red dots are towns the Serbs have attacked.

(81)   The arrows show the movement of refugees – north, east and south.

(82)   Already, this movement is threatening the young democracy in Macedonia, which has its own Albanian minority and a Turkish minority.

(83)   Already, Serbian forces have made forays into Albania from which Kosovars have drawn support.

(84)   Albania is a Greek minority.

(85)   Let **a fire burn** here in this area and **the flames will spread**.

(86)   Eventually, key U.S. allies could be **drawn into** a wider conflict, a war we would be forced to confront later – only at far greater risk and greater cost.

The purpose is evidently this time not simply to locate Kosovo geographically, historically, ethnically, ideologically and in other ways, as it was the first time but to demonstrate the likelihood of events in the Balkans having an impact on American interests. Sentence (78) introduces the assertion to be 'proved', along with a concept of 'natural' national boundaries. Sentences (79–84), combined with visual images, rest on two basic image schemata: *container* and *path*. The mental picture projected appears to be one of a contiguous boundary containing spaces with penetrations ('attacks' on 'red dots', 'forays into'), evacuations and extractions ('arrows', 'movement of refugees', 'draw from').

Thus far the map and its accompanying verbal conceptualisation serve presumably as a demonstration that there are no 'natural national boundaries'. The cognitive frame for the nation state is presumed, and further inference from frame-based knowledge seems to be required to make sense of why refugee movement should 'threaten [. . .] young democracies' (83). But the claim that all these represented actors and activity impact on the country's interests is not made until (86). The precise political, international relations and military events that could lead to America being involved in a war on the scale of the First or Second World Wars are not spelled out. The argument is instead made by way of metaphor. Metaphorical transposition facilitates reasoning, including the making of predictions. In this instance, it is easier to project one's thinking schematically into a familiar think-space (that of fire and its effects), and then map the results back into the domain one started from (Kosovo and the Balkans):

the conflict is a fire
fires are intensified by gasoline
fires spread
fires draw combustible material into them
fires damage or destroy the things they burn

thus:

fire could spread to America?
America could be forced to enter the conflict
America would be damaged.

Figure 8.3 shows some of the coordinate shifts, and some of the inferencing involved in (31) and (85). The referents in (31) have coordinates in a recent past on t and at somewhat remote points on s, but they are represented as truth claims by the speaker, hence at the positive end of m. However, linguistic elements in (31) imply, albeit inferentially, a causal relation between events as described above and a hypothetical 'major war' in the unspecified (but presumably not too far distant) future. There is a sort of mirror-image structure in (85), where the phrase 'here this area' locates the ontological space in play at the same point as in (31). The non-finite 'let' establishes the antecedent part of a conditional sentence (i.e., 'if you let . . .'), whose consequent is in the future tense ('the flames **will** spread'). Conditional sentences are closely linked to causal meanings: if such-and-such a condition is met, then such-and-such will inevitably follow, and behind this is a *post hoc ergo propter hoc* reasoning schema. The link, however, is inferable rather than explicitly coded. In (86) 'eventually' indexes a more remote t in the conditional m space.

The workings of historical analogy

Above we have taken it that metaphor functions access conceptual source domains that are not deictically coordinated: they are, as it were, outside space and time. But are there no source domains that *are* fixed in relation to points in space and time? We could define *analogy* as a relation between spaces that *do* have deictic coordinates. The inferential processes with which analogy is associated are similar to those of metaphor.[3]

Following the *ingredients*, *centre*, *gasoline* and *flames* metaphors of (31), there is a lengthy portion of text (sentences (32–47)) that shifts the focus of argument from geographical space-based reasoning to time-based reasoning. In parallel, not metaphors but rather analogies are employed. One of the striking features is the effort that goes into bringing the Balkans 'closer to home' in historical terms, just as (8) to (10) do in geographical terms.

Here, however, we shall just zoom in on sentences (32–5), already considered above, which establish a complex set of ontological spaces and interrelations:

(32)   Sarajevo, the capital of neighboring Bosnia, is where World War I began.
(33)   World War II and the Holocaust engulfed this region.
(34)   In both wars Europe was slow to recognize the dangers, and the United States waited even longer to enter the conflicts.

(35)   Just imagine (35′) if leaders back then had acted wisely and early enough, (35″) how many lives could have been saved, how many Americans would not have had to die.

In this part of the text, the conceptualisations generated by sentences (28) to (30) are already in play (integrated in the conceptual 'common ground' built up by the communicative cooperation of speaker and hearer, one assumes). The speaker uses his visual aid, the map, to move metonymically from the geographical location *Sarajevo* to the historical frame of the First World War and thence to the Second World War. The analogy is a separate cognitive operation. It is not pointed out in so many words, but left to inference. Sentences (34) and (35) draw more explicit inferences, but the processing is still complex.

Figure 8.4 shows the structure along *t* for the metonymic relations and the potential analogy inference; the position on *s* is assumed to be relatively remote from the United States and Europe. In Figure 8.4 sentence (34) is omitted for clarity, but note that both of the conjoined sentences in (34) involve (a) movement from the self's home space to the other's alien space and (b) a counterfactual space at the very remote end of *m* in which Europe did not (at first) recognise the dangers and the United States did not at first enter the conflict. There are the further available inferences: Europe waited too long (the 'too' indicates a type of deontic meaning); the United States waited longer than Europe and this was therefore also too long.

Let us consider now the conceptually very dense (35), which starts by setting up a hypothetical space by means of the imperative: 'Just imagine'. Within this space is a counterfactual conditional sentence. Roughly, the antecedent of the sentence (the *if* part) is: 'if leaders act wisely and early enough'. There are two consequents: 'lives can be saved' and 'many Americans do not have to die'. There is an epistemic modal element in the first of the consequents ('can', though this could also have the dynamic sense, 'have ability to'), and a deontic element in the second ('had to'). Figure 8.4 does not attempt to incorporate these complex modal dimensions within the hypothetical space.

Perhaps even more important is the potential for inferencing. The following inferences are made available by the syntax of the conditional sentence: leaders back then did not act wisely; lives were not saved; many Americans had to die. Furthermore, the understanding of the conditional relation in natural-language processing (as distinct from formal logic) is well known to involve a concept of cause. So the following inferences are also potentially available: *the leaders' not acting wisely back then* caused *lives not to be saved*; *the leaders' not acting wisely back then* caused *many Americans to have to die*.

I will leave the reader to pursue these complex representations further. Suffice it to note that (36) initiates a new sub-unit of the text, explicitly generating another analogy between the two world wars and the conflict in Bosnia:

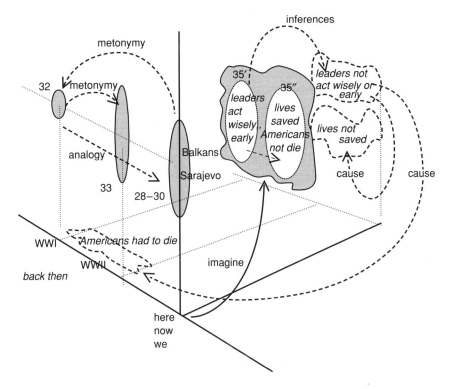

Figure 8.4 Metonymic relations and analogy inference

'we learned some of the same lessons'. A further and final analogy is then generated in (47) between the world wars, Bosnia and the present crisis in Kosovo: 'we must apply that lesson in Kosovo'. Having invoked historical and geographical analogies that are relatively remote for many of his hearers, one might assume, the speaker is obliged to redress this spatial and temporal remoteness in (40) and (41), which insist on the geographical centrality (at least to Europe) of the conflict, and at somewhat greater length on the temporal presentness of the events.

There are several complementary tendencies in the manipulation of the ontological spaces that we have started to analyse. The first is the mobilisation of conceptual schemas to represent remote effects as close or as probable encroachments on the space of the self. The second is the linking of historical episodes and the drawing of conclusions by analogy. Third, there is the linking of temporally remote spaces with the space of the present speaker and hearers. Fourth, there is the making available of the inference that inaction causes undesirable effects.

Justifying war

Although what the President is doing in this speech, in the sense that we have defined it in Chapter 3, involves a legitimising function, it would be misleading to speak of his 'legitimising war'. The reason for this is that in the general domain of discourse about war there is a presumption that war can be either legitimate or illegitimate, or, in another dimension legal or illegal. At least, this appears to be true for the language used by political elites in the political culture of many states. A war that is said to be 'legal' or 'illegal' is one whose legality is defined in relation to some system of law, for instance international law. To 'legitimise' a particular war might be understood to mean showing or claiming it to be legal, or making it legal with respect to some system of law. This of course is not the sense in which we have been using the term 'legitimise' in this book. There is a further interesting complication. In the western world at least there is a traditional set of concepts – a 'discourse' in one sense of that term – that distinguishes between 'just' and 'unjust' war with respect to ethical and to some extent religious values. The tradition, though not crucially dependent on theological concepts, has been mediated primarily by theologians.[4]

In this chapter we have spoken of 'justifying' war rather than 'legitimising' it. Using that term is not meant to imply a connection with just-war theory as such. But it would nonetheless be true to say that the President's text uses *some* concepts and self-legitimisations that draw some of their effect from the presumption in our sense of the term) of the norms of just-war concepts. It is asserted, or more often implicated, for example, that there is a moral duty for the self (the 'nation') to go to war – primarily in terms of self-preservation but to some extent in terms of rescuing others. Efforts to obtain a peaceful settlement are listed point by point. Some other themes – for, example, discrimination (the need to protect non-combatants in one's attack) and proportionality (not using excessive force to achieve the just goals) – do not seem to contribute much to the legitimising strategy.

What was the point, then, of the detailed apparatus of analysis that we applied in this chapter? One purpose was to show how language-in-use is anchored in spatial, temporal and modal dimensions defined in relation to the speaker. If that has indeed been shown, then the result is relevant to the operation of discourse of many, perhaps all kinds. The key point is that spatial representation, both in its relation to physical extension, and as a source domain for metaphorical representations, seems to be fundamental. But the point that is more relevant to our present purpose is that political discourse in particular might well have a distinctive tendency to invoke spatial representations. And, even more obviously, political discourse that has to do with defending territory and forcefully entering someone else's will involve spatial representations.

The peculiarly spatial connection with the legitimising function enters the picture in two ways. First, the general public will not have direct experience of the realities that are at issue – territories that are physically and psychologically remote. The entire burden is then on linguistic expression, which somehow has to induce hearers to make mental representations of something for which they have no, or only very indirect, sensory evidence. This is why the speaker establishes multiple coordinates within the three fundamental cognitive axes. Second, the electorate has to be persuaded that there is a significant reason for undertaking the risks of fighting war. One way to do this is to stimulate anxiety or fear. We have seen an example of this strategy (a kind of coercive strategy) in a different context (Chapter 7). It is easy to see, in general terms if not all its physiological detail, how language use can stimulate adrenaline. And one way to make the effect more likely is to encourage a representation of the danger as *near*.

The greatest discourse complexity in this presidential address seems to relate to three topics: the representation of the location of a particular territory (Kosovo) in subjective geopolitical space, the representation of potential dangers to the self (the United States), and to the representation of frightening and morally outrageous acts perpetrated by the enemy. This representational 'proximising' of the subjectively remote can obviously only be done in relation to a fixed point. In the text we have analysed both the proximising and the fixing seem to be done by way of frequent shifts in deictic coordination – scene-shifts in space, flashbacks in time and changes of focus in modality. The strictly spatial parts of the discourse world represent Kosovo as 'close' to home. The temporal spatial spaces together represent Kosovo as 'central' to a historical process. The modal spaces are conceptually marked as those of potentiality, imminence and prediction supported by metaphorical entailment.

Fixing a presumption of where the centre lies is fundamental to discourse processing. The cognitive schemas of centre-periphery and of containing spaces seem to be bound up with the close-remote system. Perhaps there is also an intimate connection with political behaviour and discourse.

9 Worlds apart

As we have indicated many times in this book, the meaning of a text is not 'contained' in the text itself. Sense is made by readers or hearers, who link their knowledge and expectations stored in long- and short-term memory to the processing of the language input. Loosely, we can call this backstage knowledge 'context'. People do the processing on the basis of minimal communicative cooperation, which leads them to apply both inferential procedures and their ability to check for inconsistency, duplicity, and the like.

This point raises the question of the selectivity, availability, and extent of knowledge. For analysts, whose analysis necessarily begins with the same processes of interpretation as any other language user, there is enormous scope for choosing what context can be applied. Actually, ordinary language users are also analysts and vice versa. This means that context, and the discourse and meta-discourse that surround its construction, is plastic and contestable. If context is crucial to discourse analysis – and it is – then it (a) has no inherent limits and (b) is constituted not only by the knowledge but also by the interests and presumptions of the hearer/reader. And this applies to the analyst also. In investigating language used around the events of September 11, 2001, therefore, we begin with some possible contexts, without any claim to completeness.

September 11, 2001: contexts

The destruction of the twin towers of the World Trade Center on 11 September 2001, and the attack on the Pentagon on the same day, took place in a period of time characterised by various forms of conflict and violence in the Middle East. The talk and text that followed these events was naturally aimed in many respects at expressing emotion, but also at explaining, understanding and formulating a policy reaction. Forming and negotiating a representation of what had happened was thus crucial. Explanation and understanding requires representing causation and agency, and this in turn requires the use of contextual information. Such contextual knowledge must mean historical knowledge – knowledge of recent and not so recent events presumed relevant to the present events. But there is considerable uncertainty and variation with respect to (a) access to historical representations stored either in personal memory or in archival memory and (b) what actually is presumed relevant. The maxim of relation emerges here in a most indeterminate and politically contestable form. The following notes on context are meant as very incomplete indications of the kinds of long-term memory background knowledge that could be, or could have been accessed in the production and interpretation of discourse following 11 September 2001. They are inevitably selective.[1]

Notes on the Middle East context

Unrest in the Palestine authority had been increasing since September the previous year, finding expression in actions. This uprising against Israeli authorities was known as the second *intifada*, and ranged from civil protest to suicide bombings. The first *intifada* had occurred between 1987 and 1993.

Part of this context is the way not only Israel but the United States was perceived by the inhabitants of the Palestine Authority. In our terms, political actors in Palestine had their representations of Israelis and Americans, which included the contexts *they* presumed relevant and, furthermore, *meta*-representations of Israeli and American mental representations. For example, their contexts, i.e., what they held in long-term memory concerning their own recent history, included beliefs and judgements about the governmental relations between Israel and the United States, about the American economic, political and military presence in the Middle East and about the wider Jewish community and its relationship with the American political process. Further, they held meta-representations about Israeli and American motives and intentions – that is to say, they had read the Israeli and American mind in a certain way. Putting things in this somewhat theoretical manner raises questions about the degree of meta-representational embedding. We do not know, for instance, whether American politicians and policymakers held representations of Palestinian meta-representations. Put simply, did one party know what the other side thought they thought?

A further part of this immediate context – and remember, we are thinking of context as representations of the world stored in the mind and accessed when presumed relevant – is the representation of the physical and social components of the United States. Among the multiplicity of details that people would have stored would be images of the World Trade Center and the Pentagon. These would be not simply visual images, but have metonymic links with representations of the American economic system, the American military institutions and other elements of perceived American culture.

Notes on less immediate context

Still considering context as relevant mental representations stored in memory, what else might have been in the mind of people, of some people at least, in the Middle East? Some people, would have the following in their contexts. In 1945 President Franklin D. Roosevelt met King Abdel-Aziz ibn Saud and agreed with him that he would protect the Saudi dynasty in return for indefinite access to Saudi oil reserves. The British initially protected American interests, but left in 1972, when the Americans took over.

Eight years later, the fundamentalist Islamic revolution took place in Iran and the Americans lost influence, later issuing 'the Carter Doctrine', which stated that the USA would repel by military force any threat to its oil interests in the Persian Gulf. Ten years on from that, Iraq's invasion of Kuwait brought the fear that Iraq would invade Saudi Arabia also – whence Operation Desert Storm, and the stationing of American troops in large numbers in Saudi Arabia.[2]

If such were the 'factual' representations, what would be the affective stance, also stored in memory? Given the religious belief system, and given what we have seen earlier about the significance of spatial representations, many people would regard the American presence and influence as a form of intrusion into their domestic space, possibly a sacrilegious intrusion by unbelievers. People of this persuasion might also have a particular representational stance towards the government of Saudi Arabia, perceiving it as protected by the United States and also as corrupt and ungodly. In this context, the attacking of buildings metonymically associated with complex representations and attitudinal stances, becomes 'relevant'.

Notes on the American context

Let us turn to the contexts that might be available to, or relevant to, American minds. This is a vast question, and here we mention only the briefest details. The principles of spatial sanctity might be as relevant here as in the contexts outlined above. Consider, for example, a number of facts that American citizens might have in mind, with varying degrees of accessibility and relevance. Strikes at the American symbolic heartland, the president's residence, took place in 1812 (Chace and Carr 1988). In more conscious historical memory, the Japanese attack on Pearl Harbor in 1941 is salient. In 1946 the question of how to deal with the perceived communist threat from eastern Europe was dealt with in terms of cognitive structures revolving around the spatial schema of containment (Chilton 1996) and an ethical–emotional stance that blended fear of attack, fear of the unknown, and, in the minds of some Americans, fear of the ungodly. The Cuban missile crisis of 1961 was still in 2001 a consciously shared memory of the penetration of America's security sphere. We have seen in Chapter 8 the role that analogy can play in reasoning about international politics. The suggestion here is that analogical conflation of stored representations of events, consciously worked out through discourse or not, can play a role in the construction of mental contexts.

Bush and bin Laden: two worlds

The US government decided on a response to the attacks of 11 September 2002 that included military intervention in Afghanistan. As in other cases of US military action, the president appeared on national television to give, in this case, a *post facto* legitimisation of the action. Texts of this type have particular characteristics that also reveal some of the fundamental operations of political language-in-use. As in Chapter 8 we shall investigate the cognitive implications by focusing on the spatial, temporal and modal spaces that appear to be bound up with the processing (both productive and interpretative) of a presidential text seeking to justify going to war, this time the address given by President George W. Bush on 7 October 2001. Using the same approach, we shall also investigate the spatial–temporal–modal structuring of a text issued by Osama bin Laden, which was translated and broadcast by the BBC, also on 7 October 2001. In Chapter 10 we shall follow this up by investigating a dimension that has not been treated before – the ways in which political leaders, whether democratically elected or self-appointed, make overt or covert appeals to supernatural participants.

The president of the USA

In earlier chapters we suggested that in processing discourse, people make mental models in working memory. More specifically, we have claimed that for many types of discourse this involves setting up a multi-dimensional model, one that involves space, time and modality. All entities (people, things) and actions have coordinates in these spaces: that is, they are positioned in relation to the self's location, time of uttering, beliefs and values. There is here a prima facie connection with our intuitions as to what politics is about: it is about space and territoriality, it is about past and future action, and it is above all about being right. Let us consider the opening of President Bush's 7 October speech:

(1)   Good afternoon.
(2)   On my orders, the United States military has begun strikes against al-Qaeda terrorist training camps and military installations of the Taliban regime in Afghanistan.
(3)   These carefully targeted actions are designed to disrupt the use of Afghanistan as a terrorist base of operations, and to attack the military capability of the Taliban regime.

(4)   We are joined in this operation by our staunch friend, Great Britain.

(5)   Other close friends, including Canada, Australia, Germany and France, have pledged forces as the operation unfolds.

(6)   More than 40 countries in the Middle East, Africa, Europe and across Asia have granted air transit or landing rights.

(7)   Many more have shared intelligence.

(8)   We are supported by the collective will of the world.

An important additional claim about the way that discourse processing works, is that the temporal sequence of reading or listening may be iconic, in such a way that the referent of a first-mentioned referring expression is conceptualised as 'closer' to the centre (i.e., self), while later mentions get 'further away', where 'further away' may have different specific meanings depending on context. Such specific meanings include: less important, less correct, less probable, but also less geographically close, less friendly, and perhaps less 'nice' or less moral. Of course, this iconic aspect only operates in conjunction with other semantic and pragmatic cues. For example, words like *close* may be used, and certainly a speaker can rely on some mutual background knowledge about what countries, peoples and regions are felt to be 'close' by his or her audience, geographically, geopolitically or culturally. In the most general terms there should be nothing very surprising about this idea – precedence, rank and hierarchy are spatial and political concepts that are embodied symbolically in events like processions, seating arrangements, the use of raised platforms and so forth.

Sentences (2–8) can be analysed in this light. If we extract the phrases that contain the first-mentioned referents, the alignment is clear:

(2)   *self* (from 'On my orders'), the United States has begun strikes

(3)   *actions of the United States* are carefully designed

(4)   *we*

(4′)   *Great Britain*

(5)   *other close friends*

(6)   *more than 40 other countries*

(7)   *many more countries* (left unspecified)

(8)   *we.*

The 'close friends' are listed in an order, a kind of verbal procession, that is politically significant on the premise of iconicity. So there is order within the rungs of the hierarchy, too. Sentence (6) might seem to run against the pattern: is not Europe closer than Africa? What seems to be happening here is that the 'centre' is displaced at that point in the discourse. Since the speaker is representing Afghanistan as the theatre of operations, what is relevant for landing rights is closeness to that country, the order is what would (perhaps subjectively rather

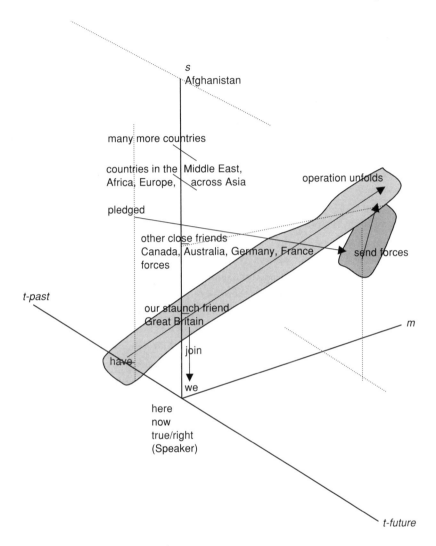

Figure 9.1 Relative distances from 'we'

than geographically) be expected. The discourse sequence for these referents corresponds to the 'distance' from 'we' on the *s*-axis in Figure 9.1.

In this type of speech by a political leader it is crucial to establish who is 'us' and who is 'them'. In fact it was an essential part of President Bush's discourse in this period to assert that there was no neutral or middle ground: leaders of other countries were told (since domestic broadcasts are directed also at non-Americans) to be either 'with us' or 'against us'. The propositional structure of the opening sentences of the speech is, we suggest, processed by setting up a discourse ontology in which the entities and the relations between them are plotted onto dimensions in terms of their relative remoteness.

The conceptual starting point is 'we'. The passive is used in (4) because 'we' is in focus, although in semantic-role terms it is merely a Goal, while Great Britain is both Theme and Agent. It is worth noting that in presenting the predicate *join* as an arrow we have suggested a representation of motion. In fact, 'our staunch friend' is not actually moving; what is interesting is that the concept of sympathetic alliance is expressed metaphorically as motion. The situation with 'other close friends' is more complex, though their location on the *s*-axis seems clear. The actions ('pledged forces') are related in the developing discourse model to the unfolding of 'the operation'. The definite article here indicates a given element in the model and alerts us to the part of the world already set up in the opening three sentences. For this reason it seems likely that the mental model for 'as the operation unfolds' involves a relation whose end point is al-Qaeda and the Taliban regime in Afghanistan and whose origin is in America (2), and where that relation stands for the process 'strikes' (2). This is a distinct space, a space in which there is ongoing activity which ends at some point in the future. Now, 'our close friends' performed an action of pledging in the recent past ('have pledged'), but this action creates a link with a more remote space – a non-definite future space, in which, we infer, Canada and the others will, or might, send forces to combine with 'the operation'. Note that 'pledge forces' could be modelled either as the forces going to the theatre of operations, Afghanistan, or to 'us', just as in (3) the (metaphorical) movement is towards 'us'. The more remote countries (the Middle East, Africa, even, it seems here, Europe) are represented as having performed supportive actions that have the same time coordinate ('have', indicating relatively recent past), but not in a hypothetical space on *m*; they do, however, get represented as performing the same causative motion – causing the transfer of 'rights' to us. Again, this movement could be modelled either as an arrow whose end point is at 'us' (we are the goal), or at the unfolding operations.

What about 'We are supported by the collective will of the world'? How is this represented in the ongoing discourse model? Two possibilities suggest themselves. One is that the hearer or reader simply does not form a representation of part of the discourse, because it is not clear how 'collective will' is to be represented in a mental model. If a representation *is* constructed, then there might be two further possibilities. The first depends on our assuming that there are two levels of mental representation, (suggested by Pavio 1971; Johnson-Laird 1983; Jackendoff 1996) and that there are in fact two decoding representations: one is essentially propositional and the other, corresponding in part to our deictic dimensions model, is essentially spatial. So a person processing (7) might deal with it at the relatively 'shallow' level that Jackendoff (1996) calls conceptual or propositional structure. Alternatively, if the processor gets any further, there are two spatial representations that we might consider. First, in (7) 'the collective will of the world' might be set up as an entity in the emergent discourse ontology, though, if so, then it is not clear where it would be positioned on the scalar dimensions relative to 'friends' and 'Afghanistan'. For this reason alone (and assuming that our underlying scalar deictic model is correct), 'the collective will of the world' might not get represented in this way at all. Second, what might happen is that discourse cohesion principles might lead to an interpretation of 'the world', such that 'the' indicates a given entity in the preceding stretches of text and emergent representation, and such that 'world' is interpreted as the superordinate of 'Great Britain, Canada, Australia' and the other named countries and regions. This emergent representation is a kind of cognitive map of the world. In this map, the world is defined as consisting of the previously named entities. Finally, we should note that at some level of processing, perhaps the propositional–conceptual one, there is a presupposition – namely, *the world has a collective will*.

Thus we might suppose that the discourse processor superimposes a containing entity, 'the world', on the already constructed deictic model. A question that this raises, however, is whether the predicate 'supports' is represented as a spatial process, parallel to 'join' (3) and whether it is represented as a material action at all. The syntactic and conceptual parallel between (3) and (7) is, however, noteworthy. Without trying to depict the superimposition in detail on paper (the mind is more malleable), we can view the effect of (7) as perhaps being as in Figure 9.2. The places named in (2) to (5) appear lumped in one geo-spatial space, with Afghanistan on the outside at the remote end of the scale.

Let us now consider a section of the President's speech which develops this world-view further:

(22) Today we focus on Afghanistan, but the battle is broader.
(23) Every nation has a choice to make.
(24) In this conflict, there is no neutral ground.
(25) If any government sponsors the outlaws and killers of innocents, they have become outlaws and murderers, themselves.
(26) And they will take that lonely path at their own peril.

This is indeed a world 'view', expressed from a point of view, and mediated through deixis and other space-related expressions. The scalar deictic model captures this aspect well (see Figure 9.3). The text clearly anchors the point of view (the point from which the world is viewed) in the spatial and temporal origin, the collective self. The terms 'today' and 'we' build a specific discourse space, from which we are invited to switch in the second part of (22), where 'but' triggers a shift of focus.

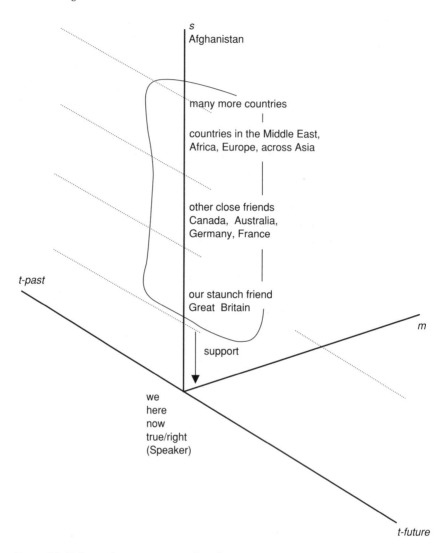

Figure 9.2 Relative distances in geopolitical space

In (22) the expression, 'the battle', signals a given entity that has already been evoked and maintained in an anaphoric chain, signalled deictically and lexically, in preceding expressions that include 'this military action', 'our campaign', 'another front in a war' (20), 'our enemies', 'this conflict' (21). And the preceding discourse has established a space where the conflict is occurring, the remote region of Afghanistan. The *but*-clause, and the following sentences (23–6) now seem to prompt the discourse processor not so much to expand the space spanned by 'we' and 'Afghanistan', but to structure it. Parts of these

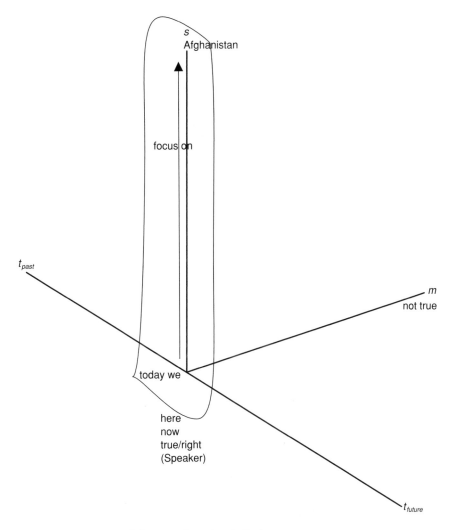

Figure 9.3 Distance and deictic polarization in Bush text

sentences may only be processed at a propositional–conceptual rather than a spatial level: e.g., the quantified 'Every nation has a choice to make' (23). But there is clearly also an important spatial and deictic underpinning, which is outlined in Figure 9.4.

Sentences (23) and (24) split the space of the global spatial model: the term 'choice' contributes to this, though it is the highly significant spatial metaphor in (24) that most obviously establishes polarisation. I have argued that the modal dimension is based on spatial distance and direction, and that it can be either epistemic or deontic. The lexical area evoked by 'choice' and the expression

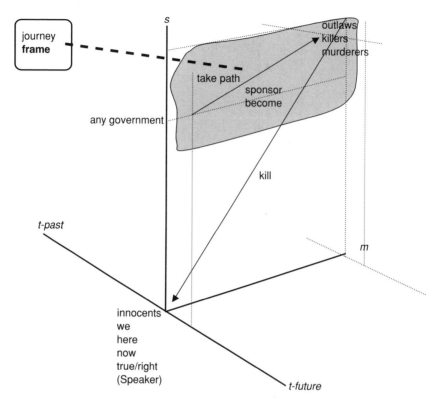

Figure 9.4 Polarisations, conditionals and metaphor (sentences 25–6)

'neutral ground' may, I suggest, be sufficient for the discourse processor to engage the *m* axis in the deontic gear, and this would be confirmed by the vocabulary of (25): 'outlaws and killers of innocents', 'outlaws and murderers'. In the context of 7 October 2001, the day of the speech, 'outlaws' appears at the extreme end of *m*, but also of *s*, while 'innocents' is diametrically opposed. Thus I take 'killers of innocents' to be inferentially represented by an arrow whose tail is at 'outlaws' and whose head is at 'us'. The entity 'any government' I take to be somewhere between the two extremes on *s*, at least until the reader or hearer comes to the consequent part of the conditional sentence (25) and (26).

In (25) the term 'if' sets up a conditional space. This is not a remote hypothetical counterfactual space on *m*; on the contrary, it seems likely that the epistemic modality of the 'if' here, in context, is close to something expressed by 'probable' or 'quite likely'. It is not in fact easy to see fully how the term 'if' should be characterised semantically in this type of context. One way of looking at it would be to suggest that (25) is processed at the relatively shallow propositional level, as a truth-conditional entailment.[3] But there may also be a spatial representation of this, in which the 'if' has simply acted to conflate 'sponsor' and 'become'. For both predicates can be seen as the same vector: 'sponsor' is an arrow linking 'any government' and 'outlaws'; 'become' lies on the same arrow. Both predicates have a possible spatial interpretation, but 'become' actually moves 'any government' from the middle ground in the mental model into the extreme place inhabited by 'outlaws'. It is not at all surprising, therefore, that the next sentence uses an explicitly spatial metaphor, which seems indeed to depend on the spatial model for 'become' which I have assumed in the analysis:

(26)   And they will take that lonely path at their own peril.

Here 'that lonely path' must be added to the unfolding discourse model as co-referring to the action already modelled, or so we have proposed, in terms of a path schema in (25). Of course, there is more than this going on here. The predicate 'lonely' can give rise to the inference in propositional form approximating to 'anyone sponsoring outlaws will be in a minority opposed by the majority of countries', though the affective element of the predicate will surely also be activated. In addition, there is an implied proposition approximating to: 'taking that path (i.e., sponsoring or becoming outlaws) is perilous', from which a hearer or reader presumably infers that the USA (and its 'friends') is threatening violence against anyone acting in this fashion. There is here speech act – a conditional threat, albeit a somewhat indirect one.

Osama bin Laden

Let us turn now to the text authored by Osama bin Laden and broadcast first by al Jazeera television. The original version was broadcast in Arabic. Strictly speaking, if we are interested in the speaker and the community in which he is embedded, it is the Arabic text that we need to analyse. However, the English translation had global dissemination.[4] Let us take a closer look at the way a person processing the translated text might build mental representations in response, always bearing in mind of course that such a model is not going to be a simple transfer of the one in the mind of the utterer that generated the original text.

The bin Laden text interweaves political and theological concepts. In contrast, American discourse, like western political discourse in general, has historically split the religious discourse from the political. The American president's text of 7 October, while incorporating some religious conceptualisation, as American political discourse expects (in contrast, say, to French political discourse), does not do so on anything like the same scale as bin Laden's. In the American (and western) context very extensive religious discourse is only sanctioned in specific settings and on specific occasions – such as President G. W. Bush's address in the national cathedral on 14 September. Another obvious difference is that any attempt to sketch a mental model derived from bin Laden's text must include 'God' as an acting entity. It is not that God does not appear in the discourse of American presidents, but the thematic roles given to this referent are different because of different background presumptions, as we shall see in Chapter 10.

Despite the differences, there are commonalities, and I want also to suggest that God, in both Islamic and Judaeo-Christian representations, is (partly at least) conceptualised on spatial axes and scales. This is clear in the opening sentences of bin Laden's text:

(1)   Praise be to God and we beseech Him for help and forgiveness.
(2)   We seek refuge with the Lord of [sic] our bad and evildoing.
(3)   He whom God guides is rightly guided but he whom God leaves to stray, for him wilt thou find no protector to lead him to the right way.
(4)   I witness that there is no God but God and Mohammed is His slave and Prophet.
(5)   God Almighty hit the United States at its most vulnerable spot.
(6)   He destroyed its greatest buildings.
(7)   Praise be to God.[5]

As a tentative first step, we might suppose that 'God' is located at the extreme end of s. Probably, this should be in the vertical dimension of s. (We have to recall that s in these diagrams is a shorthand for the three physical spatial dimensions.) If we assume that 'God' is conceptualised as remote on the vertical dimension, we can explain expressions such as 'God is above us, has power over us' and the like. Of course it may be retorted that these are abstract theological concepts; nonetheless, like many abstract expressions, they involve cognitive metaphorical mappings from physically experienced source domains, in this case the vertical-spatial one. Various theological positions and controversies may surround the positioning of God on the *near-remote* scale of the s-dimension. Interestingly, it is possible that Christian readers, especially any with a Protestant or American-fundamentalist Christian background will conceptualise 'God' at the 'close' end of s. However, I will make the assumption that for the bin Laden text, and perhaps for Islamic representations in general, God is conceptualised at the remote end. These matters really need detailed discussion, but for present purposes let us proceed on this hypothetical assumption.

There is, however, another remote entity that is referred to in the bin Laden text, namely, the USA. Clearly, we cannot place 'United States' in the same place as God (not if we are seeking a plausible modelling of bin Laden's intention, though the reverse might be true for an American representation). This is not a problem, if we recall, again, that s must be seen as a shorthand for three orthogonal axes. What I suggest here is that the 'United States' is conceptualised

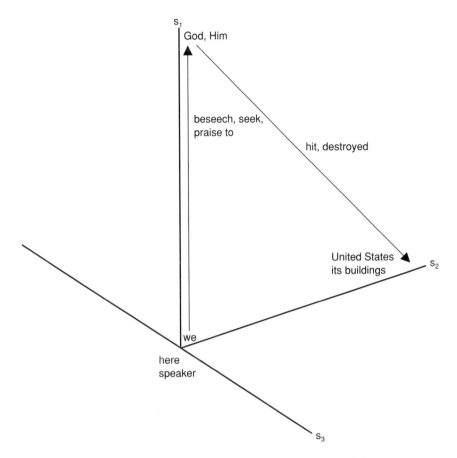

Figure 9.5 Distance and deictic polarisation in bin Laden text (spatial dimensions)

in a spatial frame that is horizontal in the 'in front of the speaker' axis (s2), and 'God' on the vertical s1.[6] Given this decision, we can sketch in Figure 9.5 a hypothetical mental representation derivable from (1) to (7), showing only the three *spatial* dimensions (leaving out *t* and *m*, in view of the exigencies of the two-dimensional page).

Figure 9.5 thus adds more detail to the *s*-axis of the diagrams discussed so far. What is important is that it is detail that is not relevant, or is far less relevant, to the discourse processing required for the American presidential text. Furthermore, Figure 9.5 suggests a link between the *we-God* relationship and the *God-United States* relationship: 'we beseech God' may appear to be causally linked to 'God hit America', though this is certainly not expressed overtly.

But how does the bin Laden text represent the *we-United States* relationship, and how is the space in between represented? Is this different from the representations prompted by the Bush text? In the case of the bin Laden text, this relationship is explicitly indicated throughout the text. Figure 9.6 is a summary of the way the entities *we* and *the United States* are located in a multi-dimensional space, in which the *m*-axis appears in its deontic guise. The relevant sentences are the following:

(12)   Our nation has been tasting this humiliation and contempt for more than 80 years.

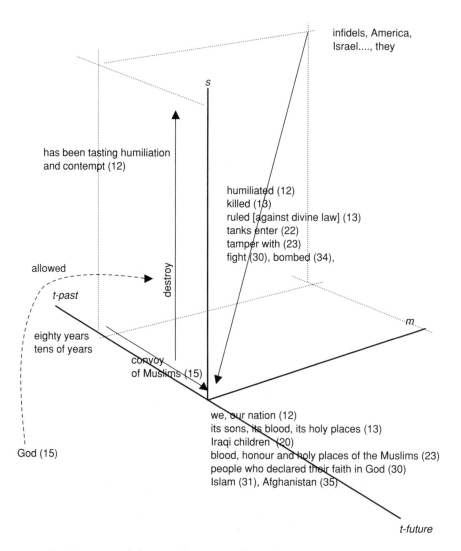

Figure 9.6 Distance and deictic polarisation in bin Laden text (spatial, temporal, modal)

(13) Its sons are being killed, its blood is being shed, its holy places are being attacked, and it is not being ruled according to what God has decreed.

(14) Despite this, nobody cares.

(15) When Almighty God rendered successful a convoy of Muslims, the vanguards of Islam, He allowed them to destroy the United States.

(16) I ask God Almighty to elevate their status and grant them Paradise.

(17) He is the one who is capable to do so.

(18) When these defended their oppressed sons, brothers and sisters in Palestine and in many Islamic countries, the world at large shouted.

(19) The infidels shouted, followed by the hypocrites.

(20) One million Iraqi children have thus far died in Iraq although they did not do anything wrong.

(21) Despite this, we heard no denunciation by anyone in the world or a fatwa by the rulers' ulema [body of Muslim scholars].

(22) Israeli tanks and tracked vehicles also enter to wreak havoc in Palestine, in Jenin, Ramallah, Rafah, Beit Jala, and other Islamic areas and we hear no voices raised or moves made.

(23) But if the sword falls on the United States after 80 years, hypocrisy raises its head lamenting the deaths of these killers who tampered with the blood, honour and holy places of the Muslims.

(24) The least one can describe these people is that they are morally depraved.

(25) They champion falsehood, support the butcher against the victim, the oppressor against the innocent child.

(26) May God mete them the punishment they deserve.

(27) I say that the matter is clear and explicit.

(28) In the aftermath of this event and now that senior US officials have spoken, beginning with Bush, the head of the world's infidels, and whoever supports him, every Muslim should rush to defend his religion.

(29) They came out in arrogance with their men and horses and instigated even those countries that belong to Islam against us.

(30) They came out to fight this group of people who declared their faith in God and refused to abandon their religion.

(31) They came out to fight Islam in the name of terrorism.

(32) Hundreds of thousands of people, young and old, were killed in the farthest point on earth in Japan.

(33) [For them] this is not a crime, but rather a debatable issue.

(34) They bombed Iraq and considered that a debatable issue.

(35) But when a dozen people of them were killed in Nairobi and Dar es Salaam, Afghanistan and Iraq were bombed and all hypocrite ones

stood behind the head of the world's infidelity – behind the Hubal [an idol worshipped by pagans before the advent of Islam] of the age – namely, America and its supporters.

(36)   These incidents divided the entire world into two regions – one of faith where there is no hypocrisy and another of infidelity, from which we hope God will protect us.

(37)   The winds of faith and change have blown to remove falsehood from the [Arabian] peninsula of Prophet Mohammed, may God's prayers be upon him.

The text works by systematically repeating an opposition between Islamic countries and the USA. The attack on the USA and the suffering of the Americans in (5–6) is opposed to the suffering of 'we' and 'our nation' (whose precise referents are by no means clear) in (12–13). The USA is not given explicitly as Agent, though it can be inferred to be one of the agents. But the agentless passives (13) leave it open for hearers to infer not only the USA, but also Israel and the government of Saudi Arabia. The dependency on presumptive context is considerable. It is therefore possible that the emerging mental model will locate Israel and Saudi Arabia at the same remote point of space and morality.

In the model sketched in Figure 9.6, the actions of which 'we', etc. are the Patient, are represented as arrows, the point being to reflect distance and direction. Words from the text are used to indicate the conceptual–spatial representation, which can be extracted by way of argument–predicate structure. In (15), note that God sanctions the destruction. As we have argued, God has to be represented (metaphorically) on a vertical-s axis, and while a flat diagram cannot depict this easily, the mind can. Sentences (16–17) are partly a dialogue between God and the speaker, and partly a propositional assertion about God. In any case, what is involved is a shift towards the kind of model given in Figure 9.5. A three-dimensional space diagram is also required to deal with (18), since the action of 'defending' is, so to speak, a lateral action: the defending is of those (sons, brothers, sisters) within the same space, namely 'Palestine' and 'many Islamic countries'. It is important to note that two different spatial representations are possible here, namely the space in which the 'convoy of Muslims' is allowed to destroy the USA, and the space in which the same 'convoy of Muslims' defends their sons, brothers and sisters. How is the discourse processor to represent 'defended'? To which actions does this refer? A likely process is that the destroying of the USA is blended with the defending of sons, brothers and sisters, though it is possible that hearers will find referents in other violent acts of the past. Some of the agency effects are inferred, but nonetheless added to the model: e.g., (20) One million Iraqi children have thus far died in Iraq.

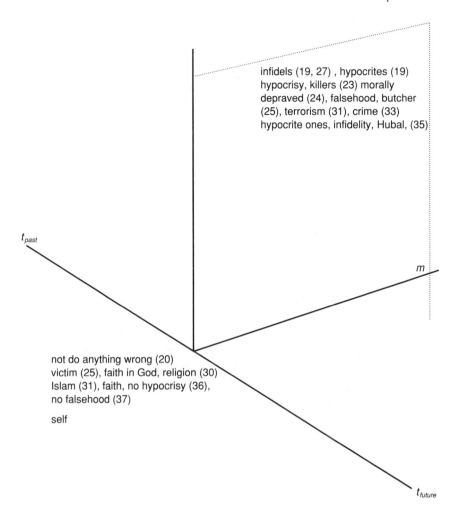

infidels (19, 27) , hypocrites (19)
hypocrisy, killers (23) morally
depraved (24), falsehood, butcher
(25), terrorism (31), crime (33)
hypocrite ones, infidelity, Hubal, (35)

t_{past}

m

not do anything wrong (20)
victim (25), faith in God, religion (30)
Islam (31), faith, no hypocrisy (36),
no falsehood (37)

self

t_{future}

Figure 9.7 Moral value vocabulary in bin Laden text

   In the next section (20–36), the text continues to list actions in which the
USA, or Israel, are the agents, Islamic peoples the victims. What is happening
here is that a kind of mental balance sheet of atrocities is being drawn up. The
purpose of this is not made explicit, but it is clear through inference. The
function is to justify and legitimise the principal action being referred to –
the massively destructive acts of 11 September. Background values seem to be
taken for granted which would sanction violence against some person if that
person had inflicted greater violence. But this is not the only way in which
moral justification is established. The entities that have a primarily geographical
representation, overlaid onto a friend-enemy scale, are also mapped onto a

corresponding moral scale. As we have argued, morality and lawfulness can have a conceptual representation in spatial terms. According to this scale, what is close to self is also morally good, and vice versa. Frequently also, such a scale is mapped onto a centre-periphery schema and a container schema – what is inside is close to the self, and what is outside is also outside the law.

Thus Figure 9.7 above is a summary of the moral value vocabulary in the translated bin Laden text that maps onto the coordinates we have been using already for Figure 9.6.

If it might appear that such antonymous lexical sets do not have any spatial basis, (36–7) should remove the doubt:

(36)   These incidents divided the entire world into two regions – one of faith where there is no hypocrisy and another of infidelity, from which we hope God will protect us

(37)   The winds of faith and change have blown to remove falsehood from the [Arabian] peninsula of Prophet Mohammed, may God's prayers be upon him.

'These incidents' are of course those whose possible mental representation are partially diagrammed in Figure 9.6. In fact, the conceptualisation of these events has already, for the discourse processor, divided up the multi-dimensional deictic space into two regions. Sentences (36–7) are likely to be processed not simply in propositional-conceptual terms, but in spatial-conceptual terms. A comparison should now be made with Figure 9.4. It would be inaccurate to ignore the serious differences between the Bush and bin Laden text. But there is a striking parallel, despite the relative explicitness of bin Laden and the relative implicitness of Bush. Both Figures 9.4 and 9.6 represent a world space – which is a geographical, geopolitical, cultural and moral space – split into two. It also appears that in some respects the two conceptualisations are mirror images of one another.

10 The role of religion

The last chapter brought us to a point where we applied a spatial model of human discourse processing to two contrasting, indeed conflicting, texts arising at a moment that will, one assumes, be judged to be of considerable historical importance. This enabled us to see the way in which language is used by political actors to communicate representations of a divided world. But this point raises more questions than it answers. So the present chapter aims to open up some of these questions for future research and thinking. What the spatial analysis of Chapter 9 showed us was the intricacy of opposing mental representations, though also some of the strange commonalities and symmetries between them. We also saw how contexts, viewed as knowledge bases, are essential to understanding communication, but also recruited in varying ways for varying ends.

In the present chapter we fix on one particular characteristic of what is now not just international politics but cross-cultural politics. This characteristic is the new role of religious belief systems. Another reason for focusing on this dimension is that it is much neglected by analysts of discourse. We shall aim simply to provoke further research and discussion rather than to advance theory or method. The main instrument will be our rather informal notion of presumptions – the varied but structured conceptual baggage that minds interacting in societies carry around with them because individual survival, social cooperation and communicative cooperation would not work without them.

The main question we are seeking to open up is: what religious entities, processes and roles are presumed semantically or pragmatically in political language-in-use, especially in that of political leaders? In order to explore this type of question, we shall examine the president's 'Remarks at National Day of Prayer and Remembrance' at the National Cathedral on 14 September 2001. In the aftermath of 11 September 2001, religious discourse was, not surprisingly used by American leaders in special ways. Equally unsurprising, religious language was used in public statements by Islamic leaders. We shall also, therefore, take another look at the bin Laden text, analysed in Chapter 9. The point of analysing side by side a text by an American president and a text by Osama bin Laden is to begin to investigate the extent to which political language and religious beliefs are intertwined.

The role of religion

The fact that we have to choose a specifically religious occasion and location in the case of the American text is in itself significant. True, American political rhetoric does include religious language, and religious speech acts. However, these are reserved to particular parts of the structure of public speeches, usually the conclusion. For example, President Clinton's speech, which we investigated in Chapter 8, concludes thus:

> Our thoughts and prayers tonight must be with the men and women of our Armed Forces who are undertaking this mission for the sake of our values and our children's future. May God bless them and may God bless America.

And in the 7 October 2001 speech, President Bush concludes with the same formula:

> May God continue to bless America.

Osama bin Laden concludes his 7 October text with a formula which, though bearing some important differences, is nonetheless similar in crucial respects, namely the 'May God . . . bless . . .' formula, which appears in both cases to assume the authority of the speaker to appeal to God to perform some action benefiting the people whom they claim to be (and may or may not be in fact) representing:

> May God's peace, mercy, and blessings be upon you.

These examples do not of course take account of many other features of the texts which evoke religious concepts and practices indirectly through lexical and syntactic selection. Nonetheless, they show how explicit invocation of a deity is located in these text types. Let us consider some crude statistics.

In the presidential address to the nation on 7 October – a primarily secular setting – the word 'God' occurs once in a speech of about 1,028 words; President Clinton in 1999 uses 'God' twice in about 2,018 words. In the specifically religious setting of 14 September, however, President Bush uses referring expressions (which include e.g., the phrase 'Lord of life') for God much more frequently. Even then there are only seven occurrences in about 950 words (approximately 0.73 per cent). On the other hand, the translated text of bin Laden has 'God' nineteen times (and one 'Lord') in about 764 words (approximately 2.6 per cent). While there are clear differences of degree, there is still much of religious significance in the American text that might repay further analysis. In general, it seems that while bin Laden (and perhaps other Muslim leaders) may make no behavioural distinction between political contexts and religious contexts, between political utterances and religious utterances, western leaders in modern democracies *will* make such a distinction, in certain cases reflecting a constitutional separation of the state and religion. There are clearly modifications one has to make about this statement. One is that in some western states politicians certainly have to take account of religious sensibilities, both in the negative direction of not *offending* any religious group and in the positive direction of *favouring* (maybe despite appearances) some particular group. Equally, I am not suggesting that in the Muslim world (or the western world for that matter) no purely religious and non-political contexts and utterances occur. The generalisation is simply that in certain Muslim states or regions, political discourse will be religious, or contain salient religious elements, though there must be differences of degree that it would be of interest to determine. While in the west, the expectation (though not necessarily always the practice) is that political utterances will be secular.

What Bush and bin Laden presume hearers presume about religion

What are the religious presuppositions that are made in the two texts? What is meant by this question is that in analysing the language of the two texts, it is possible to become aware of two aspects of religious discourse. The first aspect includes certain conceptualisations that are frequently propositional (e.g., that God is good, merciful, wise, etc.). Sometimes such propositions are linked with spatial and other experiential schemas, including the close-remote scale (e.g., God is *above* us, God is *within* us, I have seen God *face to face*). The second aspect has to do with religious actions and which actions can be authoritatively ('felicitously' in the terminology of speech act theory) be performed by whom. Thus if X performs a speech act that can be characterised as a religious speech act (consecrating, preaching, marrying, for example), then X can be assumed to be making a claim to have the power or the authority to do so. Such acts may, depending on cultural context, include speech acts resting on moral authority (say, admonishing, approving, cursing), which in western culture have become divorced from specifically religious contexts and authority.

In the following investigation, I have adopted a mixed approach, and tried to indicate the presumptions and the validity claims that are made (in the senses discussed in Chapter 3), by bearing in mind the questions: What is being presumed here about the sort of religious utterances that it makes sense, or is 'right' to make? Who has the right to make these utterances? What sort of representations of God are presupposed by a given assertion or presupposed assertion? In fact, it is useful to apply once again the terminology and approach discussed in Chapter 3. In the texts under scrutiny in the present chapter, there is, for example, a presumption created by the claim *that God exists* that the speaker means sincerely to assert this, that the speaker has the authority to assert this, and that the act of asserting this is carried out in an acceptable language or style of that language. Another example is *praying*: it is taken for granted, i.e., presumed, that *praying* exists as a recognisable and recognised form of behaviour. Similarly, there is a presumption created by the implicit claim that it makes sense, is normal or legitimate, for the speaker in the speech situation he or she is in *to ask God to do certain things*, or that it makes sense *to ask God to bless or to curse some category of persons*, where the category of persons will often be specified and sometimes restricted to exclude certain other persons. And so forth.

The American text and its presumptions about religion

In Tables 10.1 and 10.2 below, we compare the presumptions that seem, at least to the present analyst, to be driven by the text. I have included some presuppositions and potential inferences that seem to be closely related to the particular religious presumptions, for example, the president's presupposition of the reasons or motives that give rise to praying.

We now consider presumed assertions and speech acts that occur (are presumed) in bin Laden (Table 10.2) but not Bush (Table 10.1). This is not of course a straightforward matter, since a good deal of interpretation is needed, and, moreover, in the case of the bin Laden text we are begging many questions about the translation effects. Furthermore, ideas may be invoked without being verbally represented, and religious doctrines may be consistent without being identical.

The bin Laden text: presumptions, analogies and entailments

Naturally, there are doctrine-specific presumptions. The lexical structure of bin Laden's text draws on the Koran, and there is a presumption of background knowledge of the Koran. As one would expect, bin Laden's text presumes the reality of Mohammed and his relation to God (4, 37). More interestingly, bin Laden presumes the reality of *Hubal*. Here we need to consider the specific conceptual framework that is likely to be evoked for Muslim hearers throughout the Muslim world. In the Islamic narrative, Hubal is one of many Gods who, in the seventh century was worshiped by infidel Arabs, and whose stone image was set up in the *Kaaba* in Mecca, an edifice built by the monotheistic prophet Ibrahim as a special sanctuary of true belief. Hubal thus stands for infidelity and also for defilement of a sacred space. This schema is mapped onto a geopolitical representation of the world of 2001: America is the 'head of the Hubal of the

Table 10.1 Presumed knowledge in Bush text

President G. W. Bush 14 September 2001	Presumptions
(3) We **come before God** to **pray for** the missing and the dead, and for those who love them	*Move into sacred location,* ***Praying to God for beneficiary X,*** *X = those who suffer;* **God exists.**
(23) Yet our wounds as a people are recent and unhealed, and **lead us to pray**.	**Praying,** *beneficiary or goal or effect unspecified; suffering causes people to pray.*
(24) In many of our **prayers** this week, there is a searching, and an honesty.	**Praying**; *beneficiary or goal or effect unspecified.*
(25) At St Patrick's Cathedral in New York on Tuesday, a woman said, 'I **prayed to God to give us a sign**	**Praying for effect** *X, X = God give sign.*
	God gives signs; *belief attributed, not necessarily endorsed by speaker.*
that **He is still here**.'	**God might be absent from 'here'**; *attributed presumption.*
(26) Others have **prayed** for the same, searching hospital to hospital, carrying pictures of those still missing.	*As in* **(25)**, *plus possible implication that a sign of God's presence is the survival of a loved one, and possible implication of the converse.*
(27) **God's signs** are **not always the ones we look for**.	**God gives signs; we look for signs; God's signs might not be recognised**. *Possible inference, answering the converse implication above – if loved ones do not survive, this does not mean God has given no sign?*
(28) We learn in tragedy **that his purposes are not always our own.**	**God has purposes; God's purposes not always 'our' purposes.**
(29) Yet the **prayers of private suffering**, whether in our homes or in this great cathedral, **are known and heard, and understood**.	**Praying motivated by suffering; God receives such prayers**
(30) **There are prayers that** help us last through the day, or endure the night. (31) **There are prayers** of friends and strangers, **that give us strength** for the journey. (32) And **there are prayers that yield our will to a will greater** than our own.	**Praying for different beneficiaries and with different effects;** *some prayers have supportive effects on 'us'; some prayers affect relationship between 'us' and God.* **God has a will; God's will is greater than human wills.**
(33) This **world He created** is of **moral design**.	**God created world; world has moral design.**
(36) And the **Lord of life** holds all who die, and all who mourn.	**God controls (is lord over) life; God 'holds' those who suffer.**
(48) This is a **unity of every faith**, and every background. (49) It has joined together political parties in both houses of Congress.	**There are different religious faiths; different faiths currently have common ground.**

Table 10.1 (continued)

President G. W. Bush 14 September 2001	Presumptions
(50) It is evident in services of **prayer** and candlelight vigils, and American flags, which are displayed in pride, and wave in defiance.	**Praying**; *beneficiary or goal or effect unspecified. Different faiths share prayer and ritual; different faiths share loyalty to the USA.*
(58) On this national day of **prayer** and remembrance, **we ask almighty God** to **watch over our nation**, and **grant us** patience and resolve in all that is to come.	**Praying**; *beneficiary or goal or effect unspecified.* **Asking God for effects X, Y,** *X =* **God protect a particular beneficiary** *(= 'our nation'), Y = give virtues of patience, resolve (beneficiary = 'us')*
(59) We **pray** that He **will comfort and console those who now walk in sorrow**. (60) We **thank** Him for each life we now must mourn, and the **promise** of a life to come.	**Praying for effect X,** *X = God comfort those who suffer.* **Thanking for X,** *X =* **God has given individual life. There has been a promise – that there is life after death.** *God might be inferred to have made this promise. Speaker does not assert that there is life after death.*
(61) As **we have been assured**, neither death nor life, nor angels nor principalities nor powers, nor things present nor things to come, nor height nor depth, can **separate us from God's love**.	**We have been assured of X,** *X =* **God loves 'us'. The** *'assurer' is left implicit. Speaker is giving a warrant ('as we have been) but does not give source.*
(62) **May He bless** the souls of the departed. (63) **May He** comfort our own. (64) And **may He** always **guide** our country. (65) **God bless** America.	**Requesting X, Y, Z.** *X = God 'bless' the dead, Y = God comfort specifically 'us', Z = 'guide' and 'bless' specifically 'our country'.*

age'. What is important about this metaphorical mapping is the entailments. First, Hubal entails that there exist followers of Hubal. In this particular translation the followers are represented by the expression 'all hypocrite ones'. Bin Laden's hearers, or at least his Muslim hearers if not his western ones, will infer that the relevant referent here is those Arab states, such as Saudi Arabia, who have supported and been supported by successive US governments since 1945. Second, the mapping entails that America is present in a sacred space, namely here, the Arabian Peninsula. Referentially speaking, the Hubal (alias America) is present in the sacred Islamic space in the form of military personnel, advisers, manufactured goods and cultural artefacts.

But more of the narrative is potentially mapped to the present by bin Laden's text. In the narrative, Mohammed called the Arabs back to monotheism and

Table 10.2 Presumed knowledge in bin Laden text

Osama Bin Laden 7 October 2001	*Presumptions*
(1) **Praise be to God** and we **beseech** Him for help and forgiveness.	*Praising God; God exists; Beseeching (asking) God for effects X, Y, X = God help 'us', Y = God forgive 'us';*
(2) We **seek refuge** with the Lord of our bad and evildoing.	*[translation not clear]*
(3) He **whom God guides** is rightly guided but he whom **God leaves to stray**, for him wilt **thou find no protector to lead him to the right way**.	*God guides some people, but God does not guide others; God does not protect those he does not guide.*
(4) I **witness** that there **is no God but God** and **Mohammed is His slave and Prophet**.	*Witnessing; God is unique; Mohammed is God's slave and Prophet.*
(5) **God Almighty hit the United States** at its most vulnerable spot.	*God commits acts of violence X, X = hit enemy;*
(6) **He destroyed** its greatest buildings.	*God destroys buildings [people not mentioned]*
(7) **Praise** be to God . . . (10) **Praise** be to God. (13) [our nation] . . . is not being ruled according to what **God has decreed**.	*Praising God; God exists*
(14) Despite this, nobody cares.	*God decrees forms of government*
(15) When **Almighty God rendered successful** a convoy of Muslims, the vanguards of Islam, He **allowed them to destroy** the United States.	*God can cause success; God caused success of X, X = 'a convoy of Muslims, the vanguards of Islam' [inferred referent is suicide bombers]*
(16) I **ask** God Almighty to elevate their status and grant them Paradise.	*Asking God for effects X, X = God grant Paradise (beneficiary = suicide bombers)*
(17) He is the one who is **capable** to do so.	*God has power to grant Paradise.*
(26) **May God mete them the punishment** they deserve.	*Asking God for effect X, X = God punish enemy*
(35) . . . all **hypocrite ones** stood behind the head of the world's infidelity – behind **the Hubal** . . . of the age – namely, America and its supporters.	*There exist hypocrites; there exists the Hubal; Hubal is America.*
(36) . . . two regions – one of faith where there is **no hypocrisy** and another of **infidelity**, from which we **hope God will protect** us.	*The world of infidelity threatens us; there exists a world of no hypocrisy and a world of infidelity. God may protect beneficiary (= 'us') against 'region . . . of infidelity'.*

Table 10.2 (continued)

Osama Bin Laden 7 October 2001	Presumptions
(37) The winds of faith and change have blown to remove falsehood from the [Arabian] peninsula of **Prophet Mohammed, may God's prayers be** upon him.	**Asking God to favour X,** *X = Mohammed;*
(39) ... **I swear by Almighty God who raised the heavens without pillars** ...	**Swearing by God;** **God created the heavens;** **God is powerful;** **God transcends natural law;** **Asking for effect X,**
... the land of **Mohammed, may God's peace and blessing be upon** him.	*X = beneficiary (Mohammed) have God's 'peace and blessing').*
(40) **God is great and glory to Islam**.	**God is powerful; favours a particular group of people (Islam).**
(41) **May God's peace, mercy, and blessings be upon** you.	**Speaker asks God to grant favour ('peace, mercy and blessings') to hearer.**

incited them to destroy Hubal. The ruling elite, who accepted Hubal, attempted to suppress Mohammed's followers. But, regrouping in Medina, they fought a war, destroyed the idol Hubal and spread Islam around the known world. There is a particularly significant detail. During the struggle, Mohammed was challenged by the *Munafiqun*, the 'Hypocrites of Medina', who sought to preserve their tribal power by outwardly accepting Islam while secretly rejecting it and opposing the new prophet.

Now, once the Hubal-America analogy has been set in motion, more entailments are potentially activated, though in different ways by different receivers. For, Muslim and Middle Eastern receivers or for anyone who calls up the Koranic script, the implied referent of 'the hypocrites' would in all probability be Saudi Arabia, bin Laden's native land. For most western receivers, the only visible implied referent is America as an un-Islamic defiler, though this will be an inference that will not be consistent with their own mental representations of the world. There is a further possible set of entailments that arise from this conceptual merging of the two narratives. If Hubal is America, if the hypocrites are Saudi Arabia (and similar states), and if bin Laden is calling for the destruction of Hubal, then bin Laden himself is potentially available to fill the conceptual slot 'Mohammed', or at least, perhaps, 'prophet'. Indeed, the role presumed by the religious speech acts performed by bin Laden are prototypically 'prophetic', in a sense that is also known to Jews and Christians.

One final point about this transfer of the Mohammed script might be made. The Hubal is conceptualised as a stone idol, and it is this that is attacked and destroyed in the narrative of Mohammed's holy war. The World Trade Center and the Pentagon could be viewed as symbolic (metonyms for American, capital and military might), not simply functional. While it is true that the correspondence is not point for point (since Hubal stood in a sacred space and the American buildings did not), it is not unlikely that these salient American buildings somehow became semiotically blended into the metaphorically transposed Hubal–Mohammed script.[1]

Before leaving the topic of religion-specific conceptions and speech acts, it is important to note that the Muslim hearers of the text would know one other key fact – that bin Laden is associated with a somewhat diverse and widely spread sect within Islam, the Salafiyya. The Salafis' cognitive script uses concepts of purity and contamination – they believe that a previous era, that of Mohammed and the first generation of his followers was purer than the present, and that later believers have polluted it. Purity is associated in these kinds of scripts with simplicity, austerity, discipline, authority (often patriarchal) and a return to the past. In turn, the concept of purity, as suggested in Chapter 9, is constructed through more fundamental spatial concepts, including concepts of bounding.

Another ingredient of such scripts is the path concept and its metaphorical mapping onto the target domain that has to do with deontic conceptualisation. This particular metaphor is familiar in many religious systems of ideas, and is of course frequent in the Koranic text. It is a metaphor that can generate several kinds of automatic entailments. The 'right way' for example is an expression that depends on the 'behaviour is a path metaphor' and is associated with several other possible entailments – that guidance is needed, there may be a leader, the path can be lost, people can choose the wrong path, or wander ('stray') from the path, which is typically straight (rather than crooked or devious). This is the schema that accounts for sentence (3):

> (3) He whom God guides is rightly guided but he whom God leaves to stray, for him wilt thou find no protector to lead him to the right way.

Many similar reformist movements, and precisely the same metaphors, have emerged over the centuries also within Christendom. There is a distinctive feature of the script presumed by bin Laden that is not hinted at in President Bush's text, although the presumed notion is not entirely foreign to certain strands of Christian thought, specifically Calvinism. In (3) it is presumed that God does not prevent people 'straying'; moreover, when they do stray, God ceases to protect them and may destroy them.

Bin Laden performs acts of *praise* (or *thanksgiving*),[2] Bush does not. This is presumably not a product of different religious concepts, since *praising God* also exists in all versions of Christianity. It is not that Bush performs the opposite of praising, though he is in the opposite situation for the purposes of the discourse (victim as opposed to victor); *dispraising God* is not a presumed speech act for either Christianity or Islam. Nonetheless, Bush perhaps comes close to it in evoking the notion that there are no 'signs' of God's existence, in order of course to deny it. One could thus claim a complementary symmetry – bin Laden praises God, Bush laments and doubts, or comes as close as coherently feasible to that act.

Sentence (39) seems to constitute an act of swearing:

(39)   I swear by Almighty God who raised the heavens without pillars that neither the United States nor he who lives in the United States will enjoy security before we can see it as a reality in Palestine and before all the infidel armies leave the land of Mohammed, may God's peace and blessing be upon him.

Swearing is a speech act that appears to function as a way of strengthening the claim to be telling the truth, and also as a way of bolstering the rightness of, the authority upon which a speech act is made. Typically a performative verb if *swearing* will embed a complement clause representing a future action of the speaker such as a promise or threat: I swear that I will do X. But the embedded clause may also, as in (39), represent a future state of affairs without mention of the speaker as agent of anything. In bin Laden's utterance, there are actually two states of affairs linked by 'before', which has the effect of implicating a conditional relationship between them – something like:

if there is no security in Palestine, there will be no security in the USA.

This has the further effect of creating a particularised implicature, on the basis of presumed knowledge about the speaker and the recent history, that counts as a speech act of warning or threatening. No Agent roles appear; it is left for hearers to make their own inferences.

So who might the agent be? In bin Laden's text the agent of destructive acts, e.g., acts expressed by the verbs of 'hit' and 'destroy', is 'God', not the suicide bombers, or al-Qaeda, or bin Laden himself. What is presumed, and directly represented by the syntactic form (at least in the English translation), in sentence (5), is that the agency is that of God:

(5)   God Almighty hit the United States at its most vulnerable spot.
(6)   He destroyed its greatest buildings.

Implicitly, it is presumed that it is an attribute of God that he has the will and power to destroy an enemy, causing people to suffer in the process. In (15) there is a slightly different view of the causal connection:

(15)   When Almighty God rendered successful a convoy of Muslims, the vanguards of Islam, He allowed them to destroy the United States.

the agent of 'destroy' is not explicit but can be inferred as *they* ('them'), the 'convoy of Muslims, the vanguards of Islam', an expression that is relevantly interpreted as referring to the suicide hijackers of 11 September. In other words, God is not the immediate cause from the perspective of this sentence; God merely 'allows' the destruction to happen. Behind these variant representations, there are doubtless theological niceties that we cannot go into; but let us note in passing that theological uncertainties as to human and divine will and agency are not unknown to Christianity.

The sentences we have just looked at seem to be pragmatically framed as part of the act of *praising* set up in the opening sentence ('Praise be to God . . .'). But the reverse also occurs. In the belief frames that bin Laden's text appears to presume is also the proposition that God has the will and the power to punish the wicked – he does not destroy without moral legitimisation. In (26):

(26)   May God mete them the punishment they deserve,

the victim is the Arab states (indirectly referenced via the phrase 'the hypocrites'), who in bin Laden's discourse world have supported Hubal-America. This particular divine attribute is called up as part, not of a praising act, but as part of an act that is approximately an act of *cursing*. In (26) the speaker presumes the power and conditions that legitimise his making a request to God that God punish some group of people (and perhaps individuals).

Bin Laden thus makes assertions that presume the belief that God commits violent and destructive acts, and that these acts are directed, by implication, at the speaker's enemies, and by further implication, those enemies are also God's enemies. What is noteworthy is that bin Laden here selects his words to avoid direct mention of human victims and agents. This form of verbal evasion (it mitigates the face-threatening act of openly admitting responsibility for killing) is well known, widespread and not of course limited to a bin Laden. The Agent and Patient roles are not specified, i.e., assigned overtly to referring expressions. On the one hand it is God who, in bin Laden's text, is the responsible agent of destruction, rather than the suicide bombers themselves or those who col- laborated with them. A further belief system underlies these formulations, as becomes clear in (15). Taking the English translated text, it appears that the suicide bombers ('a convoy of Muslims'), were 'allowed' by God to destroy

American people (and buildings). This presupposes that they had the intention to do so and were also the agents of the action, while God removed impediments. The precise conceptual underpinning is not clear, but one interpretation a reader might have is that God had to give permission because the speaker anticipates a possible reader inference that destroying is immoral, unless divinely 'allowed'. On the other hand, the American victims are not mentioned, only the buildings, whereas the sufferings of Muslim people *are* mentioned. The motivation for this is made explicit in (11–14):

(11)   What the United States tastes today is a very small thing compared to what we have tasted for tens of years.

(12)   Our nation has been tasting this humiliation and contempt for more than 80 years.

(13)   Its sons are being killed, its blood is being shed, its holy places are being attacked, and it is not being ruled according to what God has decreed.

(14)   Despite this, nobody cares.

Here there is an implicit claim that sufferings can be compared on a scale of magnitude – that is to say, Muslim sufferings (referenced by the pronoun 'we' in (11)), bin Laden claims, are greater than American ones. This is the mirror image of the American president's representation of the situation: he too omits to mention the sufferings of the others.

Yet another attribute of God is presumed. By contrast with the examples discussed so far, it is also an attribute of God that God grants favours – or '*blesses*' – other groups of people. In (16) and (17), it is a presumed attribute of God that God can grant some individuals to enter Paradise, but it is also presumed that there is a religiously meaningful act in which the speaker, a particular authority figure, may rightly make a request to God that God grant such a favour.

The word *pray* does not occur in the translated text. However, one type of prayer is the request prayer, and the making of requests to God does occur in bin Laden's text (16) and (26). There are two kinds of requested effect. One effect requested is that God grant Paradise to a specific group of Islamic individuals, the men who killed themselves destroying buildings in New York and Washington. The other effect requested is that God bless Mohammed. The way in which praying is mentioned in the two texts is one of the striking differences between them.

The American text: pluralism, ambiguity and a hidden God

Unlike the bin Laden text the Bush text takes place in a special location, and this is presumed in (1) of the President's speech. This topographical separation of the religious and the secular is not presumed in bin Laden in the same fashion. Rather, for bin Laden the sacred space is presumed to be an entire geographical region contrasted with another region outside it that is characterised as ungodly. The American cognitive frame therefore presumes particular kinds of directed movement, into and out of local sacred spaces – for example the 'coming before God' of (3). This is a stereotypical Christian phrasing using an archaic meaning of the preposition *before*, namely 'in front of'. ('We come before God' does not mean that Bush came in first and God followed!) This meaning implies that the landmark, God, is oriented with his face towards the speaker's own face. This kind of face-to-face orientation is associated with meeting of a lesser power with a greater, typically in the feudal hierarchy (vassals come 'before' their lord).

The purpose of the movement into a special space is presumed to be specifically for *prayer*. What is noteworthy about the Bush text compared with bin Laden's is not only the recurrence of references to praying but also the extent to which the act of praying is overtly specified. The overall frame that Bush draws on presumes several components. However, Bush does not directly presume all of these components himself; and this itself is another interesting feature. In certain instances he attributes types of praying to other people or groups of people. Underlying this is a kind of religious pluralism, though a limited one. While praying is presumed to be a universal behaviour among 'us', it is also presumed that different types of prayer happen among 'us'. Bush does not present universal propositions about the nature of prayer: for example, he will say 'in *many of* our prayers . . . there is *a* searching, and *an* honesty . . .' (24). In (25) and (26) the different kinds of prayer referred to seem to be clearly attributed to others, thus not necessarily endorsed by the speaker:

(25)   At St Patrick's Cathedral in New York on Tuesday, a woman said, 'I prayed to God to give us a sign that He is still here'.

(26)   Others have prayed for the same, searching from hospital to hospital, carrying pictures of those still missing.

However, prayer per se does seem to be universally presumed. It does not seem, for example, to be presumed that there are atheists who do not pray at all. What the speaker does seem to presume generally are three attributes of prayer. Prayer can be thought of as requesting something – for example a 'sign', as in (25) and (26). There are different motives for people praying, for example, suffering, as in (23) and (29). And prayers are always 'received' by God, as asserted in (29).

However, a significant number of sentences concerning prayer are ambiguous, in the sense that a hearer may interpret the text as either endorsed or attributed, or be uncertain of which of these to select as the intended meaning. Essentially, the contrast is between *de dicto* and *de re* meanings. Sentences (30–2), which focus on the effects of prayer, are particularly striking in this regard:

(30)   There are prayers that help us last through the day, or endure the night.

(31)   There are prayers of friends and strangers, that give us strength for the journey.

(32)   And there are prayers that yield our will to a will greater than our own.

That it is the effects element that is pragmatically and semantically ambiguous is of interest. Do prayers work? This may be the underlying question that has seeped into the discourse, perhaps via a concern to admit a plurality of beliefs and points of view. The repeated formula 'there are prayers that . . .' can be processed either as the speaker presuming these variations of prayer for each individual in the relevant community of addressees, or as asserting that some people pray in one way for or with such-and-such an effect, some people in another way, etc., without the speaker himself presuming, or endorsing, these types of prayer. In any event, there seems to be something like 'distancing' here, which may have to do with American pluralistic sensitivities. Interestingly, the first type of prayer to be mentioned (30) has to do with supporting the private self. Moreover, the participant role structure of the proposition expressed is ambiguous. Sentence (30) can be understood as:

(30a)   we pray, and this praying helps the person praying

(30b)   someone prays (for us), and this praying helps us

Here (30a) seems to rest on a subjectivist concept of praying (praying does you good, whether there is an objective God or not), while (30b) would rest on an objectivist concept of prayer (praying for somebody has objective effects on that person, presumably via divine intervention). A similar, though not identical, kind of ambiguity is present in (31):

(31a)   people pray for us, we know that they pray for us and this knowledge helps us

(31b)   someone prays (for us), and this praying helps us.

The claim that there is ambiguity here, does of course rest on the presumption that in the relevant culture (31a) is a possible way of conceptualising prayer. The important point is that the formulation (31) is compatible, and we are claiming intendedly compatible, with such a way of conceptualising prayer, and that this in turn arises from a culture that pluralises religious belief (while probably not admitting religious unbelief).

Sentence (32) raises particular problems because of its more specifically theological content – namely, the concept of subordination of human will to the divine will. Here too the modality can be either *de dicto* or *de re*. Is Bush making a truth claim about the varieties of prayer? Or is he making a truth claim about the various types of prayer that different people (or groups of people) presume? Because (32) involves a theological presupposition that could, given the pluralistic culture, be contestable (some Christian groups may not hold quite this version of the hierarchical relationship between the individual will and the will of God), it is doubly unclear what meanings will be constructed by hearers, or what hearers might see as the intended meaning. There is a degree of inexplicitness in the concept of prayer that seems to be closely linked with the fact that secular pluralism combines in complicated ways in the USA with presumptions about religious belief in public discourse.

The sentences just discussed are part of a sequence that continues through to (36). The logical links are not explicit; any coherence depends on background assumptions and inferences. We can consider sentence (33) in this regard:

(33)   This world He created is of moral design.

How does one relate this to the mental model being built up on the basis of the President's words? Sentence (33) may depend on, or imply, a background proposition which has been established in the context in various textual and extra-textual ways – a proposition amounting to:

the events of 11 September imply that the world is *without* moral design.

Sentence (33) serves to deny this background proposition and additionally to assert, by presupposition, that God has created the world, which, in turn, simultaneously presupposes God's existence. The subsequent sentences, (34–6), can then be read as cohering with (33), and responding to the background proposition doubting moral design.

If one turns now to the speech acts of prayer that Bush seems to be performing, these involve making requests in the form 'ask for' (or 'pray for' in the same sense). What is it presumed to be acceptable to pray for? The president does not pray for the destruction of the nation's enemy. His requests do, however, appear to be more numerous than bin Laden's. There also appear to be two kinds of formulation – one in which requests and thanksgivings are made by a collective 'we' (58–61), and one in which requests are made in the persona of the President. The 'we' formulation is common in forms of Christian ritual where a cleric is making supplications on behalf of a congregation. The sorts of things presumed acceptable to request here include benefits that are unclear in their precise referents, but which fall into broad semantic categories: that God protects ('watches over') some specific group of people, that these people receive certain virtues or psychological attributes in vague future difficulties ('patience and resolve in all that is to come'), and that God gives emotional consolation to those who suffer, by implication those who suffer as a result of the attacks of 11 September.

Thanksgiving is scarcely likely to be the kind of speech act performed in the circumstances. The act of thanksgiving (its close partner being *praising*) is not, however, omitted altogether. While bin Laden asks God to bless the suicide bombers, and praises/thanks God for them and their actions, Bush thanks God for the lives of their victims. While bin Laden asks God to give Paradise to the suicide bombers, Bush thanks God for 'the promise of a life to come'. These are approximate mirror images; both men presume prayers of request, the power of God to grant life after death (a felicity condition that is part of both the speech act *requesting* and the speech act *promising*, spelled out by bin Laden explicitly), and the existence of life after death. It may be that the President's formulation 'the promise of a life to come' (60) is interpretable as unfulfilled, thus somehow intended with less epistemic certainty than in bin Laden's formulation.

Some prayer formulations seem to be the preserve of the president alone. Presidential addresses to the nation customarily conclude with '(may) God bless America' (as in the last sentence (65) of Bush's address), but on this special occasion there is an expansion of the requests. In (62) there is a request for God to bless the souls of the dead, a speech act reserved uniquely to priests in some forms of Christianity. Sentence (63) is a request for God to give comfort to 'our own', a phrase that is presumably interpreted by hearers as 'all Americans', with the possible implication that other humans are excluded from this specific request. Sentence (64) is remarkable in that it ends the speech by evoking a metaphor based on the path schema – the same metaphor that bin Laden used to open *his* speech (3). Bush's sentence presupposes that in the past the USA has continuously been the recipient of God's guidance.

In looking at the bin Laden text in Chapter 9, we suggested as a hypothesis that God was represented as a remote entity. We can ask in a similar fashion what sort of spatial representation is suggested by the presidential text. The use of the expression 'is still here' in (25) presumes a number of rather elusive meanings. The sentence embeds the proposition 'God is not here' in the mental representations of 'a woman'. It is thus not (necessarily) endorsed within the speaker's own world, but it is nonetheless *presumed* as a meaningful proposition in itself – that is, meaningful to represent God as being present in or absent from a location, or, conceivably, being 'still there' but hidden. However, the President does make some interesting overt presumptions about God within his own discourse world. In (27, 28) it is presumed to be normal to presuppose that God 'gives signs' and that these signs are sometimes not recognised by 'us':

(27) God's signs are not always the ones we look for.
(28) We learn in tragedy that his purposes are not always our own.

Sentence (28) associates 'signs' with the presupposition that God has purposes, that God's purposes cannot be known, and that these purposes are sometimes different from human purposes. There is an additional presumption, again linked with established Christian conceptualisations, to the effect that humans can and do 'learn', and learn through suffering, that God's purposes are unknowable. Further, there is a potentially paradoxical assertion, presumed valid by the speaker for the cultural context, that private prayer is actually received (known, heard and understood) by God.

These presumptions are approaching the assertion of doctrine, a role normally carried by clerical authority. This does not necessarily mean that a president is here taking on a priestly role, since the American religious culture could accommodate the notion that any lay person has the right and the knowledge to make assertions of belief. What is happening appears to be that the President, confronted by a devastating event, reaches for discourse that locks into opposing concepts of hope and despair and somehow seeks to reconcile them. But there is more than that; the speech is an act that both draws on and consolidates a politico-religious community. President Bush (or his script writers), in this particular passage and elsewhere, could be seen to be drawing on the collective resources of a current of Christian teaching that has historical discourse antecedents in the origins of the American state. Similar doctrinal strands are suggested by the mention of subordination of the self's will to a higher will (32).

Reflections

It is easy for western readers of bin Laden's translated text to assume that it is directed only at them. It is possible that some such assumption even affects the translation process itself, though this is impossible to judge without detailed comparison of source and target texts. What we can say, however, is that close inspection of even the translation shows that bin Laden's discourse world is one in which the USA is not the sole or even the primary enemy. This of course is not to say that bin Laden does not target the West, or that his targeting of the West is not morally repugnant. The point is that targeting the West is manifestly just part of a larger view of the world. From a discourse-analytic point of view the lesson is that intended meanings are relative to readers/hearers, and that politically significant meanings can get overlooked without careful scrutiny of the presumptive contexts relevant to such readers/hearers. From a political point of view, widening the context, one then has to consider the purpose in the bin Laden or Salafi universe of the attacks on the World Trade Center and the

Pentagon, and this includes the possibility that the purpose is to provoke the West to confirm the myth of Hubal-America, and, further, to do so in order to unify *internal* Islamic opposition against the *internal* enemies of true Islam, namely the 'hypocrite' regimes of Saudi Arabia, Egypt and other states who have accommodated the West in varying degrees.

What does our scrutiny of President Bush's speech tell us? Comparison with bin Laden is suggestive, but should be done cautiously. We suggested in Chapter 9 that if we try to model the conceptualisations that may have given rise to or may be prompted by bin Laden's text, then we are led to include a vertical dimension of space, in order to accommodate the theological dimension that is closely woven into the text. The same cannot be said of Bush's cathedral speech to anything like the same extent.

If we turn to the representation of time and history in the two texts, there are several observations we might make. As we have seen, the bin Laden text gives rise to analogical conceptions of contemporary political realities. Specifically, the narrative of Mohammed's struggle against Hubal and 'the hypocrites' is mapped onto present political circumstances. There are other examples in extremist Salafi discourse. The role of the European Crusaders in the Middle East in the eleventh and twelfth centuries is mapped onto contemporary America. The historical narrative of the Mongol invasion of the Middle East in the thirteenth century is also mapped onto contemporary America, entailing a potential mapping of the historic defender of Islam, ibn Taymiyya, onto bin Laden himself (Doran 2001: 36–43).

This kind of analogical historical reasoning should be distinguished from the forms of historical memory and argumentation that are found among other critics of the West's dealings with the Muslim world. In particular, the evocation of wider historical contexts – for example, public memory of western fragmentation of the Middle East after the First World War, and of the western stake in the oil fields in Saudi Arabia, Kuwait and Iraq – is cognitively a different process. It is found among critics and protest movements across the Middle East and among those in the West.

But to return to analogical reasoning from historical narratives, can one say that this mode of cognition is entirely absent from American discourse about international conflict? In Chapter 8 we found clear cases in the speech of President Clinton. Whether these instances of analogical historical reasoning are of the same kind as those of bin Laden text is a question we leave open, but on the face of it the cognitive processes appear to be similar.

In President Bush's speech of 7 October, given in the aftermath of appalling events, we do not find any overt analogical reasoning about history. Nor, unsurprisingly, do we find the evocation of historical contexts that would give an explanatory account of the events. Nonetheless, 'history' is evoked:

(16)   Just three days removed from these events, Americans do not yet have the distance of history.

(17)   But our responsibility to history is already clear: to answer these attacks and rid the world of evil.

What do hearers, and we as analyst–hearers, make of such assertions? Discourse analysis itself does not answer the question; it merely draws attention to the materials to work on. Here are some points that could be made.

Notice that a whole concept of history is presumed by the phrase 'the distance of history'. At various points in this book we have proposed that the spatial concept of relative distance from the self is a fundamental cognitive resource that is recruited, via metaphor, in other conceptual domains. In sentences (16) and (17) we have an interesting case. The view of history presumed in these sentences is not like the one that seems to be presumed in the bin Laden text, where the very distant past is brought close in the present. President Bush and his American audience, by contrast, presume almost the opposite – that 'history', by implication, is something in the past, which is by definition a more or less 'distant' relative to 'us'. Such 'distance' is also presumed to be desirable. The two sentences make sense only against the background of such accepted cultural assumptions.

The well-known spatial metaphor for time (see e.g., Lakoff and Johnson 1980) underlies the semantics of the English expressions used here ('remove', 'distance'). It involves a linear conception, according to which 'we' are moving and leaving the past 'behind'. The use of the term 'history' itself seems to presume several rather unclear conceptualisations. Sentence (16) might be understood as the writing of history in retrospect, or simply as the passing of a stretch of time. But in (17) the notion of history is even more vague. Perhaps hearers would understand it in connection with the idea of preserving a certain American reputation for subsequent generations. In the overall argumentation the function of the first part of (17) may be that it constitutes an appeal to some form of higher moral authority (not, one should note, God). The purpose of the appeal seems to be to legitimise two propositions, two policies – namely, 'answering these attacks' and 'ridding the world of evil'. It is taken for granted that there is a moral duty to 'answer these attacks', however that phrase may be construed by hearers.

The phrase 'rid the world of evil' induces a moral justification in itself, resting on implied meanings supported by a presumed conceptual framework. It presupposes that evil exists (as a sufficient explanation of the atrocities of 11 September); it implicates that the 'responses' will lead to the 'ridding'; and it also possibly implicates that that the USA will perform this task for the entire world. In the religious setting, this is a large claim with further interesting implications. One such implication, for example, is that the USA is in some sense an agent of good and perhaps of God. If so, then the separation of the religious and the political is not a fully psychologically real one. Public presidential discourse may include some degree of assimilation of religious and political functions.

We are not quite done with the invocation of history in the President's cathedral address. To conclude this chapter we speculate about the linkage between historical evocation and religious presumptions within the framework of presidential discourse on special occasions in situations of crisis. It may well be the case that while the example is particular there are general conclusions to be drawn about leadership behaviour in general. What is the nature of the religious presumptions Bush makes, presumptions that are probably not to be taken as personally *his*, but as those arising from the *role* of president in this political culture? We have seen that some utterances in the cathedral speech come close to those of the priestly role – blessing America and, more strikingly, blessing the souls of the dead. And there is a continuous presumption that God can rightly be asked to give special protection to 'the nation', the collective self, a presumption that in the circumstances has to be given sense and plausibility by invoking the discourse of the God who hides himself.

The broadest political purpose becomes clear in (47) to (52), in the evocation of Roosevelt's phrase 'warm courage of national unity', in the evocation indeed of Roosevelt himself, and in the claim to unity in diversity:

(47)   Today, we feel what Franklin Roosevelt called the warm courage of national unity.

(48)   This is a unity of every faith, and every background.

(49)   It has joined together political parties in both houses of Congress.

(50)   It is evident in services of prayer and candlelight vigils, and American flags, which are displayed in pride, and wave in defiance.

(51)   Our unity is a kinship of grief, and a steadfast resolve to prevail against our enemies.

(52)   And this unity against terror is now extending across the world.

(53)   America is a nation full of good fortune, with so much to be grateful for.

(54)   But we are not spared from suffering.

(55)   In every generation, the world has produced enemies of human freedom.

(56)   They have attacked America, because we are freedom's home and defender.

(57)   And the commitment of our fathers is now the calling of our time.

The evocation of America's founding constitution – 'the commitment of our fathers' in (57) – depends on presumed knowledge that we cannot go into here. In the text it is connected, with (56) and (55) which have presumed another set of beliefs related to political and cultural identity. The immediate function seems to be that these concepts provide an explanation of the events of 11 September and simultaneously conceptualise a group identity. The concept in question is the idea that the self's territory is the unique locus ('home') of supreme values, which automatically have enemies. Here those values are identified as 'freedom'. A further premise is already in place in (55), a historical truth claim. The causal claim in (56) then follows.

This mode of argumentation rests precisely on the spatial model we have been exploring in the past few chapters – one in which the self is defined at the origin of intersecting coordinates of space, time and rightness. This is a descriptive and theoretical point, arising from the close scrutiny of language in use, and does not necessarily imply any ethical judgement.

Part IV

Concluding thoughts

11 Towards a theory of language and politics

In each chapter of this book we have elaborated our theoretical framework by following two broad tracks. On the one hand we have focused on human interaction and on the other hand focused on the way that humans represent the world in their minds in the process of linguistic communication. Following each of these two paths we have come not quite to the end of the road, but to the point where the horizon opens to the research and thinking that needs yet to be done.

In analysing the interactive aspects of discourse, we looked at small-scale dialogues and conversations, moved to the interactions between political parties in parliament, and on to political leaders addressing their local electorates, mass electorates and even global audiences. We asked what was the nature of the micro-interaction and what were the strategic functions of their uses of language? By the time we reached Chapter 10, the question broadened to become more challenging. In the new world of the early twenty-first century, what does it mean to communicate across societies, cultures and languages? How is communicative interaction possible? What does it mean to cooperate at the fundamental human level of linguistic communication, the precondition for all other forms of human cooperation?

In terms of cognitive representation, we began by seeing how our minds might set up and communicate different worlds of actors and actions, and we have suggested a theoretical framework for understanding the way the self and its group mentally positions itself. But the world contains other minds, and we found that it was necessary to incorporate an account of how we read the minds, intentions and motives of others. And if we push further along this road, we end up asking another pressing question. How do we read the minds of other humans who speak different languages and have different social political and cultural experience stored in long-term memory? Or rather, how do we make it possible for them to communicate with us?

We have reached the point where we have to recognise that interaction and representation converge – we have only separated them in this book for analytical convenience. This is a theoretical crossroads because we are standing before a research field that is only just starting to be cultivated – a field in which cross-cultural and cross-linguistic interactions and representations among human groups have to be seriously examined.

Towards a theoretical framework

I began this book with a quotation from Aristotle's *Politics* that suggested a link between the human faculty of language and the human propensity to live in a *polis*. Humans are not the only species to live in groups, establish boundaries, engage in bonding rituals, build hierarchies and behave in a machiavellian manner. But, and it is a big 'but', we are the only species to have language and the communicative, reflective and cultural peculiarities that go with it. This raises the question: just how close is the relationship between language ability and political ability?

To my knowledge, current linguistic approaches to political discourse do not look at things this way. The tendency has been to view political discourse in terms of some social group or elite exploiting, controlling or distorting language in order to preserve its own position. Language in the service of power has thus been a central concern, and perhaps rightly so. But if one is seeking a theory of language and politics, it is not enough. Why not? For one thing, politics involves cooperation as well as conflict. For another, one has to ask not only what is 'power' – a standard question for political scientists – but also how do the manifestations of power, language, conflict, cooperation come into being? Many discourse analysts have been content to regard these phenomena as somehow out there 'in society'. But society is merely the interaction of human individuals, and the actions of human individuals are motivated, planned and executed first of all by neural networks in their skulls. The cognitive sciences are beginning to grasp these complex issues, and it would be unwise for scholars of political discourse to stand aside from them. That is why this book has adopted a broadly cognitivist perspective.

Let us go back to Aristotle for a moment:

> Speech, on the other hand, serves to indicate what is useful and what is harmful, and so also what is just and what is unjust. For the real difference between man and other animals is that humans alone have perception of good and evil, just and unjust, etc. It is the sharing of a common view in these matters that makes a household and a state.

Remarkably he does not just say the function of 'speech' (that is, *logos*, what we have called language$_L$ in this book) is to convey information in the sense of true or accurate information. Rather, what he says appears to infuse the use of language with human social meaning. He does not tell us what he has in mind by 'useful' and 'harmful', but these terms are certainly not the same as 'true' or 'accurate'. One assumes, from the context, that 'useful' and 'harmful' can be understood in a social framework. For Aristotle, to serve a social purpose means a 'political' purpose in the sense that people live in a 'polis'. It is possible that Aristotle's aphoristic summary matches the modern idea that the evolution of language can only be explained (barring some genetic mutation) because language was *adaptive*. A cooperative social group needs its members to be able to tell one another about, for instance, the location of food, of dangerous animals, of group members, of rival groups.

What is more remarkable is that Aristotle says that 'speech' also serves to indicate what is 'just' and 'unjust', and goes on to suggest that humans are unique in having a 'perception' (*aisthesis*, so perhaps 'sensation' would be better, or 'intuition') of good and evil, right and wrong, just and unjust. We don't know what Aristotle meant by 'etc.' in the quotation above, of course, but we could take up the hint and assume that humans operate with a range of related ethical concepts that pop up as dichotomies.[1] One more step in the argument: having a *shared* view in matters of justice and injustice, good and evil is what makes a 'household' (*oikos*, the smallest unit of human association) and state (*polis*). We can understand this in terms of agreed value systems communicated, through language, among members of a group.

The reason for bothering with Aristotle is that this passage links together in a concentrated fashion the main ingredients of a theory of politics and language that will serve as a framework for practical analysis of political discourse. To summarise our interpretation of Aristotle:

(1) Language$_l$ has the function of indicating to members of the group what is harmful or useful. We can understand this further in terms of social intelligence issues, reciprocal altruism and communicative cooperation, discussed in Chapter 2.

(2) Language$_l$ has the function of indicating what is good and evil or just and unjust. Humans have conceptions, or intuitions, of good and evil, justice and injustice.

(3) The producing and sharing of a common view regarding these concepts is an intrinsic part of constituting a social or political group.

Throughout this book we have seen examples of the very detailed way in which, in political situations, political actors fix on what we have called 'legitimisation'. What this means is that humans using language politically seem to feel a strong pressure to justify their actions or proposals for action in terms of oppositions between right and wrong. At the heart of what we call 'politics' is the attempt to get others to 'share a common view' about what is useful–harmful, good–evil, just–unjust. Language is the only means for doing this. It is not surprising that languages$_l$ have structural and lexical resources for communicating these concepts.

This story we have told so far excludes much. It makes everything seem positive, cooperative and final. Yet in Chapters 1 and 2 we encountered the apparent contradiction of the cooperative and the exploitative in human communication. At a fundamental level, however, we have argued that

cooperation is the necessary premise for non-cooperation.

In the evolutionary story, we set aside the possibility that language evolved by accident. We adopted the assumption that it evolved because it was useful to individual survival, where individual survival also means working in groups for individual advantage. You can work more successfully in groups if you can trust people's communications about what is 'useful' and 'harmful' to you. So you need a minimal, or fundamental, principle for cooperative communication. Then you can meaningfully lie, deceive or dominate. Taking the next step, we have accepted and adapted the ideas of theorists such as Leslie (1987), Cosmides and Tooby (1989, 2000) and Sperber (1994, 2000), the gist of which is that humans probably have developed the abilities to:

  'read' the intentions of others, checking for deception,
  to check and remember a reliability value for information that has been communicated,
  to monitor the logical and rhetorical aspects of verbal communications.

Aristotle has set us off on a line of thinking that poses the question: Is there a connection between the innate political tendencies of humans and their innate linguistic tendencies? This question can be interpreted in two ways. First, it might mean that language$_l$ is intrinsically designed, has adaptively evolved, to communicate and challenge the political cognitions of humans living in social groups. It may also have evolved to work indexically as a political signalling system, e.g., signalling group membership or rank, bonding and dominance. Second, the question might mean simply that it is language$_{l/u}$ that serves political interaction and communication, while the language faculty itself, language$_l$ remains quite apolitical.

This book does not answer these questions – the aim has been to pose them for further investigations into language, the human mind and political discourse. Without answering them, we may still put forward some hypotheses, based on our descriptive and explanatory analyses of political texts, concerning (a) the specific political purposes of language-in-use and (b) the specific linguistic means that are used by people speaking politically. We have analysed examples of language$_{l/u}$ and we stay on that level, without prejudice to the bigger questions regarding language$_l$.

Some propositions regarding political discourse

Political discourse is the use of language in ways that humans, being political animals, tend to recognise as 'political'. We can try to separate out aspects of language (structure and lexicon) that are frequently or typically found in association with what we, again as political animals, interpret as particular types of political behaviour.

Political discourse operates indexically

By indexical I mean that one's choice of language$_1$, or features of it, can implicitly signal political distinctions. Examples would be: choosing to speak one language rather than another, choosing a regional accent, or accent associated with a social class, choosing words associated with particular political ideologies, choosing forms of address (and in some languages, pronouns) that express distance or solidarity. Group boundaries and bonding can thus be expressed indexically.

Political discourse operates as interaction

While indexicality is clearly an interactive mode, there are many other forms of interaction facilitated by the structure of human language. Chapters 5 and 6 used techniques of fine-grain transcription to show the micro-timing of verbal interactions, and to point out the ways in which these interactions are 'political'. Verbal interaction is often indexical: for example, interruptions and overlaps can implicate conflict or cooperation, depending on often complex factors in the ongoing exchange. Again, interactions often signal boundaries and bonding, as well as rank and role.

Interaction functions to negotiate representations

By representations I mean the use of language oriented to the communication of conceptualisations of 'the world'. People communicate among themselves partly in order to coordinate their world conceptions – this is what being in a polity is about, as Aristotle suggested. Shared representations may be *presumed*. For example, speakers take it for granted (that is, presume) that certain presupposed meanings are shared by the relevant community, or that a local maxim of quantity, for example, is accepted and that a certain implicature will be generated by the hearer. I have left the notion of 'presumption' relatively undefined in this book, but it seemed to be a necessary one. The reason is that, in analysing political texts, it is often very clear that hearers could not make sense of the language-in-use, unless they were expecting, and expected, to adduce pre-existing knowledge stored in memory concerning roles, institutions, values, etc., current in a particular polity. Implicatures in particular require them. They are cognitive 'frames' of various kinds, but they are of a special kind and I have called them 'presumptions' because of their normative and sometimes coercive characteristics. Many of the analyses in this book have shown that representations of the world are the focus of promotion or challenge, and that their intelligibility in the first place depends on prior representations. These also may have had to be negotiated, promoted or imposed in the past.

Recursive properties of language$_L$ subserve political interaction

Political actors need to guess what their rivals are up to. Without a 'theory of mind' ability – which is a language-independent cognitive ability – this would be impossible. Human individuals have to decouple the representations of the world that they have stored as 'true' or 'real' from those that they reckon other people have. They can do *meta-representation*. Essentially, they have to be able to think the mentalese equivalent of 'Niccolò thinks that *p*', without accepting *p* as true, and that is exactly the case in natural language. Using human language also permits rather complex political calculations by multiple embedding: 'Niccolò thinks that Lorenzo believes that Piero suspects that. . . . *p*'. Meta-representation is essential for truly machiavellian behaviour.

Modal properties of language subserve political interaction

Probably all languages have grammaticalised modal expressions attached to concepts such as: social obligation–compulsion, certainty–doubt, evidence with credible–incredible source. If they do not have a grammaticalised system (e.g., modal auxiliaries), then there are plenty of ways in which any propositional attitude can be formulated. English, for example, has grammaticalised concepts of social obligation, etc., degrees of certainty and straightforward ability ('she can swim'). It also has ways of decoupling propositions and putting them in an 'irreal' or 'hypothetical' mental space, for the sake of various kinds of reasoning process (uses of 'if', 'unless', 'in the event that', and the like). It does not, like some languages, have 'evidentials', compulsory morphemes tagging the source of a truth claim. But it has equivalents. Moreover, we have seen (for example in Chapter 7) that establishing 'credibility', claiming 'rightness' and 'legitimising' truth claims constitute a political strategy that recruits many available linguistic mechanisms.

Binary conceptualisations are frequent in political discourse

Although the lexical potential can communicate scales of probability–possibility, social acceptability and legality, for example, the tendency in much political discourse is towards antonymous lexical choices, and other lexical choices that must lead to hearers making mental models that are binary in character. We have seen the binary tendency at work in representations of party politics, in political interaction itself, in the formation of group identity and the fear of foreigners, and in the later chapters of this book in the representations of the global political universe.

Political representations are sets of role-players and their relations

Political text and talk involve assuming, negotiating or imposing discourse ontologies – representations of the people, objects, places, etc., that exist, and the relations among them, that is, who does (did, might do, will do) what to whom, when and where, who or what caused what, etc. Language seems inherently designed to enable us to communicate such representations, by enabling us to assign semantic roles to referring expressions. One of the essential features of coherent language use is that it enables us to maintain continuities in which players 'exist' along with their roles, by linguistic phenomena such as anaphora, and conceptual abilities that search for and detect convergent reference across sentences. All coherent discourse works in this way, but the achievement of coherence is heavily dependent on cognitive frames and political discourse relies on presumptive frames of particular kinds.

Political discourse draws on spatial cognition

Not exclusively, of course. However, the analyses in this book have been predicated on, and perhaps have demonstrated, that the perception and conception of space is of major significance. On the anthropological level this claim involves the suggestion that territoriality is an intrinsic part of the socio-political instinct. On the psychological and neurological level, it involves the fact that humans have complex sensory-motor and proprioceptive systems, the ability to construct and store topographic maps, and other spatial abilities. On the level of linguistic and cognitive science it involves the evidence that metaphorical transfers from spatial (and other) base domains are important in the conceptualisation of abstract domains.[2]

Political discourse involves metaphorical reasoning

Cross-domain metaphorical mappings make it possible to draw inferences that could not be drawn on the basis of direct evidence or the basis of direct experience. In political discourse metaphors are often not just embellishments of literal propositions, but modes of reasoning about, for example, the future and about policies.

Spatial metaphors make concepts of the group and identity available

Certain source domains from spatial cognition are found again and again in political discourse. Particularly prominent ones are the container image schema and the path schema. The former is fundamental to the conceptualisation of groups of all sizes, from families to states. In Chapter 7 we saw its presence among speakers representing racial groups; in Chapters 8 and 9 we saw how spatial projections are made on the global scale. The latter (the path schema), because it is involved in the conceptualisation of time and also of action, appears in political discourse as a means of representing policies, plans, national history and grand ideas like 'progress'.

Political discourse has specific connections to the emotional centres of the brain

This hypothesis emerged during our investigation of texts in Chapter 7, but is relevant to others as well. Whether there are indeed *specific* emotions that could be called 'political' remains arguable. However, some politically relevant feelings, such as territorial belonging and identity ('home'), love of family, fear of intruders and unknown people have certainly shown up in our analyses. Such emotions might have an innate basis and be stimulated automatically in the political use of language.

Political discourse is anchored in multi-dimensional deixis

One of the major claims made in this book is that political discourse rests on the intersection of several deictic dimensions. These are cognitive dimensions, tapped by language-in-use. The model we have sketched is derived from the practical analysis of political text and talk. It is particularly detectable in political discourse that is oriented to the international arena, presumably because the wider the arena, the greater the need to identify one's 'position' (Chapters 8 and 9). To make things manageable, we proposed the intersection of just three axes, space, time and modality, though in reality the model must be multi-dimensional. The space dimension, for instance, has several forms, derived metaphorically from one another. The central claims are these:

> discourse worlds require entities in it to be relativised to the self,
> the self is the speaker, but the speaker may claim identity with the hearer and third parties,
> role-players in the discourse world are 'positioned' more or less close to 'me' or 'us',

the self is positioned at the intersection that is conceptualised not only as 'here' and 'now' but also as 'right' and 'good'.

There is a corollary to this claim that has not so far been mentioned. It answers the question: Where does identity come from? The human nervous system has its innate ways of producing the sensation of personal identity. But some component of the subjective experience of individual identity, and possibly the whole of that of group identity, depend on communication, largely linguistic communication. Identity unfolds in discourse by positioning others on the axes of space, time and rightness, presuming the centrality and fixity of the self.

Envoi

Discourse analysis is a kind of microscope: it focuses in on different objects at different levels of magnification, at the whim of the analyst. Discourse analysis has its own version of the uncertainty principle: at the level of sub-textual analysis, 'observers' (i.e., people reflecting more than casually on texts and talk) cannot exclude themselves from their observations (i.e., interpretations), these being selective and potentially influenced by their 'position' and interests. Such effects cannot be avoided if the aim is an understanding of the links between discourse and social processes at large, but they can be made explicit.

Discourse analysts too are political animals. Some of us in the past have felt it important to give prominence to this point, to the extent almost of treating critical discourse analysis as a mode of political action in itself. This approach has focused on language as a part of society. My own feeling now is that a primarily critical approach is not going to give us new insights into language and the human mind. However, one's political standpoint cannot be entirely decoupled, nor should it be. In fact, one could argue that it is impossible to analyse political language behaviour unless one does exercise one's political intuitions, which are by definition critical. There are two implications of this line of thinking. One is that the approach I am advocating should focus on the processes of our minds in order to enhance our understanding of human nature, including our political nature. The second is by implication guardedly optimistic. If people are indeed political animals, at least to some degree, and depending on how they define 'political', then they are also in principle, *capable* of doing their own political critique. The important question is whether they are free to do so.

Appendix

Notation

(.)	smallest significant hesitation, in most cases a beat
(..)	approximate length of hesitation relative to smallest significant hesitation (.)
.	end of normal falling intonation curve
,	end of normal falling–rising intonation curve
?	end of normal rising-intonation curve (not necessarily a question)
↑s	relatively marked pitch rise over following syllable *s*: the syllable starts relatively low with pitch raising markedly over its duration
↓s	relatively marked pitch fall over following syllable *s*: the syllable starts relatively low with pitch falling markedly over its duration
↑ *s* ↓	relatively marked rising–falling intonation over syllable *s*
↑↓ *s* ↑	rising–falling–rising intonation over syllable *s*, often implying surprise, indignation, etc., in English.
/	step pitch rise in following *stretch of talk*
\	step pitch fall in following *stretch of talk*
|	vertical bars mark approximate point of interruption
*	approximate alignment of end of interruption
>	tempo decreases significantly
<	tempo increases significantly
=	continuity marker where required by page layout; latching between utterers
(( ))	vocalization (e.g., syllable beats) not or only partially transcribed; or unclear but inferable word
(2.5)	approximate duration of pause in seconds and tenths of seconds
:	lengthening of vowels and some consonants phones
er	lengthened schwa
s, **s**	perceptible syllable, relative intensity indicated by bold
.hh	perceptible in-breath
hh	perceptible out-breath
@	laugh
'	glottal stop

Notes

1 Politics and language

1 This account leaves out relations between states – the international arena. It is often argued that beyond the state the international sphere lacks differentiated institutional functions and is anarchic in the technical sense. Such a model does indeed characterise the foreign policy of most states. Opponents of this view of international relations point to the development of international law, the increasing porosity of state boundaries, and global economic and communication networks, all of which increasingly lead to world politics. This dimension, though arguably continuous with domestic politics, does require separate treatment and is not dealt with directly in the present volume.
2 The Rackham (1932: 11) translation makes the point even more clearly: 'why man is a political animal . . . is clear. For . . . man alone of all the animals possesses speech . . . Speech is designed to indicate the advantageous and the harmful, and therefore also the right and the wrong . . .'.
3 For discussions of these issues, see Hurford *et al.* (1998).
4 *Guardian* 13 January 1999.
5 'Sur la nécessité et les moyens d'anéantir les patois et d'universaliser l'usage de la langue française', see de Certeau *et al.* (1975).

2 Language and politics

1 According to some accounts, a 'social language' could have evolved in *homo habilis* about one and a half million years ago (Mithen 1996: 158ff.).
2 Chimpanzee behaviour appears to include machiavellian deception, though on a relatively limited scale (Byrne and Whiten 1988; Byrne 1995).
3 True, some groups of chimpanzees appear to show intentionality and cooperation in hunting, but there is disagreement on how to interpret this behaviour, and what they do is vastly outdistanced by human anticipatory planning (see Mithen 1996: 87–8).
4 It is important to note that Cosmides and Tooby (1989) provide experimental evidence as well as arguments from evolutionary theory.
5 See, for example, 'Notes on Anarchism' (1970) published in Chomsky 1973 and his 1972 Russell Lectures 1972, published as *Problems of Knowledge and Freedom*, which draw on Kropotkin.

3 Interaction

1 In other terms, any language$_i$ has lexical and syntactic devices to facilitate this, thus indicating that it is a property of language$_L$.
2 It is possible, of course, to *exclude* someone from human intercourse by force or by silencing through censorship.
3 There are many theoretical issues involved here that exceed the subject of the present book. For revisions to Grice's maxims see e.g., Horn (1984) and Levinson (2000). The most radical revision is relevance theory (e.g., Sperber and Wilson [1986] 1995), which proposes a theory of cognitive effects dependent entirely on relevance and the principle of least effort–maximum benefit. For criticisms of relevance theory, see, for instance, Levinson (1989), Werth (1999: 137ff).
4 This sort of example raises the question as to how distinct quantity and relevance really are, but this issue need not detain us here.
5 He actually claims to be reading this story from a letter allegedly sent to him by a member of his constituency, but we ignore this extra layer of complexity for present purposes. I neglect also phonological features, in particular intonation, that could have contributed to the production of implicatures.
6 Some of these points are made in Chilton and Schäffner (2002: 14–16).
7 There are some similarities between the notion of a legitimising strategy and the study of 'account' in social psychology, ethnomethodology and conversation analysis and of excuses and apologies in ordinary conversation (Austin 1962; Semin and Manstead 1983; Potter and Wetherell 1992: 74–94). There have also been studies of justification in formal contexts, specifically legal proceedings (Atkinson and Drew 1979). Self-legitimisations, unlike excuses, do not presuppose that a given action is wrong or deny agency or responsibility. Rather they claim a given action is right, performed deliberately, for good purposes, or at least that it is permissible in the circumstances or with respect to certain values (Austin 1962). It has been argued that the various types, or components, of justifications include: denial or minimisation of injury, claiming the victim deserved injury, comparison with other actions allegedly not censured, appeal to higher authority and to law and order, claiming that benefits outweigh harm, appeal to political, moral or religious values, appeal to the need to maintain credibility or honour (Semin and Manstead 1983: 91–2).

4 Representation

1 Although the sense-reference distinction invokes Frege, we here part company, since he held that *Sinn* is, like objective *Bedeutung* (reference), independent of the human cognitive constitution.
2 See Saeed's formulation (1997: 23–5).
3 This approach was that of Fowler *et al.* (1979); Kress and Hodge ([1979] 1994); Fowler (1991, 1996).
4 See among cognitive scientists, Minsky (1975, 1986); Charniak (1978); Schank and Abelson (1977); and among linguists Fillmore (1968, 1977, 1982, 1985); Lakoff (1987, 1993, 1996); Lakoff and Johnson (1980, 1999); Langacker (1987, 1991); Fauconnier (1985).
5 See Hawkins (2001).
6 Deciding what roles and the number of roles is a controversial matter. Fillmore (1968, 1977) on 'semantic cases', Dillon (1977) on 'semantic roles', Gruber (1976),

Jackendoff (1972) and Frawley (1992) offer different criteria and terminologies; Halliday (1970 and 1985) has yet another perspective.

7 The term *indexical* is also used in a broader sense, following the distinctions between different types of signs devised by C. S. Pierce. Gumperz and Levinson (1996: 225) explore the probability that 'indexicality is rampant through language'. See also van Dijk (2002) on the indexing of context, roles, etc., by political speakers.

8 The way I am using this term should not be confused with Levinson's (2000) *presumptive meanings*.

5 Political interviews

1 See, for instance, 'Hague plays on landslide fears', Nicholas Watt, political correspondent, *Guardian*, 5 June 2001.

2 BBC online 12 March 2001 (http://news.bbc.co.uk/hi/english/uk_politics/newsid_1216000/1216410.stm).

3 Maud's words quoted as reported in 'Vaz accused of lying about five homes' (http://www.conservatives.com).

4 There are a number of studies on news interviews that reveal both the verbal and the political complexities: Heritage and Greatbatch (1991), Heritage (1985), Harris (1986, 1991, 2001), Jucker (1986), Bavelas *et al.* (1988), Bull and Mayer (1988), Clayman (1992), Greatbatch (1986, 1988, 1992), Bull (1994), Fairclough (1989: 172–6 and 1995b), Ekström (2001).

5 In cognitive science the ability to infer other people's intentions and representations is known as 'theory of mind' (Leslie 1987). This innate ability is obviously an element of 'machiavellian' social intelligence (see Chapter 2 in this volume) and exists in a developed form in political behaviour.

6 Parliamentary language

1 Parliamentary questions are discussed in Wilson (1980, 1990) and Harris (2001). Wilson distinguishes different approaches: formal-logical, functional and 'sequential' (that is, ethnomethodological or conversational analysis (CA) approach). He is also justifiably critical of a purely functional account, and his own account attempts to combine formal-linguistic with the sequential and the functional. Using Harris (1986) and Dillon (1990) Wilson describes question-making as consisting of 'units' (effectively, propositions and presuppositions) that contribute to 'establishing a specific universe of discourse (or knowledge frame) within which the question will be assessed' (Wilson 1990: 136); answering the question involves accepting the propositions and presuppositions that make up that 'universe'.

2 S = Speaker, M = Members of Parliament, P = Prime Minister. The BBC commentary is in a smaller font. The transcripts here are based on what is heard by a TV audience, given by the positioning of microphones.

3 See Erskine May (1989: 392).

4 In fact Hansard does not favour 'would' but 'will'.

5 Erskine May (1989: 392) says cries of 'hear, hear' have to come at the end of sentences. Usually there has also to be some other signal such as a pause and falling intonation. See also Atkinson (1984).

6 See Cruttenden (1986: 101).

7 This is a feature of low-fall contours (Cruttenden 1986: 100).

8 An example is Blair in the question time of 14 July 1999: 'Madam Speaker well I can see why the Conservatives wanted to shout the question down . . .'.

7 Foreigners

1 There is a good deal of important work on this type of discourse: see in particular van Dijk (1984, 1987, 1993b).
2 See Smithies and Fiddick (1969). The text of Powell's speech analysed below is the version given in this work.

3   Bella, horrida bella,
     Et Thybrim multo spumantem sanguine cerno.
     I see wars, horrible wars,
     and the Tiber foaming with much blood.
                              (*The Aeneid*, Book 6, l. 86)

4 Phonetic and prosodic features, together with paralinguistic features such as gesture and voice quality are also neglected. However, it is worth noting that Powell's pronunciation preserves features of Midlands or Birmingham English, and that his style of delivery is highly formal, and that this is a combination that is not irrelevant to the types of audiences targeted on this occasion. In particular, the accent creates common ground and group identity between an elite political actor and a working-class constituency.
5 The terms 'epistemic' and 'deontic' are generally used in connection with modal expressions, especially the meanings of modal auxiliaries like *must* and *might*. In these paragraphs I am in effect extending this dichotomy to a third category often discussed in connection with modals, namely, *evidential* expressions. What we are examining here is a variety of linguistic expressions for the 'evidence' given by speakers in legitimising their assertions, and suggesting that such evidentials can be either epistemic or deontic, and sometimes both at the same time.
6 On the 'container' schema and its role as a source for cognitive metaphor, see e.g., Johnson (1987), Lakoff and Johnson (1999), and for its role in political discourse Chilton (1994, 1996). The fluid and container metaphors recur in discourse about foreigners. From Powell's utterances, consider the following: 'As towns and cities are transformed by the automatic expansion of what Lord Radcliffe once called 'the alien wedge', a volume of mutual fear, mistrust and resentment builds up **like water filling a cistern**. It is not the sum of antagonisms between individual and individual. It is collective instinctive, human, the imperative of territory, possession and identity' (Powell writing in the *Sun* after riots in Brixton, London, July 1981; emphasis added).
7 The technical term for patients that change location.
8 Sequence 11, pp. 9–10, *Stephen Lawrence Inquiry*, Appendices.
9 Stephen Lawrence Inquiry, Appendix 10, Sequence 11, 3 December 1994, 23:25:28 to 23:28 (http://www.official-documents.co.uk/document/cm42/4262/sli-ap10.htm). Transcription conventions are as in the published report: text in rounded brackets denotes unclear speech open to individual interpretation; dashes represent unintelligible speech; text within square brackets clarifies sequence.
10 First, some caveats. The text is the transcript given in the *Stephen Lawrence Inquiry* derived from a police surveillance videotape, so some linguistic details of interest to

discourse analysts will not have been included. The exact nature of the physical setting is not evident. The text is an extract produced for the purposes of legal evidence. Because of these factors, care needs to be exercised, but, within the limits of the transcription method, the accuracy of the text itself cannot reasonably be doubted.

11 The intonation would be relevant here, were it indicated in the transcription.

12 Seeing Africa was not a part of Powell's arguments for immigration control and repatriation, but the fact that the youths are inventing this detail may confirm the suspicion that they are searching for some form of 'evidence' to legitimise their beliefs.

13 It is worth repeating that this tabulation is not along strict syntactic, but semantic lines. Thus 'it gets on ya nerves' is analysed as a proposition in which the predicate is represented by something like 'get on nerves' and the argument in patient role is equivalent to 'you' (or 'one'); the fact that a prepositional phrase is involved is relevant to syntax but not relevant here to semantics.

8 Distant places

1 Some of the analyses in the present chapter appear in an earlier form in Chilton (2003).

2 Evidence for some such metaphor in English: *raw facts, cook up a new theory, half-baked ideas*.

3 Given ArB, where A, B are deictically specified spaces and r is a relation of discursively claimed similarity, then discursive analogy argues that if a' holds in A then b' holds in B.

4 Principally Augustine, Thomas Aquinas, and the seventeenth-century philosophers Grotius and Pufendorf. Four well-known normative criteria from this body of thought are having a just cause, discrimination (to protect non-combatants), proportionality (of the force used to the ends sought) and reasonable chance of success.

9 Worlds apart

1 There are limits in the attempt to be objective in discourse analysis. In case there can be any doubt, the present author personally condemns all acts of terrorism. Some of the points made in the following sub-sections are revisions of Chilton (2002).

2 See Klare (2001).

3 This would be consistent with the possible representation of the strange use of the perfective 'have become'. This can be understood if we treat, as suggested, the meaning of 'if' here as expressing an entailment: it is 'already' (hence perfective tense) part of the definition of 'sponsor of outlaw' that they are 'outlaws'. The natural language expression of logical relations involves the temporal axis; see also *post hoc ergo propter hoc* ('after this therefore because of this') arguments.

4 It is important to remember that translation itself is an interpretation process, and that the text is, to that extent, a constructed western representation of bin Laden's original utterances. These are issues that we cannot address here and the analysis proceeds on the assumption that translation preserves the conceptualisations, especially the spatial representations that we are interested in. There were different translations of the text: Associated Press, http://www.guardian.co.uk (accessed 20 November 2001); ABS-CBN News, http://www.abs-cbnnews.com (accessed 20 November 2001); Agence France Presse (http://www.afp.com (accessed 20 November 2001)). The

version used in this chapter is the BBC's (http://www.bbc.co.uk/hi/english/world/south-asia/newsid–158000/1585636.stm (accessed 20 November 2001)).

5 In (2) 'of' seems to be an error; maybe we should read it as 'for'.

6 On spatial frames and axial conceptualisation, see Jackendoff (1996).

10 The role of religion

1 This analysis is based on Doran (2001), but couched in terms of discourse analysis.

2 The Associated Press translation has 'thank God for that' where the BBC version has 'praise' in (7) and (10). The CBN translation has 'grace and gratitude to God' (7) and 'thanks be to God' (10).

11 Towards a theoretical framework

1 See Rackham's (1932) translation: 'man . . . alone has perception of good and bad and right and wrong and the other moral qualities'.

2 Jackendoff (1993: 204–22) makes some similar points in a cognitive perspective.

Bibliography

Abraham, L. A. (1964) *A Parliamentary Dictionary*, London, Butterworths.

Adonis, A. (1993) *Parliament Today*, second edition, London, Manchester University Press.

Anderson, B. (1991) *Imagined Communities: Reflections on the Origin and Spread of Nationalism*, revised edition, London, Verso.

Aristotle (1932) *Politics*. With an English Translation by H. Rackham, London, Heinemann.

—— (1992) *The Politics*, translated by T. A. Sinclair, revised and re-presented by Trevor J. Saunders, Harmondsworth, Penguin.

Atkinson, M. (1984) *Our Masters' Voices*, London, Methuen.

Atkinson, J. M. and P. Drew (1979) *Order in Court. The Organisation of Verbal Interaction in Judicial Settings*, London, Macmillan.

—— and J. Heritage (eds) (1984) *Structures of Social Action: Studies in Conversation Analysis*, Cambridge, Cambridge University Press.

Austin, J. L. (1962) *How to Do Things With Words*, Oxford, Clarendon Press.

Axelrod, R. (1984) *The Evolution of Cooperation*, New York, Basic Books.

Barbour, S. and C. Carmichael (eds) (2000) *Language and Nationalism in Europe*, Oxford, Oxford University Press.

Bavelas, J. B., A. Black, L. Bryson and J. Mullett (1988) 'Political equivocation: a situational explanation', *Journal of Language and Social Psychology*, 7 (2): 137–45.

Bickerton, D. (1990) *Language and Species*, Chicago, University of Chicago Press.

Birch, A. (1993) *The Concepts and Theories of Modern Democracy*, London and New York, Routledge.

Blommaert, J. and C. Bulcaen (eds) (1997) *Political Linguistics*, Amsterdam, Benjamins, special issue of *Belgian Journal of Linguistics*, 11, 1997.

—— and J. Verschueren (1998) *Debating Diversity*, London, Routledge.

Bloom, P., M. A. Petersen, L. Nadel and M. F. Garrett (eds) (1996) *Language and Space*, Cambridge, Mass., MIT Press.

Boden, D. and D. H. Zimmerman (eds) (1991) *Talk and Social Structure. Studies in Ethnomethodology and Conversation Analysis*, Cambridge, Polity Press.

Brown, P. and S. Levinson (1987) *Politeness: Some Universals in Language Usage*, Cambridge, Cambridge University Press.

Brubaker, R. (1999) *Nationalism Reframed: Nationhood and the National Question in the New Europe*, Cambridge, Cambridge University Press.

Bull, P. (1994) 'On identifying questions, replies and nonreplies in political interviews', *Journal of Language and Social Psychology*, 13 (2): 115–32.

—— and K. Mayer (1988) 'How Margaret Thatcher and Neil Kinnock avoid answering questions in political interviews', paper presented to the British Psychological Association, London.

Byrne, R. (1995) *The Thinking Ape: Evolutionary Origins of Intelligence*, Oxford, Oxford University Press.

—— and A. Whiten (eds) (1988) *Machiavellian Intelligence: Social Expertise and the Evolution of Intellect in Monkeys, Apes and Humans*, Oxford, Clarendon Press.

Camilleri, J. A. and J. Falk (1992) *The End of Sovereignty? The Politics of a Shrinking and Fragmenting World*, Aldershot, Edward Elgar.

Carmichael, C. (2002) '"A people exists and that people has its language": language and nationalism in the Balkans' in S. Barbour and C. Carmichael (eds), *Language and Nationalism in Europe*.

Charniak, E. (1978) 'On the use of framed knowledge in language comprehension', *Artificial Intelligence*, 11: 225–65.

Chace, J. and C. Carr (1988) *America Invulnerable: The Quest for Absolute Security from 1812 to Star Wars*, New York, Summit Books.

Chilton, P. A. (1994) '"La plaie qu'il convient de fermer . . ." Les métaphores du discours raciste', *Journal of Pragmatics*, 21 (6): 583–619.

—— (1996) *Security Metaphors: Cold War Discourse from Containment to Common House*, New York, Lang.

—— (2000) 'Participant roles and the analysis of leadership discourse: British and American leaders explain the Kosovo crisis' in I. Plag and P. Schneider (eds), *Language Use, Language Acquisition and Language History*, Trier, Wissenschaftlicher Verlag.

—— (2002) 'Do something! Conceptualising responses to the attacks of 11 September 2001', *Journal of Language and Politics*, 1 (1): 181–95.

—— (2003) 'Deixis and distance: President Clinton's justification of intervention in Kosovo' in D. Nelson and M. Dedaic (eds), *Words at War*, Berlin, de Gruyter.

—— and G. Lakoff (1995) 'Foreign policy by metaphor' in C. Schäffner and A. Wenden (eds), *Language and Peace*, Aldershot, Ashgate.

—— J. Mey and M. Ilyin (eds) (1998) *Political Discourse in Transition in Europe 1989–91*, Amsterdam, John Benjamins.

—— and C. Schäffner (1997) 'Discourse and politics' in T. van Dijk (ed.), *Discourse as Social Interaction*, London, Sage: 206–30.

—— and C. Schäffner (eds) (2002) *Politics as Text and Talk: Analytic Approaches to Political Discourse*, Amsterdam, John Benjamins.

Chomsky, N. (1966) *Cartesian Linguistics*, New York, Harper & Row.

—— (1968) *Language and Mind*, New York, Harcourt, Brace & World.

—— (1969) *American Power and the New Mandarins*, London, Chatto & Windus.

—— (1972) *Problems of Knowledge and Freedom*, London, Fontana.

—— (1973) *For Reasons of State*, New York, Pantheon.

—— (1975) *Reflections on Language*, New York, Pantheon.

—— (1985) *Knowledge of Language*, New York, Praeger.

—— (1989) *Necessary Illusions: Thought Control in Democratic Societies*, London, Pluto.

—— (1999) 'A letter to Santa Claus?', Amnesty Lecture, Sheldonian Theatre, Oxford, reproduced in *Times Higher Education Supplement*, 19 February 1999: 23–4.

—— (2000) *New Horizons in the Study of Language and Mind*, Cambridge, Cambridge University Press.

—— and Herman, E. S. (1988) *Manufacturing Consent: The Political Economy of the Mass Media*, New York, Pantheon.

Clayman, S. (1992) 'Footing in the achievement of neutrality: the case of news–interview discourse' in P. Drew and J. Heritage (eds) (1992): 118–46.

Clerks in the Table Office (1979) *Questions in the House of Commons: A Short Introduction to their History and Procedure*, London, Her Majesty's Stationery Office.

Cosmides, L. (2000) 'The evolution of decoupling' in D. Sperber (ed.), *Metarepresentations*.

—— and J. Tooby (1989) 'The logic of social exchange: has natural selection shaped how humans reason? Studies with the Wason selection task', *Cognition*, 31: 187–276.

Cruttenden, A. (1986) *Intonation*, Cambridge, Cambridge University Press.

De Certeau, M., D. Julia and J. Revel (1975) *Une politique de la langue: la Révolution française et les patois*, Paris, Gallimard.

Deutsch, K. (1953) *Nationalism and Social Communication*, Cambridge, Mass., MIT Press and John Wiley.

Dillon, G. (1977) *Introduction to Contemporary Linguistic Semantics*, Englewood Cliffs, NJ, Prentice-Hall.

Dillon, J. T. (1990) *The Practice of Questioning*, London, Routledge.

Dirven, R., R. Frank and C. Ilie (eds) (2001) *Language and Ideology. Volume II: Descriptive Cognitive Approaches*, Amsterdam, John Benjamins.

Doran, M. S. (2001) 'Somebody else's civil war' in Hoge and Rose, *How Did this Happen? Terrorism and the New War*.

Douglas, M. (1970) *Purity and Danger: An Analysis of Concepts of Pollution and Taboo*, Harmondsworth, Penguin.

Dowty, D. (1991) 'Thematic proto-roles and agreement selection', *Language*, 67: 547–619.

Drew, P. and J. Heritage (eds) (1992) *Talk at Work*, Cambridge, Cambridge University Press.

Dunbar, R. (1993) 'Coevolution of neocortical size, group size and language in humans', *Behavioral and Brain Sciences*, 16: 681–735.

Dworkin, R. (1977) *Taking Rights Seriously*, London, Duckworth.

Ekström, M. (2001) 'Politicians interviewed on television news', *Discourse and Society*, 12 (5): 563–84.

Erskine May (1989) *Erskine May's Treatise on The Law, Privileges, Proceedings and Usage of Parliament*, 21st edn (ed.) C. J. Boulton, London, Butterworths.

Fairclough, N. (1989) *Language and Power*, London and New York, Longman.

—— (1992) *Discourse and Social Change*, Cambridge, Polity.

—— (ed.) (1992) *Critical Language Awareness*, London, Longman.

—— (1995a) *Critical Discourse Analysis: the Critical Study of Language*, London, Longman.

—— (1995b) *Media Discourse*, London, Edward Arnold.

—— (2000) *New Labour, New language?* London, Routledge.

Fauconnier, G. (1985) *Mental Spaces*, Cambridge, Mass., MIT Press. Revised edition, Cambridge, Cambridge University Press, 1994.

Fetzer, A. (2002) ' "Put bluntly, you have something of a credibility problem": Sincerity and credibility in political interviews' in P. Chilton and C. Schäffner (eds), *Politics as Text and Talk*.

Fillmore, C. (1968) 'The case for case' in E. Bach and R. Harms (eds), *Universals in Linguistic Theory*, New York, Holt, Rinehart & Wilson.

—— (1977) 'The case for case reopened' in P. Cole and J. Sadock (eds), *Grammatical Relations, Syntax and Semantics*, 8, New York, Academic Press.

—— (1982) 'Frame semantics' in the Linguistics Society of Korea (ed.), *Linguistics in the Morning Calm*, Seoul, Hanshin Publishing Co.

—— (1985) 'Frames and the semantics of understanding', *Quaderni di Semantica*, 6 (2): 222–53.

Fowler, R. (1991) *Language in the News: Discourse and Ideology in the Press*, London, Routledge.

—— (1996) *Linguistic Criticism*, Oxford, Oxford University Press.

—— R. Hodge, G. Kress and T. Trew (1979) *Language and Control*, London, Routledge & Kegan Paul.

Franklin, M. and P. Norton (eds) (1993) *Parliamentary Questions*, Oxford, Clarendon Press.

Frawley, W. (1992) *Linguistic Semantics*, Hillsdale, NJ, Erlbaum Associates.

Frege, G. (1980) *Translations from the Philosophical Writings of Gottlob Frege*, edited by P. Geach and M. Black, Oxford, Blackwell.

Gallie, W. B. (1956) 'Essentially contested concepts', *Proceedings of the Aristotelian Society*, New Series 56, 1955–6: 167–98.

Gärdenfors, P. (2002) 'Cooperation and the evolution of symbolic communication', *Lund University Cognitive Studies*, 91; http://lucs.fil.lu.se/Abstracts/LUCS_Studies/LUCS91.html (accessed 5 May 2003).

Gelber, K. (2002) *Speaking Back: the Free Speech versus Hate Speech Debate*, Amsterdam, John Benjamins.

Goffmann, E. (1967) *Interaction Ritual*, New York, Doubleday.

—— (1974) *Frame Analysis*, New York, Harper & Row.

Greatbatch, D. (1986) 'Some standard uses of supplementary questions in news interviews', *Belfast Working Papers in Language and Linguistics*, 8: 86–123.

—— (1988) 'A turn-taking system for British news interviews', *Language in Society*, 17: 401–30.

—— (1992) 'The management of disagreement between news interviewees' in P. Drew and J. Heritage (eds), *Talk at Work*: 268–301.

Grice, H. P. (1975) 'Logic and conversation' in P. Cole and J. Morgan (eds), *Syntax and Semantics: 3: Speech Acts*, New York, Academic Press.

—— (1989) *Studies in the Way of Words*, Cambridge, Mass., Harvard University Press.

Gruber, J. (1976) *Lexical Structures in Syntax and Semantics*, Amsterdam, North-Holland.

Gumperz, J. J. and S. C. Levinson (eds) (1996) *Rethinking Linguistic Relativity*, Cambridge, Cambridge University Press.

Habermas, J. (1971) 'Vorbereitende bemerkungen zu einer theorie der kommunikativen kompetenz', in J. Habermas and N. Luhmann (eds), *Theorie der Gesellschaft oder Sozialtechnologie*, Frankfurt, Suhrkamp.

—— (1973) *Legitimation Crisis*, London, Heinemann.

—— (1979) *Communication and the Evolution of Society*, London, Heinemann.

—— (1981) *Theorie des kommunikativen Handelns*, Frankfurt, Suhrkamp.

Hague, R., M. Harrop, and S. Breslin (1998) *Comparative Government and Politics: An Introduction*, Basingstoke, Macmillan, 4th edn.

Halliday, M. A. K. (1970) 'Language structure and language function' in J. Lyons (ed.), *New Horizons in Linguistics*, Harmondsworth, Penguin.

—— (1985) *Introduction to Functional Grammar*, London, Arnold.

Hansard (1999) *House of Commons Daily Debates*, July 1999.

Harris, S. (1986) 'Interviewers' questions in broadcast interviews', *Belfast Working Papers in Language and Linguistics*, 8: 50–86.

—— (1991) 'Evasive action: how politicians respond to questions in political interviews' in P. Scannell (ed.), *Broadcast Talk*, London, Routledge: 76–99.

—— (2001) 'Being politically impolite: extending politeness theory to adversarial political discourse', *Discourse and Society*, 12 (4): 451–72.

Haugen, E. (1966) 'Dialect, language, nation', *American Anthropologist*, 68: 922–35.

Hawkins, B. (2001) 'Ideology, metaphor and iconographic reference' in Dirven *et al.* *Language and Ideology*.

Heritage, J. (1985) 'Analysing news interviews: aspects of the production of talk for an overhearing audience' in T. van Dijk (ed.), *Handbook of Discourse Analysis*, vol. 3: 95–117.

—— and D. Greatbatch (1991) 'On the institutional character of institutional talk: the case of news interviews' in D. Boden and D. H. Zimmerman (eds), *Talk and Social Structure*: 93–137.

Hirschfeld, L. and S. A. Gelman (eds) (1994) *Mapping the Mind: Domain Specificity in Cognition and Culture*, Cambridge, Cambridge University Press.

Hobsbawm, E. J. (1990) *Nations and Nationalism since 1780*, Cambridge, Cambridge University Press.

Hockett, C. (1960) 'The origin of speech', *Scientific American* 203 (3): 88–96.

Hoge, J. F. and G. Rose (eds) (2001) *How Did this Happen? Terrorism and the New War*, Oxford, Public Affairs.

Horn, L. (1984) 'Toward a new taxonomy for pragmatic inference: Q-based and R-based implicative' in D. Schiffrin (ed.), *Georgetown Round Table on Language and Linguistics 1984*, Washington, D.C., Georgetown University Press: 11–42.

Humphrey, N. (1976) 'The social function of intellect' in P. P. G. Bateson and R. A. Hinde (eds), *Growing Points in Ethology*, Cambridge, Cambridge University Press.

Hurford, J. R., M. Studdert-Kennedy and C. Knight (eds) (1998) *Approaches to the Evolution of Language: Social and Cognitive Bases*, Cambridge, Cambridge University Press.

Irwin, H., A. Kennon, D. Natzler and R. Rodgers (1993) 'Evolving rules' in M. Franklin and P. Norton (eds), *Parliamentary Questions*.

Jackendoff, R. (1972) *Semantic Interpretation in Generative Grammar*, Cambridge, Mass., MIT Press.

—— (1993) *Patterns in the Mind: Language and Human Nature*, New York, Harvester Wheatsheaf.

—— (1996) 'The architecture of the linguistic–spatial interface' in P. Bloom, M. A. Petersen, L. Nadel and M. F. Garrett (eds), *Language and Space*.

—— (2002) *Foundations of Language: Brain, Meaning, Grammar, Evolution*, Oxford, Oxford University Press.

Johnson-Laird, P. (1983) *Mental Models*, Cambridge, Cambridge University Press.

Johnson, M. (1987) *The Body in the Mind. The Bodily Basis of Meaning, Imagination, and Reason*, Chicago, University of Chicago Press.

Jones, B. (ed.) (1994) *Politics UK*, 2nd edn, New York, Harvester Wheatsheaf.

Jucker, A. (1986) *News Interviews: a Pragmalinguistic Analysis*, Amsterdam, John Benjamins.

Klare, M. (2001) 'Asking why', *Policy Forum Online*, September 20 (www.nautilus.org/ for a/Special-Policy-Forum/09) (accessed 27 September 2001).

Kress, G. and R. Hodge [1979] (1994) *Language as Ideology*, London, Routledge & Kegan Paul; revised as Hodge R. and G. Kress, 1993, *Language as Ideology*, London, Routledge.

Lakoff, G. (1987) *Women, Fire and Dangerous Things. What Categories Reveal about the Mind*, Chicago, University of Chicago Press.

—— (1993) 'The contemporary theory of metaphor' in A. Ortony, *Metaphor and Thought*.

—— (1996) *Moral Politics*, Chicago and London, University of Chicago Press.

—— and M. Johnson (1980) *Metaphors We Live By*, Chicago, University of Chicago Press.

—— and M. Johnson (1999) *Philosophy in the Flesh: the Embodied Mind and its Challenge to Western Thought*, New York, Basic Books.

—— and M. Turner (1989) *More than Cool Reason*, Chicago, University of Chicago Press.

Langacker, R. (1987) *Foundations of Cognitive Grammar. Volume I Theoretical Prerequisites*, Stanford, Stanford University Press.

—— (1991) *Foundations of Cognitive Grammar. Volume II Descriptive Application*, Stanford, Stanford University Press.

Leech, G. N. (1983) *Principles of Pragmatics*, London, Longman.

Leslie, A. (1987) 'Pretence and representation: the origins of "theory of mind"', *Psychological Review*, 94: 412–26.

Levinger, J. (1998) 'Language and identity in Bosnia-Herzegovina' in P. A. Chilton, M. V. Ilyin and J. Mey (eds), *Political Discourse in Transition in Europe 1989–91*, Amsterdam, John Benjamins.

Levinson, S. C. (1983) *Pragmatics*, Cambridge, Cambridge University Press.

—— (1989) 'Relevance', *Journal of Linguistics*, 21: 455–72.

—— (2000) *Presumptive Meanings: the Theory of Generalised Conversational Implicature*, Cambridge, Mass., MIT Press.

Lewis, D. (1979) 'Scorekeeping in a language game' in R. Bäuerle, U. Egli and A. von Stechow (eds), *Semantics from Different Points of View*, Berlin, Springer-Verlag.

Lucy, J. (1996) 'The scope of linguistic relativity: an analysis and review of empirical research' in J. J. Gumperz and S. C. Levinson, *Rethinking Linguistic Relativity*.

Mey, J. (1985) *Whose Language? A Study in Linguistic Pragmatics*, Amsterdam, John Benjamins.

—— (2001) *Pragmatics: An Introduction*, 2nd edn, Oxford, Blackwell.

Miller, D. (1991) 'Politics' in *Blackwell Encyclopaedia of Political Thought*, Oxford, Blackwell: 390–1.

Milroy, L. (1987) *Language and Social Networks*, 2nd edn, Oxford, Blackwell.

Minksy, M. (1975) 'A Framework for Representing Knowledge' in P. H. Winston (ed.), *The Psychology of Computer Vision*, New York, McGraw-Hill.

―――― (1986) *The Society of Mind*, New York, Simon & Schuster.

Mithen, S. (1996) *The Prehistory of the Mind*, London, Thames & Hudson.

Nelson, D. and M. Dedaic (eds) (2003) *Words at War*, Berlin, de Gruyter.

Ortony, A. (1993) *Metaphor and Thought*, 2nd edn, Cambridge, Cambridge University Press.

Orwell, G. (1949) *Nineteen Eighty-Four*, London, Martin Secker & Warburg.

Pavio, A. (1973) *Imagery and Verbal Processes*, New York, Holt, Rinehart & Winston.

Pinker, S. (1994) *The Language Instinct*, London, Penguin.

Potter, J. and Wetherell, M. (1992) *Discourse and Social Psychology: Beyond Attitudes and Behaviour*, London, Sage.

Reisigl, M. and R. Wodak (2001) *Discourse and Discrimination: Rhetorics of Racism and Anti-Semitism*, London, Routledge.

Russell, B. (1905) 'On denoting', *Mind*, 14: 479–93.

Sacks, H., A. E. Schegloff and G. Jefferson (1974) 'A simplest systematics for the organisation of turn-taking in conversation', *Language*, 50 (4): 696–735.

Saeed, J. I. (1997) *Semantics*, Oxford, Blackwell.

Salkie, R. (1990) *The Chomsky Update: Linguistics and Politics*, London, Unwin Hyman.

Sapir, E. (1970) *Edward Sapir. Culture, Language and Personality. Selected Essays*, edited by D. G. Mandelbaum, Berkeley and Los Angeles, University of California Press.

Schank, R. C. and R. P. Abelson (1977) *Scripts, Plans, Goals and Understanding*, Hillsdale NJ, Lawrence Erlbaum.

Schegloff, E. A. (1972) 'Sequencing in conversational openings' in J. Gumperz and D. Hymes (eds), *Directions in Sociolinguistics*, New York, Holt, Rinehart & Winston.

―――― Jefferson, G. and H. Sacks (1977) 'The preference for self-correction in the organisation of repair in conversation', *Language*, 53: 361–82.

―――― (1979) 'The relevance of repair to syntax for conversation' in T. Givon (ed.) *Syntax and Semantics, 12: Discourse and Syntax*, New York, Academic Press.

Searle, J. (1969) *Speech Acts: An Essay in the Philosophy of Language*, Cambridge, Cambridge University Press.

Semin, G. R. and A. S. R. Manstead (1983) *The Accountability of Conduct: a Social Psychological Analysis*, London, Academic Press.

Smithies, B. and P. Fiddick (1969) *Enoch Powell on Immigration*, London, Sphere.

Sperber, D. (1994) 'The modularity of thought' in L. Hirschfeld and S. A. Gelman, *Mapping the Mind*.

―――― (ed.) (2000) *Metarepresentations: A Multidisciplinary Perspective*, Oxford, Oxford University Press.

―――― and D. Wilson (1986) *Relevance: Communication and Cognition*, Cambridge, MA, Harvard University Press, 2nd edn: 1995.

Stephen Lawrence Inquiry (1999) Appendices Presented to Parliament by the Secretary of State for the Home Department by command of Her Majesty, February.

Sweetser, E. (1990) *From Etymology to Pragmatics: Metaphorical and Cultural Aspects of Semantic Structure*, Cambridge, Cambridge University Press.

Talmy, L. (1988) 'Force dynamics in language and cognition', *Cognitive Science*, 2: 49–100.

Turner, M. (1991) *Reading Minds*, Princeton, Princeton University Press.

van Dijk, T. A. (1984) *Prejudice in Discourse. An Analysis of Ethnic Prejudice in Cognition and Conversation*, Amsterdam, John Benjamins.

—— (ed.) (1985) *Handbook of Discourse Analysis*, 4 vols, London, Academic Press.

—— (1987) *Communicating Racism. Ethnic Prejudice in Thought and Talk*, London, Sage.

—— (1990) 'Social cognition and discourse' in H. Giles and W. P. Robinson (eds), *Handbook of Language and Social Psychology*, New York, John Wiley.

—— (1993a) 'Discourse and cognition in society' in D. Crowley and D. Mitchell (eds), *Communication Theory Today*, Oxford, Pergamon.

—— (1993b) *Elite Discourse and Racism*, London, Sage.

—— (1997a) 'What is political discourse analysis?' in J. Blommaert and C. Bulcaen (eds), *Political Linguistics*: 53–67.

—— (ed.) (1997b) *Discourse as Social Interaction*, London, Sage.

—— (1998) *Ideology: An Interdisciplinary Approach*, London, Sage.

—— (2002) 'Ideology: political discourse and cognition' in P. A. Chilton and C. Schäffner, *Politics as Talk and Text*.

—— and W. Kintsch (1983) *Strategies of Discourse Comprehension*, New York, Academic Press.

Verschueren, J. (1999) *Understanding Pragmatics*, London, Arnold.

Walker, R. B. J. (1988) *One World, Many Worlds: Struggles for a Just World Peace*, Boulder, Lynne Rienner and London, Zed Books.

Werth, P. (1999) *Text Worlds: Representing Conceptual Space in Discourse*, London, Longman.

Whorf, B. L. (1973) *Language, Thought and Reality. Selected Writings of Benjamin Lee Whorf*, edited by J. B. Carroll, Cambridge, Mass., MIT Press.

Wilson, J. (1980) 'Why answers to questions are not enough in social discourse', *Belfast Working Papers in Language and Linguistics*, 4: 70–101.

—— (1990) *Politically Speaking. The Pragmatic Analysis of Political Language*, Oxford, Blackwell.

Wilson, D. and D. Sperber (2002) 'Truthfulness and relevance', *Mind*, 111 (443): 583–632.

Wodak, R. (ed.) (1989) *Language, Power and Ideology*, Amsterdam and Philadelphia, John Benjamins.

—— (1996) *Disorders of Discourse*, London and New York, Longman.

—— (2002) 'Fragmented identities: redefining and recontextualising national identity' in P. A. Chilton and C. Schäffner, *Politics as Talk and Text*.

Wright, S. (ed.) (1996) *Language and the State: Revitalisation and Revival in Israel and Eire*, Clevedon, Multilingual Matters.

—— (ed.) (2000) *Community and Communications: The Role of Language in Nation State Building and European Integration*, Clevedon, Multilingual Matters.

Name index

Abelson, R. P. 208
Adonis, A. 92
Adorno, T. W. x
Anderson, B. 11
Aristotle 4f, 16, 26, 198f, 200, 201
Atkinson, M. 41, 208, 209
Augustine, Saint 211
Austin, J. L. 31, 118
Axelrod, R. 21

Barbour, S. 11
Barrere, B. 11
Bavelas, J. B. 209
Beckett, M. 69ff
Benjamin, W. x
Bickerton, D. 16
bin Laden, Osama 157, 165ff, 173ff, 211
Birch, A. 12
Blair, T. 99f
Blommaert, J. x
Bourdieu, P. x
Brown, P. 40
Brubaker, R. 12
Bulcaen, C. x
Bull, P. 209
Bush, George W. 157ff, 165f, 168, 172, 174ff, 181f
Byrne, R. 207

Camilleri, J. A. 137
Carmichael, C. 10
Carr, C. 156
Carter, J. 155
Chace, J. 156
Charniak, E. 208

Chilton, P. x, 45, 51, 54, 156, 208, 210, 211
Chomsky, N. x, 17, 23ff
Clayman, S. 209
Clinton, W. 55, 138, 141, 174
Cosmides, L. x, 21, 22, 200
Cruttenden, A. 105

de Certeau, M. 207
Deutsch, K. 11
Dillon, G. 208, 209
Dirven, R. x
Doran, M. S. 190, 212
Douglas, M. 129
Dowty, D. 53f
Drew, P. 208
Dunbar, R. 17
Dworkin, R. 12

Ekström, M. 209

Fairclough, N. x, 27, 209
Falk, J. 137
Fauconnier, G. x, 57, 61, 63, 143, 208
Fetzer, A. 32, 65
Fiddick, P. 110
Fillmore, C. 208
Fowler, R. x, 60, 208, 209
Frege, G. 208

Gallie, W. B. 48
Gärdenfors, P. 18, 22
Goffman, E. 40
Greatbatch, D. 69, 75, 209
Gregoire, l'abbé 11

Subject index